Regions, Spatial Strategies Sustainable Development

With its mandate for promoting sustainable development and supporting economic development, regional planning has been the centre of some of the most important policy debates in English regionalism. This book focuses on recent regional policy and planning debates in all the English regions, using a range of theoretical insights to examine major controversies such as: resistance to new housing on greenfield sites, sustainable urban development and policies for 'urban renaissance', whether to redirect or constrain economic growth in pressure areas, how to support economic development in declining areas, how best to protect environmental assets for the future.

Graham Haughton is Professor of Human Geography at the University of Hull. **David Counsell** is a planner working as a research fellow in the Department of Geography at the University of Hull.

Regional Development and Public Policy Series
Published with the Regional Studies Association
Series editor: Ron Martin, University of Cambridge, UK

Regional Development and Public Policy is an international series that aims to provide authoritive analyses of the new significance of regions and cities for economic development and public policy. It seeks to combine fresh theoretical and empirical insights with constructive policy evaluation and debates, and to provide a definitive set of conceptual, practical and topical studies in the field of regional and urban public policy analysis.

The Regional Studies Association uses its networks and publications to promote, develop and disseminate quality theoretical and empirical research on regional problems. Membership is open to all.

Social Exclusion in European Cities
Processes, experiences and responses
Ali Madanipour, Goran Cars and Judith Allen (eds)

Regional Innovation Strategies
The challenge for less-favoured regions
Kevin Morgan and Claire Nauwelaers (eds)

Foreign Direct Investment and the Global Economy
Nicholas A. Phelps and Jeremy Alden (eds)

Restucturing Industry and Territory
The experience of Europe's regions
Anna Giunta, Arnoud Lagendijk and Andy Pike (eds)

Community Economic Development
Graham Haughton (ed.)

Out of the Ashes?
The social impact of industrial contraction and regeneration on Britain's mining communities
David Waddington, Chas Critcher, Bella Dicks and David Parry

Geographies of Labour Market Inequality
Ron Martin and Philip S. Morrison

Regions, Spatial Strategies and Sustainable Development

Graham Haughton and
David Counsell

Routledge
Taylor & Francis Group

LONDON AND NEW YORK

First published 2004
by Routledge
11 New Fetter Lane, London EC4P 4EE

Simultaneously published in the USA and Canada
by Routledge
29 West 35th Street, New York, NY 10001

Routledge is an imprint of the Taylor & Francis Group

Typeset in Bembo by Wearset Ltd, Boldon, Tyne & Wear
Printed and bound in Great Britain by TJ International Ltd, Padstow,
Cornwall

British Library Cataloguing in Publication Data
A catalogue record for this book is available from the British Library

Library of Congress Cataloging in Publication Data
Haughton, Graham.
   Regions, spatial strategies, and sustainable development /
Graham Haughton and Dave Counsell.
      p. cm. – (Regional development and public policy series)
Includes bibliographical references and index.
      1. Regional planning – Great Britain. 2. Sustainable development
– Great Britain. I. Counsell, Dave. II. Title. III. Series: Regional
development and public policy.
HT395.G7H38 2003
338.941–dc21
                                                          2003013492

ISBN   0–415–31464–X (pbk)
          0–415–31463–1 (hbk)
          0–203–56124–4 (e-book)

Contents

6 Towards an urban renaissance   140

7 Regional economic development, regional planning and sustainable development: divergences and convergences in approach   169

Illustrations

Tables

Boxes

Preface and acknowledgements

This book comes at a time of rapidly growing interest in English regional-scale governance, with central government in the United Kingdom having introduced far-reaching measures towards policy devolution, most notably with the creation of the Scottish Parliament and the Welsh Assembly. In England too, there have been substantial moves to increase policy devolution to the regional scale. Key features are the strengthening of the role of regional planning, the creation of Regional Development Agencies (RDAs) which are required to produce regional economic strategies, the development of Regional Sustainable Development Frameworks, and the emergence of regional chambers of key stakeholders, including local authorities, to provide a form of accountability mechanism for the rapidly expanding realm of regional strategic work. In 2002 the government announced its intention to create a process which could lead to formal elected regional governments (Cabinet Office and DTLR 2002), adding further strength to the devolution project in England.

The main empirical focus of the book is on the issues surrounding the production of English regional planning guidance (RPG) in the period between 2000 and 2002 – that is, the new round of RPGs produced following the election of Labour in 1997. However, our ambitions are much broader than this in scope, as we aim to examine how the current approach to regional planning has grown out of previous practices, how it links into other forms of regional strategy, in particular regional economic strategies, how the strengthening of regional planning has impacted on planning at the local and national scales, and how the recent renaissance of regional planning is connected to wider changes in English governance.

Our overall aim is to provide a theoretically informed, empirical analysis of the ways in which the current regional experiments are taking place. We focus particularly on the reawakening of interest in regional spatial planning which gathered pace through the 1990s and into the early years of the present century. Something of this is captured in some of the article titles which began to appear in planning and related journals, initially usually with cautionary question marks: 'The renaissance of strategic planning?' (Breheny 1991), 'Rediscovering regional planning?' (Thomas and Kimberley 1995),

'Rediscovering the regional approach' (Baker 1996), 'The revival of regional planning' (Simmons 1999).

Renaissance, rediscovery and revival – after twenty years in the wilderness, regional planning was somehow back on the agenda. There were some changes, however. Compared to practice in the 1960s and 1970s, in its early 1990s reincarnation, regional planning had become a narrower form of policy process, aimed at land use issues in particular. In essence, regional planning was a non-statutory guidance process which lay between the statutory system of structure and local plans, and national planning guidance.

The preparation of RPG, which had been introduced in the early 1990s, was strengthened under Labour in the late 1990s, creating a form of strategy which was separate from, but linked to, the Regional Economic Strategies. Central government also required regional partners to develop Regional Sustainable Development Frameworks, which were intended to be high-level documents setting out principles for other regional strategies to follow. In effect, RPG provided the long-term spatial strategic framework for physical development in each region, which was intended also to help guide the work of preparing Regional Economic Strategies.

The research described here was undertaken in all eight English standard regions between 2000 and 2002. The advantage of covering all regions is that it allows us to undertake a comprehensive analysis of the remaking of regional planning in England. There is a specific focus on how sustainable development was dealt with in regional planning, which allows the book to cover environmental, social and economic aspects of regional planning and policy. The environmental focus is essentially twofold. First, we look at the struggles to interpret 'integrated' approaches to sustainable development through regional planning, which raised considerable concern about whether this meant environmental issues were being down-graded in importance. Second, and related, we look at struggles over the techniques being introduced for assessing the environmental impacts of the new policy. The social focus of our work concerns debates over future housing development, often the single most contentious issues during the development of regional planning guidance. Not surprisingly, many of the issues were not purely social, as environmental and economic issues were also central to the housing debates. The economic focus is achieved through an assessment of the relationship between the regional economic and regional planning systems, with a particular focus on the sometimes heated debates on where future employment should be directed towards and, in particular, decisions about land release for future employment uses.

In undertaking this project we have benefited from two sources of funding. The main funding for the project was provided by the Economic and Social Research Council (ESRC) under grant R000238368. Without this financial assistance, the project could never have been undertaken, and we want to record here our gratitude to the ESRC and its reviewers for their support. In addition, we were fortunate to receive additional funding from the then Department of Transport, Local Government and the Regions, now the Office of the Deputy Prime Minister (ODPM). This allowed us to extend our ESRC research to look at the early use of the sustainability appraisal methodology in RPG, and also progress with monitoring systems for RPG. Not only did this work extend our remit, it also allowed us a closer engagement with central government policy makers than we might have otherwise expected. We are grateful to the ODPM for its support at all stages of the project.

Some further acknowledgements are also in order. Study leave was granted by the Department of Geography at the University of Hull to allow Graham Haughton time to work on this book. Further assistance was provided by the University of Otago, which awarded a William Evans Visiting Fellowship for September–October 2002. His hosts in the Department of Geography offered considerable support during the visit, especially Dr Claire Freeman. Following the sun, Graham next benefited from a Visiting Research Fellowship at the Flinders University of South Australia for the period November 2002–January 2003, hosted by the Department of Geography, Population and Environmental Management. Again, he would like to acknowledge the valuable support of colleagues there, particularly Associate Professors Andrew Beer and Alaric Maude.

Garreth Bruff worked with us on this project for its first sixteen months, before moving on to a job with the Leeds Initiative. His input was invaluable to the early stages of this work, including helping devise questionnaires and sample frames, working on documentary analysis, and undertaking some of the interviews.

We would also like to acknowledge the support of our team of regional correspondents who helped us to identify key regional issues and people we should speak to, while also offering to comment on our draft regional summaries. They were:

North East: Tim Shaw, Newcastle University
Yorkshire and the Humber: Ted Kitchen, Sheffield Hallam University
North West: Joe Ravetz, Manchester University
East Midlands: Colin Williams, Leicester University
West Midlands: Graham Pearce, Aston University
East Anglia: Tim O'Riordan, University of East Anglia
South East: Mike Breheny, University of Reading
South West: Colin Fudge, University of the West of England

Thanks are also due to Tim Marshall and Tim Shaw for their support early on as we were developing our ideas for the project. We would particularly like to thank John Garner of the Department of Geography, University of Hull, for his work on the graphics in this book, Sandra Counsell for the photos of the North East, and Paul Nicholson for the photographs of East Anglia. Graham Haughton took all the remaining photos. We also want to thank a number of people who commented on early drafts of chapters or related conference papers which were later used in producing this book. These include Phil Allmendinger, Sally Eden, David Gibbs and Andy Jonas. Particularly valuable were the incisive comments of Aidan While, who kindly agreed to read the whole draft manuscript. Naturally, all these friends and colleagues are totally blameless for any errors of fact, interpretation and omission in this book.

Abbreviations

AEP	Area of Economic Pressure
ANEC	Association of North East Councils
BAP	Biodiversity Action Plan
CASE	Case Against Stevenage Expansion
CBI	Confederation of British Industry
CPRE	Council for the Protection of Rural England
DETR	Department of the Environment, Transport and the Regions
DoE	Department of the Environment
DTLR	Department for Transport, Local Government and the Regions
EERA	East of England Regional Assembly
EiP	examination in public
EMDA	East Midlands Development Agency
EMEL	East Midlands Environmental Link
EMRA	East Midlands Regional Assembly
EMRLGA	East Midlands Regional Local Government Association
ESDP	European Spatial Development Perspective
ESRC	Economic and Social Research Council
EU	European Union
GDP	gross domestic product
GLA	Greater London Authority
GLC	Greater London Council
GOEE	Government Office for the East of England
GOEM	Government Office for the East Midlands
GONE	Government Office for North East
GONW	Government Office for North West
GOSE	Government Office for South East
GOSW	Government Office for South West
GOYH	Government Office for Yorkshire and the Humber
HBF	House Builders Federation
HTC	high-technology corridor
IRS	Integrated Regional Strategy
KWNS	Keynesian welfare national state

LDF	Local Development Framework
LGA	local government association
MMS	multi-modal study
MUA	major urban area
NIMBY	Not in My Back Yard
NWDA	North West Development Agency
ODPM	Office of the Deputy Prime Minister
OECD	Organisation for Economic Cooperation and Development
ONS	Office for National Statistics
OSC	'other strategic corridor'
PAER	Priority Area for Economic Regeneration
PPG	planning policy guidance
PUA	Principal Urban Area
RAYH	Regional Assembly for Yorkshire and the Humber
RCEP	Royal Commission on Environmental Pollution
RDA	Regional Development Agency
REPC	Regional Economic Planning Council
RES	Regional Economic Strategy
RIBA	Royal Institute of British Architects
RICS	Royal Institute of Chartered Surveyors
ROSE	Rest of the South East
RPAA	Regional Planning Association of America
RPG	regional planning guidance
RSDF	Regional Sustainable Development Framework
RSPB	Royal Society for the Protection of Birds
RSS	Regional Spatial Strategy
RTP	Regional Transport Plan
RTPI	Royal Town Planning Institute
SAC	Special Area of Conservation
SCEALA	Standing Conference of East Anglian Authorities
SDOS	Strategic Development Options Study
SEEDA	South East England Development Agency
SERPLAN	London and South East Regional Planning Conference
SNCI	Site of Nature Conservation Importance
SSSI	Site of Special Scientific Interest
SWPR	Schumpeterian workfare post-national regime
SWRPC	South West Regional Planning Conference
TCPA	Town and Country Planning Association
TVA	Tennessee Valley Authority
VAT	value added tax
WCED	World Commission on Environment and Development
WMLGA	West Midlands Local Government Association
WSCC	West Sussex County Council
YHRA	Yorkshire and the Humber Regional Assembly

1 The re-emergence of the regions in spatial planning

> Britain has one of the most centralised systems of government in the western world. Decisions affecting our regions are often taken far away from the people and places they will affect. But there must be real doubt whether this has led to better government.
>
> (Cabinet Office and DTLR 2002, p. 1)

Once we were visionaries

Regional planners were once the grand visionaries of planning, attempting to create ambitious long-term plans for the future of large areas and all those who lived in them. From the high hopes and grand designs embedded in the regional planning efforts of Lewis Mumford and his Regional Planning Association of America (RPAA) colleagues in the United States in the 1920s and early 1930s, to Abercrombie's 1944 Plan for London, regional planning sought to offer large-scale solutions to large-scale problems. And though the reality rarely matched the vision of the plans (Hall 2000), from the Tennessee Valley Authority (TVA) with its massive infrastructure projects to London new towns such as Stevenage and Harlow, major changes did emerge out of some of these efforts. Today, though, the lofty aspirations of such planning pioneers seem almost quaint, anachronistic even, in an era which often seems to value pragmatism over vision, individualism over collectivism, and the short-term over the long-term.

It can sometimes seem as if low aspirations and expectations are the norm in much that today passes for regional planning and policy – but actually the grand ambitions and lofty rhetoric still remain. They live on in planning's new-found conviction that it can make a genuine difference to the agenda for sustainable development. It lives on too in the Regional Economic Strategies still being produced, where many regions aspire to be among the 'top twenty regions' in Europe or in the world. Regional plans and strategies still aim to make a difference.

Searching for 'new regionalism'

'Regions' tend to go into and out of fashion, academically and in terms of policy practice. Moreover, the dominant approaches to studying regions have also tended to change over time (Wheeler 2002; see also Table 1.1) from the emphasis on natural regions in the pioneering work of Geddes and Mumford, through to recent work on 'new regionalism'. The various approaches to regional studies are not wholly separate bodies of work, having developed from each other in many ways, nor were they chronologically discrete or internally coherent in their evolution. To add further complexity, while it is helpful to note some of the main thinkers who were associated with each approach, there are some key commentators, such as John Friedmann (e.g. Friedmann and Weaver 1979; Friedmann 1998) and Peter Hall (e.g. Castells and Hall 1994; Hall 1988, 1998, 2000), whose work transcends such categories. The intention is not to review all these approaches in this chapter, but rather to provide an overview of the evolving practice of regional development, with a particular emphasis on England, while Chapter 2 provides a more focused review of recent theoretical work on the institutional aspects of regionalism.

The main features prompting the current rise in interest in regionalism have sometimes been grouped together in the academic literature under the banner of 'new regionalism'. But as Wheeler's (2002) review of the 'new regionalism' in US planning notes, not only has the term been in usage over several decades in different contexts, but its contemporary usage has also involved different meanings in different national, disciplinary and professional contexts. For US planners, 'new regionalism' tends to be associated with the rise of 'new urbanism', with its attention to principles of sustainable development, especially social and environmental equity concerns, plus an emphasis on strategic approaches to planning and better urban design (e.g. Hough 1990; Calthorpe and Fulton 2001). 'New regionalism' in US planning is also associated with the need to address the political and administrative fragmentation found in many US metropolitan areas. A distinctive feature of the approach is its normative stance, where clear principles are set out as a central feature of the new strategies, almost invariably linked to the wider sets of discourses surrounding sustainable development.

The other widely noted usage of 'new regionalism' is that associated with the practice and academic critique of regional economic development. Here the concern is with the way in which regions are claimed to be an essential building block in economic management, as a consequence of profound changes in the nature and institutional shape of capitalist development. In academic terms, this is sometimes linked to critical debates about the nature of the transition of capitalist economies from previous 'Fordist' or Keynesian welfare national state approaches towards some form of 'after-Fordist' regime (Jessop 1990, 2002; Amin 1994; MacLeod 2001). The ability of national governments to exercise control over their national economies was seen to

Table 1.1 Eras of regional planning

Era	Key figures	Characteristics
Ecological regionalism, early twentieth century	Geddes, Mumford, Howard	Balancing countryside and city. Relatively holistic, normative and place based.
Regional science, late 1940s to present	Isard, Lösch, Wilson	Regional economic development, rooted in quantitative social science. Attempted to present analyses as value neutral, lacking normative framework. Spatial analysis rather than place oriented.
Critical regional geography, late 1960s to present	Cooke (1983), Harvey, Holland, Massey	Developed analysis of power and social movements within the region. Normative.
Planning's 'new regionalism', 1990s to present	Calthorpe, Hough, Rogers	Concerned with environment, physical planning and design, in addition to economic development. Normative. Place oriented.
Economic development's 'new regionalism', 1990s to present	Porter, Storper, Scott, Morgan, Cooke	Focused on institutions, non-traded relationships (trust etc.), democratic systems, economic development oriented. Concern with global competitiveness, mainly lacking an explicit normative agenda.

Source: Adapted from Wheeler (2002).

Note
See bibliography for key texts associated with each figure.

have been weakened by the increased internationalisation of economies associated with the deregulation of financial markets, improved transport and communications, and more porous national boundaries resulting from changes to protectionist trade barriers. Responding to these challenges, many governments radically changed their approach to economic management, moving to emphasise the need to develop regulatory environments more attractive to mobile capital, typically involving lower taxation levels, the provision of skilled workforces, and the reduction or remodelling of state regulation to meet business demands.

In consequence of such trends, for some commentators the nation-state has become increasingly less important as the key 'scale' of economic management. By contrast, reports of successful regions which are deemed to be competitive in the new global economy hold out hope of regions forming an essential building block within capitalist economies. Citing influential management (Porter 1990; Leadbetter 2000) and economic (Krugman 1997) thinkers, MacLeod (2001, pp. 804–805) summarises this viewpoint as meaning that 'far from signalling the "end of geography", the territoriality of globalization leads capital, institutions and technologies to be ever more intensely motivated by and stimulated through localized geographical agglomeration and spatial clustering'.

One of the most striking things about the current policy concern with regional competitive positions is that, in part at least, it is rationalised on academic and consultancy studies which have emphasised the importance of strengthening regional economic and democratic institutions. In particular, politicians and policy makers appear to have been attracted by accounts of a small number of regional success stories, which it is hoped might hold the secret for other regions to become more successful. These include Silicon Valley in California, Emilia-Romagna in Italy, and Baden-Württemberg in Germany (DiGiovanna 1996). In the United Kingdom too, apparent regional success stories have been identified and scrutinised for possible lessons for other regions, with the Welsh valleys, Silicon Glen in Scotland, and the M4 corridor and Cambridge in England all at various times held up as exemplars for other regions.

Academics, consultants and practitioners who have sought to identify, codify and critique elements of such success stories have had *selective* aspects of their work taken up by policy makers and used to justify attempts to adapt and replicate the ingredients said to be important in achieving successful regional economic development. This form of policy transfer has stimulated considerable academic controversy, initially in respect of the 'transition fantasies' associated with the literature on 'new industrial districts', and more recently in respect of the 'new regionalism' (see Amin 1994; Lovering 1999; MacLeod 2001). For instance, 'new regionalism' has been critiqued as a powerful new orthodoxy with shaky empirical and analytical foundations, representing 'the triumph of fashion and the influence of academic authority figures over social science' (Lovering 1999, p. 386). In addition, there is growing concern that failing to take into account the 'path-dependent regional economic and political geographies' of regional transformation runs the risk of repeating previous rushes to judgement about success models, only to find that their transferability is limited because of lack of attention to local, regional and national contexts (Jones and MacLeod 1999, p. 295). MacLeod's (2001) sympathetic critique of these debates suggests that some of the criticisms of the 'new regionalism' are well founded, whereas others are themselves based on a selective reading of the literature.

In short, there are lively and important academic and practitioner debates about the saliency of 'the region' as a key building block in the new global economy, and in particular about the types of strategy which are being pursued in order to promote regional success. In this chapter the emphasis is on developing an understanding of how regionalism has arisen as a policy area within the United Kingdom, focusing on regional planning.

Europe and the regions

The rise of regionalism in the United Kingdom owes much to the influence of European politics, including the emergence of stronger regional governance frameworks, for example in France, Denmark and Portugal, and the role of the European Union (EU) and European Commission in promoting the cause of regionalism. For much of the past two decades the European Union has been promoting greater political and economic integration between regions within Europe, working in ways which transcend national boundaries. The Commission's promotion of the concept of a 'Europe of the Regions' has been particularly important, politically acting as a means for it to work directly with local and regional governments rather than through their national governments, involving an approach based more on subsidiarity than on sovereignty.

As part of a growing emphasis on creating a 'Europe of the Regions', a Committee of the Regions was established with the Maastricht Treaty in 1991. One of the main rationales for this development was that the majority of the European Commission's policies require active local and regional government involvement, but the existing machinery did not encourage direct communication between sub-national governments and the European Commission. The role of the Committee, which comprises local and regional members nominated by each member state, is to comment on policies developed by the European Commission or the Council of Ministers which have regional or local impacts.

In addition, the European Commission has been active in seeking to identify and indeed bring into being a range of new transnational 'regions' as a way of creating new territorial connections within Europe. The Commission provides funding for a series of transnational, transboundary programmes to back selected regional approaches. For instance, the programme for the Atlantic Area covers parts of the United Kingdom, Portugal, France, Spain and the Republic of Ireland, seeking to develop integrated planning and management of coastal areas, the protection of natural areas and management of natural resources.

Particularly important in the context of this book was the growing interest in spatial planning coming out of the European Commission during the 1990s. This resulted in moves to promote a more integrated spatial development framework for the whole of the European territory (Shaw and Sykes 2001; Faludi 2002), with sufficient consensus among member states for them to agree to work together to produce the European Spatial Development Perspective (ESDP). This task was given to the Committee on Spatial Development, which produced a first public draft in 1997, the final document being approved by the Ministers responsible for spatial planning at Potsdam in May 1999.

The ESDP provides a non-statutory framework for spatial development in the EU, including influential statements on the scope and practice of 'spatial planning'. This concept of spatial planning is wider than traditional land use planning, typically involving:

- urban and regional economic development;
- influencing urban and regional population balance;
- planning, transport and communications infrastructure;
- protection of habitats, landscapes and resources;
- land use and property regulation; and
- coordination of the impacts of other sectoral spatial strategies (Tewdwr-Jones 2001).

The ESDP emphasises the adoption of integrated spatial development strategies at all scales, but in particular at the regional scale. These strategies are intended to be wide-ranging in scope, providing a long-term framework for all other activities which have spatial dimensions. In the UK context, integrated strategic spatial planning is now being carried forward principally through the regional planning system.

A short introduction to the emergence of English regional planning

While European politics help us to understand the recent rise of regionalism in England, over the longer term it has been national concerns which have been the dominant shaping force. Regional planning and the wider field of regional policy have played a fluctuating role in the management of the UK space economy over the past sixty years or so. In more general terms, the planning system has played a pivotal yet uneven role in British politics. In a relatively short period, planning has emerged as a central part of the formal regulatory apparatus for the state, particularly in relation to controlling land use. Alternatively, its parameters have been subject to continuing challenge, becoming increasingly involved in social and economic planning during the 1960s, only to experience a popular and political backlash before retreating to more of a land use function during the 1980s and early 1990s. In more recent years, the scope of planning has once again started to broaden, in part encouraged by the central role it has been allocated by central government in its pursuit of sustainable development (see Chapter 3). The important theme here is that planning is an important aspect of the state's approach to economic, social and environmental management, but that this has been pursued in different ways in different periods, and arguably in different ways in different parts of the country (Brindley *et al.* 1989, 1996).

Interestingly, in revisiting their classic study of six types of approach to planning, Brindley *et al.* (1996) began to argue that some of the distinctiveness which they had identified between different types of areas and their approaches had been lost, in part as a result of the rise of social and environmental agendas. Nonetheless, they felt that two distinctive approaches were still in evidence, broadly covering areas where growth management pressures were highest and areas where urban regeneration was a priority. These broad tendencies are still in evidence, though with the rise in the 'regional' approach, causal connections are increasingly being emphasised between the issues confronting both growth areas and problem areas, not least as the flight of capital and people out of inner cities is being linked to urban problems and to wider processes of globalisation (see Chapters 2 and 6). More than this, contemporary regional planning is being radically reworked by the way in which particular interpretations of sustainable development have been worked into it unevenly across the English regions, the key theme of this book. Any analysis of contemporary regional planning therefore needs to be conscious that it is inextricably linked to international, national, regional and localised economic and political structures and dynamics.

It is perhaps worth emphasising here the problematic nature of defining regions, which has been a constant recurring theme in the regional planning and geographical literatures (Glasson 1974; Powell 1978; Allen *et al.* 1998). The current 'regional scale' is largely a product of the creation of the wartime civil defence regions, which were then 'retained as an administrative convenience to assist post war reorganisation by bridging the gap between central government and local organisations' (Powell 1978, p. 5). The broad outline of the current English 'standard regions' used for government purposes was established in 1974, although there have been some boundary changes since. Indeed, even within the three years on which this book concentrates (2000–2002), three substantial counties were transferred from the South East region to the East of England region for planning purposes. In recent years too, Cumbria has passed from the North East to the North West region. To add further complexity, in some official documents Greater London is now treated as a region separate from the South East, having its own remit for producing 'regional' economic and spatial planning strategies (see p. 27).

What quickly emerges from this discussion is how fluid regional definitions are, even when simple administrative definitions of regions are adopted. Indeed, the widespread official use of the government's boundaries for 'standard region' disguises the underlying uneven and fragile awareness and acceptance of these regions, not least among the general public, whose place loyalty is often strongest towards localities, counties and sub-regional levels of consciousness (Powell 1978). Part of the problem faced by all forms of regional governance structures is, in fact, gaining acceptance by others that they operate at a meaningful scale. This means that, in effect, efforts to build regional strategies and plans also necessarily need to be directed to complex processes of place making, in the sense of trying to develop a wider acknowledgement and even ownership of particular definitions of what constitutes a 'region'.

Recent research on the South East region of England (Allen *et al.* 1998) highlighted the problematic nature of identifying a 'region'. The problematic nature of regions reflects both the multiplicity of possible regional boundaries and also the more deep-seated problem of isolating 'the region' as a scale for analysis, given the increasingly cross-scalar, interdependent nature of economic, social and environmental processes. Taking into account such issues, it is important to emphasise that the use of 'regions' is not unproblematic, with analysis needing to take account of the multiple scales within which 'regions' operate. Because regional planning in England is based on the official definitions of regions, we necessarily focus on these as our main regions for analysis, but seek to do this in ways which position regions within broader multi-scalar dynamics.

The history of the waxing and waning of interest in English regional planning and policy can be told in a number of ways: as an oscillation guided by shifting national party politics; as the story of planning visionaries and influential politicians, professionals and academics; or as a failing attempt to cope with some of capitalist crises of accumulation (see 'critical regional geography' in Table 1.1). Each of these approaches contains some explanatory value, but each is unsatisfactory on its own, variously paying too little account to individual agency, local and national politics or broader structural dynamics.

Take the issue of British party politics over the past fifty years. Throughout this period the Labour Party has tended to support regional approaches, reflecting its strong electoral support in the declining regions. By contrast, the Conservative Party has tended to regard regional institutions as an unnecessary addition to state bureaucracy, while regional government tends to be perceived as a political threat to the powers of Conservative-controlled shire counties. Valuable though it is to be aware of the party politics of enthusiasm for regionalism, on its own this is not enough to explain the different ways in which the regional approach has been pursued at different periods of time. In particular, party politics needs to be seen in relation to the waxing and waning of enthusiasm for regionalism in relation to periods of relative national economic growth.

Peter Hall (1988) provides a good example of linking key personalities and thinkers to a wide-ranging overview of developments in planning thought. But perhaps the clearest example of emphasising the role of individuals in explaining the changing fortunes of regional planning is the work of Simmons (1999), the London Planning Advisory Committee's Chief Planner. His useful overview links the development of regional planning to a number of professional, academic and political personalities. He argues that Abercrombie's work, especially the Greater London Plan of 1944, marks the 'first real flowering' of regional planning, while academic Peter Hall and Chief Planner Wilfred Burns are credited with providing the visionary inputs for plans for the South East in the 1960s and early 1970s. The arrival of the Thatcher era is said to have 'heralded a dark age for regional planning' (p. 160), with Michael Heseltine and Nicholas Ridley as successive Secretaries of State held particularly responsible. Simmons likewise attributes regional planning's revival since 1987 in part to politicians caving in to pressures from constituencies concerned about the future of the environment and housebuilders concerned about their own future.

Intertwining aspects of politics, people and the evolution of planning as a professional discipline, Wannop and Cherry (1994) provide a particularly robust overview and periodisation of regional planning. According to their review of both the professional and the academic literatures, it is possible to identify five key periods: the pioneering years (1920–1948), the fallow years (1949–1961), the regional revival (1962–1971), regional resource and economic planning (1972–1978), and regional planning 'scorned but enduring' (1979–1990s). Other useful overviews of the development of regional planning can be found in Glasson (1974), Alden and Morgan (1974), and Wannop (1995), all of which inform the overview provided here of planning since the 1960s. A separate case study is provided of regional planning in the South East, the most prosperous region in the country. The political economy context for the changing approaches to regional planning is returned to in Chapter 2.

Regional revival: the 1960s to the 1970s

Regional policy can be traced back to the 1930s, though it was only in the post-war period that regional policy moved from its very limited early geographical coverage of 'distressed areas' towards more of a national system (Wannop and Cherry 1994). The post-war regional policy system sought to address the North–South divide by linked policies for constraining growth in prosperous parts of the country and a system of incentives to induce employers to move to less prosperous areas (Glasson 1974; Alden and Morgan 1974). Though planning in the immediate post-war period was largely a local and central government activity, it did contain elements of a regional approach, most notably with the development of new town policy. However, there was no formal separate regional planning apparatus during this period, only central government's own regional apparatus.

Strong national growth and political changes during the 1950s meant that quite quickly, enthusiasm for strong regional interventions waned, with policies remaining on the books, but only weakly implemented. Rather than rehearse the detail of the evolution of regional policy in this period (see instead Table 1.2), in this section the focus is on the key policy changes since the 1960s.

After the first 'fallow' period for regional policy in the 1950s, a combination of change in national government and the economic slowdown saw regional policy strengthened from the early 1960s. Regional policy during that period involved a series of interventionist approaches for redistributing growth within the UK space economy, essentially from the growth regions in the south of England to the 'peripheral regions' in the north of England, parts of the South West, Wales, Northern Ireland and Scotland. The resulting mixture of direct and indirect support for industrial employment in the

Table 1.2 Active and less active periods of regional policy and planning

	Dominant regional institutional architecture	Dominant themes
Pioneering phase, 1920s–1948	• Appointed regional commissioners, central government ministries	• Post-Blitz plans for rebuilding cities, green belt policy, new town policy, decentralisation of the 'industrial population'
The fallow period, 1950s	• Central government ministries and New Town Commission	• Implementation of first phase of new towns • Limited application of regional policy tools
Regional revival, 1960s and 1970s	• Government ministries, regional industrial development associations • Creation of Regional Economic Planning Councils (REPCs) and Boards	• Industrial and population relocation • Regional corporatist bodies establishing non-statutory economic and physical strategies • Growing interest in sub-regional planning • Limited funding to regional bodies
The second fallow period, 1980s.	• Dissolution of both REPCs (1980) • Abolition of metropolitan county councils (1986)	• Rapid weakening of regional policy, with reined-in scope, financing and areal coverage • Growth in localised, short-term, business-led approaches
The second regional revival, 1990–	• Introduction of regional planning guidance (RPG) (1990) • Growth of regional partnerships for EU programmes, 1994 • Strengthening of RPG, 1998 • Regional Development Agencies, 1998 • Regional assemblies, 2000 • Regional Spatial Strategies (2003–)	• Gradual re-emergence of regional approach to 1997, then rapid expansion in regional institutions and number of strategies • Key themes: policy integration, sustainable development and competitiveness

declining regions amounted to the strongest form of policy interventions up to that date. In broad terms, the approach was to expand, strengthen and better fund the existing tools for redirecting growth from the prosperous regions to the peripheral regions (see Figure 1.1). With the Industrial Development Act 1966, the areas eligible for assistance increased to cover 40 per cent of the area of the United Kingdom. The creation of a new category of assisted areas in 1970, the 'intermediate areas', saw a further increase in coverage of the UK space to 50 per cent by 1972, covering a population of around 25 million (Glasson 1974; Burden and Campbell 1985).

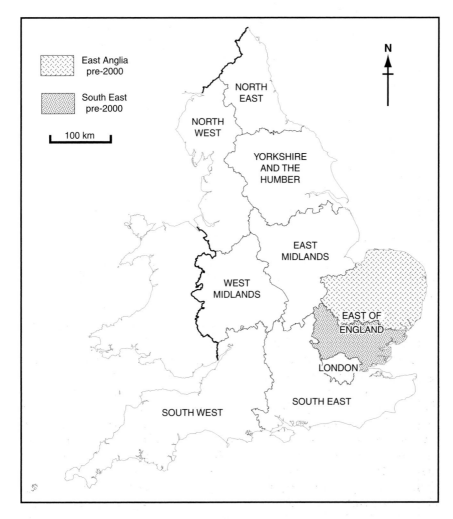

Figure 1.1 Standard regions in England. (Source: Based on ONS 2000. Crown copyright material reproduced with the permission of the Controller of HMSO and the Queen's Printer for Scotland (licence number C02W0002008).)

Reflecting the prevailing belief in national planning, the government became more interventionist in other aspects of industrial policy, many of which had a clear regional dimension, from the nationalised industries to the Industrial Reorganisation Corporation (Massey and Meegan 1978). Regional impacts were also felt from government policies for the retraining and movement of workers, plus a selective expansion of regional infrastructure, for instance new motorways, new town expansion and new industrial estates in the North East (Glasson 1974). During this period, regional industrial development associations and boards also began to emerge in the main assisted regions, helping to campaign on behalf of local authorities in the regions and to coordinate efforts to develop local businesses and to attract new ones.

Regional planning began to find favour too during the 1960s, largely as a response to projected substantial population increases. Regional and subregional planning exercises during the 1960s in part reflected the consequent search for potential new city locations, particularly in the major estuaries of the Humber, Severn and Tay, although by the early 1970s, as population growth slowed down, the search eased off (Wannop and Cherry 1994). During this period the dominant approach to regional planning remained top-down, with policies devised, largely funded and mainly delivered by central government departments and their agencies.

In institutional terms, the most significant developments was the spread of a variant of the tripartite corporatism of national industrial policy to the regional level, with the creation of the Regional Economic Planning Councils and Boards in 1965–1966. Located in each of the eight English standard regions, the councils were to assess the potential of each region, develop regional plans and to advise ministers on the regional implications of national policies (Glasson 1974; Thomas 1975). Each council had around twenty-five members, nominated by the government, coming from industry, local government, unions and a smaller representation from education and civil society groups. With a strictly strategic remit, the councils had few staff and little funds other than for analysis and the production of strategies. The Regional Economic Boards comprised fifteen to twenty civil servants from the main government departments, working to coordinate interdepartmental work and to advise on regional plans (Alden and Morgan 1974).

Despite their names, the Economic Planning Councils essentially produced physical planning analyses, though there was some variability between them in the attention they paid to economic and social issues. National political support for their work dwindled during the late 1960s, but in a later show of interest they were asked to assist in preparing regional plans during the early 1970s. In part drawing on the work of these councils, by the mid-1970s seven regional strategies emerged: four produced as tripartite efforts, one by local authorities and two by Economic Planning Councils themselves (Powell 1978). The Economic Planning Councils were soon subject to criticism for producing descriptive documents linked to population and other forms of forecasts, with only limited attention being paid to strategic development. Moreover, their essentially advisory role left them vulnerable to being ignored by local authorities and others (Glasson 1974; Alden and Morgan 1974). Indeed, one of the positive outcomes of the Economic Planning Councils, it was sometimes said at the time, was their inadvertent role in stimulating greater regional cooperation between local authorities, particularly in the planning sphere, as they sought to ensure that local government interests were not ignored.

So what happened to the 'strong' approach to regional planning and policy during the 1960s and 1970s? One explanation is that regional policy for redirecting industry had developed during a period of resurgent national economic growth, but it became hard to sustain this approach once growth faltered (Hall 1980). We return to the political economy aspects of these changes in Chapter 2, not least the rise of New Right thinking, with its challenging of the general interventionist approach of the state and emphasis on reducing the 'burden' of tax. The resulting policy changes meant that less government money was made available for pursuing interventionist regional policies. These changes were also linked to the increasing ability of businesses to move their investments across national boundaries, which meant that it became increasingly untenable to use planning powers to restrain industrial expansion in the South East, for fear of simply promoting factory closures or moves overseas. In effect, regional policy lost its 'stick', while the 'carrot' of subsidies came under increasing scrutiny in terms of its cost-effectiveness. In addition, planning at all levels was experiencing a substantial and long-lasting public and political backlash, as the system was charged with bureaucratic delays and insensitivity, not least in respect of the approach to slum clearance and the forced removal of existing residents (Healey 1998; Hall 2000).

Urban problems also started to rise up the policy agenda from the late 1960s, with London's inner-city problems in particular highlighting the folly of 'regional' efforts to subsidise the movement of jobs away from the capital's older industrial areas while starting to pour in 'urban' aid to attempt to revitalise them. In a very short period of time, policy attention shifted from the broad 'North–South' divide of previous regional policy approaches, to a recognition that growth regions such as the South East embraced inner urban and seaside areas with major economic problems, while some of the declining standard regions had within them areas of substantial economic well-being. The broadbrush approach to regional policy never quite recovered.

The second fallow period: the 1980s

From the early 1970s, regional aid was whittled down in scale, the areas deemed eligible were reduced in size, and aid became increasingly conditional, dealt with at national government level according to national priorities. This process was accelerated from 1979 when Margaret Thatcher and the Conservative Party came to power, motivated by a new intellectual and political agenda (see Chapter 2) which included a rapid dismantling of much of the apparatus of regional policy and planning as part of the Conservatives' reforms. Levels of regional assistance were further cut back, as were the eligible areas, while the Regional Economic Planning Councils, though not much loved, found themselves 'executed apparently without trial' (Hall 1980, p. 253). These were followed in 1986 by the abolition of the Greater London Council (GLC) and the metropolitan counties, which, apart from their political differences with the government, were deemed to be too remote and unpopular with their resident populations. For ten years, arguably longer, regional strategic planning was banished into the political wilderness (Breheny 1991).

By the early 1990s things began to change, only partly as a result of the replacement of Margaret Thatcher by John Major as Prime Minister. Regional economic policy began to be strengthened from the early 1990s in response to the opportunities afforded by access to European structural funds (Haughton *et al.* 1999). For planning too, the early 1990s saw considerable change, as controversies surrounding the overheating of the housing market in the South East in particular, linked to local political opposition to the development of new housing in many parts of the region, put regional planning back on the national political agenda. Linking to the growing concern with local and global environmental degradation, increasing public pressures emerged to prevent the loss of countryside and other open spaces to housing developments, leading to calls for more rather than less planning. With problems emerging from the lack of strategic planning for land use and physical infrastructure, business leaders too started to lobby for improvements to the system (Breheny 1991; Roberts 1996). In May 1990 a national system for regional planning was introduced, with a planning policy guidance note which emphasised the government's expectation that regional planning guidance (RPG) documents would be produced for most regions by the early 1990s (Roberts 1996).

Planning for the South East, 1940s–1980s

To provide a stronger sense of historical context for regional planning prior to the introduction of RPG, it is useful to examine the emergence of different approaches to planning for the South East region between the 1940s and the 1980s. Though not all the proposals from these earlier plans were put into action, enough were to make a major contribution to the changing post-war urban geography of the South East, not least new towns such as Stevenage, Crawley, Basildon and Milton Keynes.

It is worth noting here that the definition of 'the South East' tended to change quite dramatically over this period (see Table 1.3), and there have been changes too during the past few years, as we noted earlier.

Containment and planned overspill, 1945–1969

Patrick Abercrombie (1945) produced his *Greater London Plan, 1944* at the request of the Standing Conference on London Regional Planning, seeking to help guide the rebuilding of London after the heavy bombing of the capital during the Second World War. A landmark study in British planning, the report provided strong support for urban containment through the use of the metropolitan green belt, plus proposals for building better-quality homes in London at lower densities, requiring the dispersal of 'surplus' population to new satellite towns beyond the city's boundaries.

Over the next fifteen years, many of these policies were set in place, including the building of an initial ring of eight new towns around Greater London at a distance of 21 to 35 miles (34 to 56 kilometres), broadly in accordance with Abercrombie's approach, though using only two of his suggested locations. Long regarded as pioneering town planning experiments, these new towns were designed to be self-sufficient in terms of facilities and employment. Building on pre-war initiatives, the county councils in the region worked together to establish a metropolitan green belt within which development would be resisted in an attempt to prevent London's outward sprawl.

Twenty years later, responding to growing concerns about rapid population increases, a government team in 1964 produced the South East Study, and soon afterwards, in 1967, the South East Strategy was produced by the newly created Regional Economic Planning Council for the region. Though different in some respects (see Table 1.3), both proposed large-scale urban expansions outside the capital, plus continuing constraints on London's outward expansion (Figure 1.2). Although not all these proposals came to anything, three new towns were subsequently designated in 1968 – Milton Keynes, Northampton and Peterborough – and during the same period the metropolitan green belt was extended (Self 1982).

Moving away from decentralisation: the 1970s

The South East Strategy of 1970 was commissioned from the South East Joint Planning Team to reconcile some of the contradictions between the 1967 strategy and a draft regional planning framework produced by local authorities in 1968 (Buchanan 1972; Powell 1978). Led by the government's Chief Planner, the work was a collaboration between local authority and national planners, producing a massive five-volume report which, thanks to its strong central steer, was quickly adopted the next year (Powell 1978; Breheny 1991). The government's strategy review of 1976 updated these proposals in the light of major downward revisions for both population and economic growth. To get a sense of the confusion facing local planners looking for regional guidance during this period, it is worth noting Powell's (1978, p. 11) synopsis of the position:

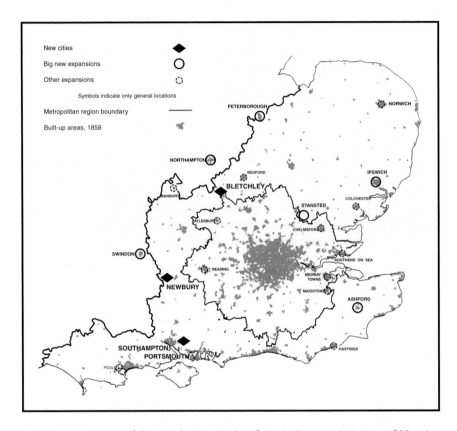

Figure 1.2 Key map of the South East Study of 1964. (Source: Ministry of Housing and Local Government 1964. Crown copyright material reproduced with the permission of the Controller of HMSO and the Queen's Printer for Scotland (licence number C02W0002008).)

> [T]he approved strategy for the South East following the 1976 review is the current response [to the strategic review of 1976] read together with the original plan [of 1970], the 1971 response to it and the development of the plan as contained in the 1976 review.

Small wonder, then, that planning came at that time to be perceived as bureaucratic, cumbersome and time-consuming.

The main change embodied in the plans for the 1970s was that policies for population decentralisation fell out of favour, partly following arguments that decanting surplus population might be adding to rather than solving the problems of inner areas in London. GLC planners were particularly prominent in drawing attention to the need to address the deindustrialisation and related unemployment problems of parts of the capital (Eversley 1975). But

Table 1.3 Principal regional plans for the South East, 1945–1976

Plan	Coverage	Main innovations	Spatial strategy
Greater London Plan, 1944	Circa 30 miles (50 kilometres) around London	Rebuilding post-Blitz and slum clearance demands major housing programmes. Creation of metropolitan green belt and dispersal from London of employment and people.	Constraint in London, plus dispersal of industry and population to eight new towns, c. 30 miles (50 kilometres) from London, around 30,000–50,000 population
South East Study, 1964	Massive extension, line from Wash to south coast, c. 100 miles (160 kilometres)	Planning for major population increase. Proposed major expansions of development plan allocations, plus more town expansions.	Constraint for London. Decentralisation on a larger scale: counter-magnets 50–100 miles (80–160 kilometres) from London, three new cities, six major expansions and twelve smaller expansions.
South East Strategy, 1967	Contracted boundaries, losing much of East Anglia (but not Ipswich) and some areas on south and west rim	Wider remit, as economic issues coming more to the fore. Produced by Regional Economic Planning Council.	Constraint for London. Growth concentrated in a few distant large counter-magnets, creating corridors: e.g. Ipswich–Colchester, Northampton–Milton Keynes, Southampton–Portsmouth.
South East Strategic Plan, 1970	Further contraction of boundaries – Ipswich no longer included	Still promoting employment dispersal from London, while Greater London Council plan is trying to stem it.	Constraint for London, plus mix of major and minor growth nodes outside the capital. The three largest were to grow to 1 million by 2001: S. Hampshire, S. Essex, and Reading–Aldershot–Basingstoke.
South East Strategic Plan Review, 1976	Uses 1974 'standard region'	Reversing decentralisation theme, introduces policies to stem population and employment loss in London	No further new town proposals. Constraint still in Rest of South East (ROSE).

more than this, as previously noted, the economic and political climate had changed by the mid-1970s, with costly interventionist policies increasingly frowned upon and policies to reduce state expenditure in the ascendant.

The 1980s and the 'deregulation' of planning

The decline of regional planning for the South East is reflected in the shift from the substantial analysis contained in the 1960s and 1970s to the increasingly slender documents of the 1980s. By 1980, regional planning for the South East was effectively reduced to a two-page letter from the then Secretary of State, Michael Heseltine, to the head of the regional planning conference, up-graded in 1986 to a six-page letter from his successor, Nicholas Ridley (Breheny 1991; Simmons 1999).

In the absence of a strong regional strategic planning system, through most of the 1980s developers were left to gauge for themselves how the planning system might respond to initiatives for new major development in the region. A consortium of private builders, Consortium Development Limited, which had been established in 1983, set out to pursue around thirty new settlement initiatives, believing that it had support from the government (Hall and Ward 1998). To the developers, the political climate appeared right for larger-scale private initiatives, with the government keen to see new houses built, keen to support the development industry but not at all keen to commit any of its own money to such major ventures. The proposals would have seen new country towns developed, with initial populations of at least 5,000. They were intended to have good public transport links, employment sites and a range of local facilities, such as shops and schools, to help encourage a degree of self-containment (Ward 1994).

Of the four major detailed proposals worked up by Consortium Develoment Limited, the most controversial was at Foxley Wood in Hampshire, a mixed-use scheme which, its promoters argued, would also provide jobs for a third of the resident workforce (*The Planner*, 6 October 1989). The government found itself caught between the lobbying of developers and the opposition of local residents within Conservative political heartlands (Thornley 1993). After initially accepting the proposal, following a change of Secretary of State the government eventually turned down the Foxley Wood scheme, along with two others. In reaching its decision, the government argued that the future distribution of new houses in Hampshire should be determined by the County Structure Plan rather than private housebuilders. Essentially these new settlement schemes reflected a fundamental contradiction in Thatcherism, which was that 'despite the ideological enthusiasm of the Thatcher government for such initiatives, they proved politically unacceptable for local voters' (Hall and Ward 1998, p. 63). None of the major, detailed schemes was to come to fruition.

First-generation regional planning guidance, 1990–1998

It is more than a semantic point that the new regional planning documents were called 'guidance', since they were not statutory plans, although local authorities were formally required to have regard to them when revising their structure and local plans. Potentially, RPG documents could be used in evidence by those objecting to local authority plans, which in itself meant that local planners had to be concerned about their contents. Because the process is central to later discussion in this book, the basics of the RPG system are introduced here.

In the early phase of producing RPG, local authorities were encouraged to join together in standing conferences to prepare *advice* on which the Secretary of State would base the *guidance*. In this process, then, the final version of RPG was produced and published by central government, through its regional offices. In other words, the process started off as a relatively 'bottom-up' affair, but in its final incarnation it became the product of a potentially centrally imposed approach.

As Breheny (1991) noted at the time, the fact that local planners worked on producing only 'advice' rather than draft guidance sent a signal that their suggestions would not necessarily be heeded. Though it was unlikely that a standing conference's advice would have been wholly rejected and replaced by a central government version, the possibility for this created tensions and a tendency to reduce the potential for conflict by producing rather minimalist and conformist forms of advice. Moreover, the requirement for local authorities to work together to produce their advice tended to result in a process which avoided conflict and hard choices by providing rather vague and short 'lowest common denominator' documents which lacked clear spatial direction on, for instance, where developments would or would not be permitted. Their main functional role was in allocating figures for new housing development for the main planning authorities within each region.

Reviews of the first generation of RPG point to the fact that the documents produced later in the sequence tended to be richer in their analysis, and more strategic in their content, and in the case of the West Midlands, the RPG started to move beyond narrowly defined land use issues and to link to other strategic documents and funding programmes (Thomas and Kimberley 1995; Roberts 1996; Simmons 1999). To turn momentarily to our earlier case study of the South East, it is perhaps worth noting that when RPG for the South East (RPG9) was released in 1994, it amounted to thirty-six pages plus six maps, a considerable improvement on the six pages of 1986 guidance, but still a thin, rather unsatisfactory document (DoE 1994d). (The second version of RPG9, released in 2001, grew to 102 pages plus thirteen pages of appendices.)

For all the improvements which took place after 1990, taken overall the first generation of RPG documents tended to be bland, lacked clear strategic content, focused too heavily on land use issues, and for much of their content tended to reproduce in modified form aspects of existing national planning guidance. In governance terms, this round of RPG was criticised too for being overly centralised, with central government involvement meaning that some of the regional detail found in the initial advice provided by local authorities was lost in the final documents (Baker 1996; Simmons 1999).

Devolution and the emerging regional institutional architecture of England, 1997–2003

With the election of a New Labour government in 1997, political devolution in the United Kingdom has become a central policy concern. In its first term the new government introduced political devolution in Scotland and Wales, while substantial efforts have been made to achieve a more durable form of devolution in Northern Ireland, although political tensions mean that these arrangements have been suspended by the national government. In addition, London has been given a new democratic forum, with the creation of the Greater London Authority (GLA).

A number of new regional institutions and strategies in England have emerged in the period since 1997 (Figure 1.3), the most important aspects of which are outlined here.

Regional chambers and assemblies

A central part of the emerging system of regional governance in England has been the growing influence of regional chambers, some of which were also known as regional assemblies. These initially developed as consortia of local authorities in the run-up to the national elections of 1997. Following the election of a Labour government in 1997 they began to grow rapidly in profile, responsibilities and resources. More recently, as the government's plans for devolution have progressed, they have been encouraged to broaden

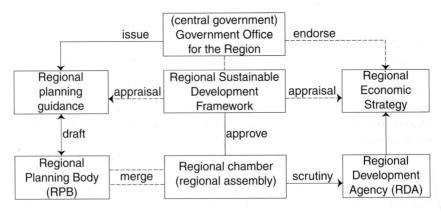

Figure 1.3 Principal regional bodies and strategies post-1998.

out in membership, becoming more like public–private partnerships, drawing heavily on the indirect electoral legitimacy of nominated local councillors, plus other key regional stakeholders (Newman 2001).

In their early incarnation, the role of regional chambers was mainly consultative, involving requirements that they be involved in consultations over all major regional strategies, though without the power of veto (Deas and Ward 2000; Jones 2001). As their remit has been expanded by central government, regional chambers have become more directly involved in producing regional documents in their own right, and the government has made them the principal body for holding to account the largest of the new regional institutions, the Regional Development Agencies (see p. 24).

The devolution White Paper *Your Region, Your Choice: Revitalising the English Regions* (Cabinet Office and DTLR 2002) suggested that Britain still had one of the most centralised government systems in the world. In proposing to move towards elected regional chambers, to be renamed regional assemblies, the government argues that the decision about whether actually to move towards this position should be left to individual regions. National government would provide a framework, but it would be for each individual region to consult about whether and, if so, when it should adopt an elected regional assembly, before moving to a regional referendum on the issue.

All the new assemblies are expected to provide a strategic vision for improving the regional quality of life, with a particular emphasis on economic performance. They will all benefit from money provided from central government finances, while those which opt for elected status will have a capacity to levy additional finance through supplements to the existing local authority tax system, provided all authorities agree. The functions of the assemblies will include economic development, skills and employment, housing, sports, culture, tourism, land use planning, environmental protection, biodiversity, waste and transport.

Government Offices for the Regions

A network of Government Offices for the Regions was created in 1994, under the government of John Major, which sought to develop stronger regional coordination between some of the main spending central government departments, including those responsible for regional policy, planning, transport, European structural funds and urban regeneration (Murdoch and Norton 2001; Newman 2001). The integrated government offices remain a central part of the current regional institutional architecture, not least in terms of regional planning, where it is Government Office officials who play the main role in representing central government interests and in producing the final version of RPG. However, the Government Offices have seen some diminution of their role with the rise of Regional Development Agencies (RDAs) in particular. In 2001, responsibility for coordinating the substantial funding for social exclusion initiatives under the Neighbourhood Renewal

Fund was given to Government Offices rather than to the RDAs. This development suggests that the government is not attempting to disempower Government Offices through creating new regional bodies; rather, it appears to be keen to keep its options open in terms of how regional policies might best be directed, delivered and monitored.

Regional planning guidance and Regional Planning Bodies

New arrangements for RPG were introduced from 1998, representing a reaction to criticisms of the previous RPG system plus the government's desire for a stronger system of regional planning (DETR 1998a, 2000a). The second generation of RPG documents were required to have a clearer strategic content, a stronger spatial component, and much greater consultation with stakeholders. With sustainable development introduced as a core objective for regional planning, the new approach was to be more sectorally integrated than previously, covering environmental, social and economic issues as well as land use matters. A summary Regional Transport Plan was also required in the new RPG documents, ensuring integration with this particularly important sectoral function. Sustainability appraisal (see Chapter 3) was introduced into the new arrangements, requiring that policies be assessed not only for their potential environmental impacts, but also for their social and economic implications.

Regional Planning Bodies, based largely on the standing conferences of local authorities, are charged with producing *draft* RPG under the new arrangements but are expected to engage in much closer consultation with other stakeholders than previously, in a marked shift from the previous arrangements for RPG. In some regions, stakeholders sometimes worked as part of the regional planning bodies, and in all regions stakeholders became involved in the sub-groups which sought to develop specific aspects of the draft document. As part of the government's wish to promote regional capacity in advance of regions' bidding for elected regional government status, Regional Planning Bodies are expected to merge with regional chambers/assemblies over time, with responsibility for producing draft RPG shifting to the merged body.

A new requirement was introduced for a formal public examination of the draft RPG (Figure 1.4). Written submissions on the content of draft RPG were invited from any interested bodies, and on the basis of these, the government-appointed public examination panel could choose the topics to be debated in public and the main protagonists whose views it wanted to hear further elaborated. Following the public examination, each panel produced its own report. At this stage, responsibility for revising the draft RPG passed from the Regional Planning Body to the Secretary of State (central government), being carried forward mainly by the relevant Government Office for the Region.

It is this second round of RPG which lies at the core of the analysis in this

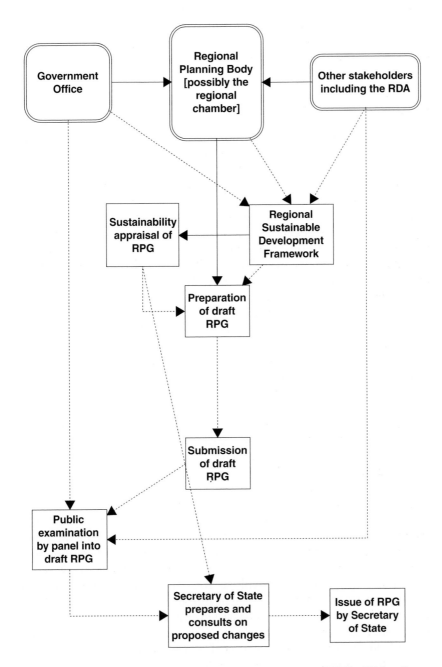

Figure 1.4 The regional planning guidance systems. (Source: DETR 2000a. Crown copyright material reproduced with the permission of the Controller of HMSO and the Queen's Printer for Scotland (licence number C02W0002008).)

book. Because the different stages of the process took place at different times in different regions, the key dates for the key stages are summarised here in Table 1.4. Recent proposals for reforming the system are dealt with in Chapter 8 on the future of regional planning.

Regional Development Agencies

The intention to create RDAs was announced in a White Paper, *Building Partnerships for Prosperity*, during December 1997 (DETR 1997). Following the Regional Development Agencies Act 1998, RDAs were established in April 1999 in each of the eight standard regions. A ninth RDA to cover London was established in July 2000 with the creation of the GLA.

Although primarily oriented towards economic development, the RDAs are expected to have regard to sustainable development in devising their policies and also to pay attention to the government's agenda on social exclusion. Each RDA is required to produce a Regional Economic Strategy (RES) in consultation with its stakeholders, which is then put forward to the government for endorsement (see Chapter 7).

The boards of the RDAs are mainly drawn from the private sector, followed by local government and other stakeholders, typically including members from the voluntary and education sectors. All the board members are appointed by *central* government, although nominations are invited in press advertisements. In the absence of a democratically elected tier of regional government in England, the RDAs are expected to consult and report on their activities with regional assemblies/chambers.

Reflecting the continuing sectoral fragmentation of policy in England (Healey 1998), RESs are separate from RPG. This said, the separate bodies responsible for RESs and RPGs are expected to consult with each other and to take account of the policies being developed elsewhere, though with neither document taking precedence over the other.

Regional Sustainable Development Frameworks

With the growing number of regional strategies set in motion by the Labour government, concerns about lack of coordination and conflicting priorities began to emerge, which probably contributed to the announcement in 2000 that each region should establish a Regional Sustainable Development Framework (RSDF). As part of its guidance on producing these documents, the government indicated that it expected that these should provide a high-level vision for sustainable development in each region which all other regional documents would be expected to take into account. The RSDFs were to be consulted upon widely within each region, setting out a range of objectives and priorities, backed up by indicators and targets. In order to ensure regional ownership, the resulting documents had to be endorsed by regional chambers, but not necessarily produced by them directly.

Table 1.4 Progress in preparing regional planning guidance (RPG), as at April 2003

Region RPG[a]	'Old-style' RPG	Draft 'new-style' RPG[a]	Public examination	Panel Report	Proposed changes	Final RPG
North East[b] (RPG1)	Sept. 1993	Dec. 1999	June 2000	Oct. 2000	April 2001	Nov. 2002
East Anglia (RPG6)	July 1991	Aug. 1998[c]	Feb. 1999	July 1999	Mar. 2000	Nov. 2000
East Midlands (RPG 8)	Mar. 1994	Nov. 1999	June 2000	Oct. 2000	Mar. 2001	Jan. 2002
South East (RPG9)	Mar. 1994	Dec. 1998	May/June 1999	Oct. 1999	Mar. 2000	Mar. 2001
South West (RPG10)	July 1994	Aug. 1999	Mar. 2000	Aug. 2000	Dec. 2000	Sept. 2001
West Midlands (RPG11)	Dec. 1998	Oct. 2001	July 2002	Oct. 2002	n.a.	n.a.
Yorkshire and the Humber (RPG12)	Mar. 1996	Oct. 1999	June/July 2000	Oct. 2000	Mar. 2001	Oct. 2001
North West (RPG13)	May 1996	July 2000	Feb. 2001	Aug. 2001	June 2002	Mar. 2003

Notes

a Dates of final drafts submitted to public examination (most regions published earlier public consultation drafts).

b Previously (old-style RPG) Northern Region (RPG7).

c Reissued following previous publication under old arrangements in February 1998.

Other regional partnerships and plans

A wide range of other regional partnership arrangements have been established and a wide variety of strategy work is under way as a result of the government's enthusiasm for regional-scale strategic thinking. These regional partnerships and plans cover topics as diverse as European funding, housing, biodiversity, energy and culture. It is important to note that regional actors have also been encouraged to establish voluntary sustainable development round tables, or similarly named bodies, to take forward work on sustainable development.

Sustainable development and regional asymmetries in approach

The central concern of this book is to examine how notions of sustainable development have been used to inform the recent development of regional spatial planning across the English regions. With the greater devolution to regional bodies, the potential has emerged for some regions to develop 'stronger' approaches to sustainable development than others. But the very notion of what might be considered a 'stronger' approach to sustainable development is itself highly problematic, given that the term has been open to substantial critique and reformulation. Whereas some analyses talk of the hijacking of the term 'sustainable development' (Davies 1997; Mittler 2001), our approach is actually to regard the way in which the term is mobilised as a political strategy, which itself becomes the subject of analysis. In our interpretation, sustainable development is less of a clear-cut, stand-alone concept; rather it is both a political resource, drawn on selectively by people, and a battleground for ideas and conflicting ideologies. In this view, selective interpretations of sustainable development are important because of how they are adopted and adapted in order to achieve legitimate broader strategic approaches to managing economic, social and environmental change. Planning is important in this largely because it has been allocated a key role in taking forward the government's work on sustainable development (see Chapter 3).

The shift towards greater regional-scale policy interventions is important because of its reworking of power dynamics within and beyond regions. Regionalism too, then, is both a political strategy and a political resource, mobilised in ways which tend to favour certain interests and certain groups more than others. So although regionalism represents a useful opportunity to break away from the competitive localism of 1980s local economic policy (see Chapter 7), it has in many ways reinvented this logic through its support for processes of competitive regionalism, in the process empowering a new set of institutional actors. Hence, regionalisation is best seen in relation to its impacts and continuous interactions with other scales of policy, from the local through the national to the international scales. This is a theme we return to in Chapter 2.

It is perhaps worth noting here that devolution in other parts of the United Kingdom has progressed much more rapidly than in England, and there has been much greater devolution of planning powers to Scotland, Wales and Northern Ireland as new, devolved political administrations were established in these territories (Allmendinger and Tewdwr-Jones 2000; Counsell *et al.* 2003). In addition, London has gained a new statutory authority, the GLA. All the post-1997 devolved administrations have started to draw up plans for restructuring their planning systems, taking the opportunity to break further away from the English-dominated planning systems of the past. By 2001 the four newly devolved administrations, in Scotland, Wales, Northern Ireland and London, had all issued statements on planning which placed sustainable development and greater integration at their heart. So, in addition to the potential for asymmetrical development of approaches to sustainable development across the regions of England, the focus of this book, there is the potential for even greater differences to emerge between the English regions and other parts of the United Kingdom.

Conclusions

Contemporary regional planning and policy is both less and more than it was in its earlier incarnations. Where once regional policy was expected to address national policy goals such as achieving a more balanced distribution of economic opportunities through directive policies to redistribute jobs and people around the country, contemporary policy makers have to come to terms with their more circumscribed powers, resources and legitimacy. Ironically, perhaps, while regional policy efforts to 'level out' in terms of national equity have been dismantled as unrealistic, regional policy is now expected to achieve even more ambitious goals, in terms of promoting sustainable development and helping regions become more competitive in global markets.

In the context of the waxing and waning of interest in regional approaches to planning and policy, the contemporary period is one of resurgent regionalism in most Western economies, not least the United Kingdom. The result has been a rapid rise in the prominence of both regional planning and regional policy, with the two still largely separate domains of activity in the case of the United Kingdom, although there is considerable evidence of an emerging shift in favour of promoting a more integrated approach towards spatial planning.

In the case of England, the rise of the regional agenda in the past decade can be summarised as the culmination of a wide variety of different concerns, including:

- structural economic and political changes associated with globalisation and the changing role of the nation-state;
- the growing influence of European thinking on regionalism;

- growing concern that a lack of strategic planning was destabilising for businesses and also contributing to environmental deterioration;
- the development of influential academic work on regional policy; and
- specific national and regional political pressures, for instance to address the housing crisis in the south-east of England.

Since the election of a New Labour government in 1997 there has been a clear trend towards political devolution and an associated proliferation of regional institutions and strategies across the United Kingdom. These developments create possibilities for growing divergence in approach across the English regions, which in theory at least has the potential to create more innovative approaches to regional policy and development. How the main spatial strategies of the new regional system work to promote sustainable development, defined broadly here as having social, economic and environmental goals, is the unifying theme for what follows.

2 Governance, institutions and regional planning

This, then, is what we have come to in four decades of planning, starting from a credo in a centralized benevolent state which was assumed to have a far-sighted and comprehensive vision of the public good to the present welter of a triumphant market economy driven by global competition, an emasculated national state in retreat, a plethora of social movements vying for our attention and support, and a burgeoning sector of voluntary organizations fiercely competing among themselves for private and public resources that are becoming ever more scarce.

(Friedmann 1998, p. 20)

From state-led planning to a more complex future

Although Friedmann's assessment of planning's recent history may not fully account for the fluctuating fortunes of regional policy and planning in England, it comes quite close to doing so. The strong central state which could oversee the implementation of some radical attempts to rework the regional and urban geography of the country, seeking to intervene directly to control the movement of jobs and people, is no longer willing and able to operate in that manner. But there is a danger of over-reading the 'strong central state' argument here, and likewise a danger in overemphasising the current supposedly hegemonic grip of the market-based approach to managing the economy.

In the case of planning's apparent shift from an era of strong government to one of strong markets, for instance, it is helpful to recall Storper's argument (1998, p. 244, drawing on Latour 1993) about the dangers of attempting to separate out pure structures: 'what we consider modern, e.g. states, civil societies, markets, has never really existed, except as convenient but wrong abstractions. What has existed are complex hybrids.' The particular value of this insight here is that it helps emphasise that rather than a simple shift from a strong state-led system to a strong market-based one, complex hybrid approaches have emerged. The difference is important, as it speaks of the complex negotiations across state, market and civil society boundaries which characterise the messiness of how planning operates and is continuously being redefined in its scope and in its approaches.

This chapter sets out to explore the ways in which the practice of regional spatial planning is linked to wider debates about governance, scale and knowledge. Following a section on changing approaches to governance, with an emphasis on the strategic and spatial selectivity of the state, the analysis turns to a wider conception of selectivity in relation to the creation and use of particular knowledges and their associated discourses in the analysis and practice of regional planning and policy. The analytical thread is the selectivities and processes of contestation involved in regional planning, in terms of how people are drawn into the process, its scope and its preferred techniques. As part of this overview, institutionalist approaches are also drawn on, as they provide further insights into the detail of how selectivity operates, especially the complex negotiations which are a central feature of contemporary plan making.

State theory and the shift from welfarism to innovation and competition

The central argument of this section is that changes in regional planning and policy need to be analysed in relation to the wider political, economic, social and environmental transformations which have been taking place in recent years. The emphasis is on the wider reworking of state powers – in particular, the emergence of new governance structures. State theory has long grappled with the problem that the boundaries of what constitutes 'the state' are fuzzy, with commentators using the term in different ways, including the widespread use of 'the state' simply to mean the political and administrative apparatus of governments. A broad definition of the state is used here: we adopt Gramsci's 'integral state', embracing both political society and civil society (Jessop 1990, p. 6).

Though there are many possible approaches to understanding the development of the capitalist state, the focus here is on regulationist-inspired work on state theory and the institutional turn in economic geography. Of particular interest is work on the strategic and spatial selectivity of the state (e.g. Jones, 1997, 2001; Brenner 2000; Jessop 2000). Much of this work draws on Jessop's strategic relational approach, which moves some way beyond more structural accounts of regulation theory in the way in which it builds in issues of political struggle and contingency (Jessop 1990, 1997, 2001). This approach is valuable because it seeks to ground an understanding of abstract tendencies in capitalism in analysis of the concrete ways in which these work out empirically in different ways in different places and at different times. The result is an increasingly sophisticated and still evolving body of work which helps in analysing many of the key political economic changes of the past sixty years or so.

It is worth emphasising at the outset that reviews of state theory have raised continuing concerns on three main accounts: assumptions about the relative autonomy of the state; a tendency to economism; and a tendency towards top-down accounts of state power, with a Gramscian emphasis on hegemony rather than resistance (see Jessop's 2001 review of recent state theory developments). It is fair to say that some of these criticisms could also apply to Jessop's strategic-relational approach to state theory (Cox 2002). We would add a fourth concern, which is the limited attention paid to the ways in which discourses of globalisation and competitiveness and debates on sustainable development and global environmental change have come to be mutually constituted. In this overview, therefore, we attempt to address these shortcomings by drawing out aspects of state theory which emphasise the contestability of state actions. In particular, our approach argues that the rhetorics of 'competitiveness', 'globalisation' and 'sustainable development' have come to be mutually constitutive, such that attempts to understand state restructuring in the UK context in particular without devoting attention to the powerful political logics of sustainable development are incomplete.

Developing an account of what he terms 'Atlantic Fordism', Jessop (2000b, 2002) argues that John Maynard Keynes was the emblematic economist associated with the rise of national state welfarism from the 1930s to 1960s in countries such as the United Kingdom, leading him to talk of the rise of the Keynesian welfare national state (KWNS). The Keynesian approach is generally identified with an emphasis on state intervention to achieve full employment within relatively closed national economies. With the much-remarked-upon breakdown of Keynesian welfarism during the 1970s came a broad-ranging critique from the 'New Right' of the failings of the mixed economy approach, as opposed to market-led economic growth. Preparing the way for neoliberal approaches to economic management, government was rhetorically recast as villain rather than saviour, and private enterprise recast as saviour rather than untrustworthy adventurer. Inspired by a variety of New Right thinking, the neoliberalist philosophies of Anglo-American governments since the late 1970s have led to political rhetorics about rolling back the frontiers of the state, deregulation and privatisation, reducing red tape, letting the market decide, and increasing personal freedoms while emphasising personal responsibilities.

Jessop (2002) argues that it is Joseph Schumpeter, with his emphasis on innovation and competitiveness, who needs to be seen as the emblematic figure for the system which is currently emerging, which he refers to as the Schumpeterian workfare post-national regime (SWPR). In this approach, creative innovation is associated with greater entrepreneurialism on the part of both individuals and businesses, with the role of the state becoming to encourage this through supportive re-regulation, and pulling out of areas where the private sector could provide products or services. Rather than entitlement-based approaches to welfare, individual responsibility and empowerment is emphasised, hence the reference to workfarism in the term 'SWPR'. The Keynesian emphasis on state planning to coordinate market activities within national economies is superseded in this approach by an emphasis on international competitiveness and the order imposed by market disciplines, regulated by a supervisory rather than an interventionist state. With the growing influence of internationalisation and the opening up of government systems, there has been a shift from the dominant institutional fix of the 'nation-state' under the KWNS, to the more broadly constructed multi-scalar governance regimes of the SWPR.

Largely missing or relegated in importance within this analysis is the way in which 'sustainable development' has been inserted into global agendas for competitiveness and globalisation. With its three inter-related themes of economic growth, social equity and environmental responsibilities, sustainable development has come to legitimate processes of global competitiveness and expansion, by neutralising opponents who would argue that growth is necessarily socially polarising and environmentally damaging. But in order to retain its legitimacy and disciplinary potential, sustainable development has also played a role in ensuring that state growth strategies have not been based simply on untramelled economic growth, providing a framework for discourses of growth management which also promote social welfare and environmental well-being. Policy makers, then, necessarily must seek to find ways of containing the tensions between economic, social and environmental goals, in the process searching for effective forms and blends of re-regulation, from fiscal policies through to formal regulatory interventions such as planning. Moreover, in seeking to work out accommodations for these tensions, decision makers need to adopt techniques which reflect changed expectations of policy processes that derive from a growing pluralisation of ideas, goals and actors.

At this stage it is worth introducing some cautionary warnings. In general, accounts informed by regulation theory, such as this, can provide useful insights into periods of capitalist economic stability, but are far less successful in explaining the shifts from one regime of capitalist accumulation to another (Amin 1994; Hay 1995; Jessop 1995). In particular, Jessop has argued that his work can help reveal *tendencies* in the development of capitalism, but that these need to be seen as descriptive and generalised, rather than explanatory or generalisable (Jessop 1995, 2000b). This links to a related concern that there are serious analytical problems in attempting to read off local responses from macro-changes in capitalist accumulation regimes (Hay 1995; Goodwin and Painter 1996). Accordingly, it is important to relate abstract tendencies in capitalism to their concrete and contingent articulation at particular times and in specific geographical contexts (Jessop 1995; MacLeod and Goodwin 1999). Moreover, broad categorisations such as 'Fordism' and 'Keynesian welfare national state' should not be used to disguise the fact that the approaches which they seek to encapsulate evolved over time, and that they often varied substantially from place to place (Peck and Tickell 1995b).

Governance and globalisation tendencies

There is now considerable work on how hierarchical and relatively closed-off systems of govern*ment* might be said to have given way to new, more porous systems of govern*ance*, bringing into the policy process a much wider range of institutional actors (Rhodes 1997; Pierre and John 2000; Newman 2001). The shift towards governance has seen a range of non-governmental actors brought closer to the centre of policy making and policy delivery, including both private-sector actors and civil society organizations. Aspects of this trend include the privatisation and contracting out of government functions, through which the role of government has increasingly been transformed from that of a direct provider of services to that of a facilitator and (re-)regulator for the competitive provision of services. The growth of governance in its many forms is also linked to a substantial growth in the number and range of institutions involved in processes of sub-national governance, with business, community action and environmental groups, plus education, crime and health institutions, all increasingly prominent in local and regional regeneration activities, for instance. Indeed, various forms of cross-sectoral partnership now represent the dominant institutional form in regeneration activities in the United Kingdom and in many other nations.

Although most attention has been paid to the growing role of businesses in sub-national governance systems (e.g. Peck and Tickell 1994, 1995a; Strange 1997; Ward 1997; Valler *et al.* 2000), the rising influence of civil society organisations also merits attention (Harding 1996; Haughton and While 1999). Since the 1960s, a rapidly expanding array of interest groups has become involved in challenging the dominant discourses and practices associated with governments, businesses and the broader apparatus of the state. This has involved both a quantitative and a qualitative shift, with some non-governmental organisations becoming influential bodies in terms of their membership and their lobbying capacity. In the field of the environment, for instance, there has been a growth in the membership of key groups plus a growing proliferation of local branches of the main organisations, and of local independent organisations. In addition, there has been a wealth of less formal groupings of activitists, sometimes pursuing particular local or short-term aims (e.g. road protestors), sometimes pursuing global, long-term aims such as the reform of the World Trade Organisation (McCormick 1995; Doyle and McEachern 2001). These groups have in varying ways sought to challenge the legitimacy of certain state actions, sometimes directly questioning the selectivity of the state in its scientific and philosophical understanding of development and environmental concerns. Responding to the political pressures mobilised by such groups, at all levels from the local to the global, governments have sought to engage more actively with civil society groups, in terms of both the strategic and the operational aspects of policy making.

For civil society groups, being drawn into the emerging systems of governance results in a continuing blurring of state–civil society boundaries, as groups are incorporated selectively into the apparatus of the state. The selectivity involved means that it is those groups most willing to endorse state actions and programmes which are accorded greatest access to state decision-making processes and also funding regimes. It is this selectivity which has led to criticisms that groups risk being incorporated into the hegemonic strategies of the state, lending their legitimacy in return for limited financial rewards and few fundamental changes to policy (Storper 1998).

One of the most important recent changes in political economy has been the shift away from the 'taken-for-grantedness' of the national economy as the focus for economic management, in favour of 'new narratives of international competitiveness, economic flexibility, entrepreneurialism, and decentralised forms of governance' (Jessop 1998, p. 39). Globalisation, in this reading, is seen to require local actors to come together to find ways of capturing and retaining mobile capital within their areas, where globalisation becomes the necessary backdrop to policies for localised pro-business growth agendas. In a related vein, sustainable development debates have focused both on the need for global agreements to address global environmental issues, and on the need for 'new localism' discourses premised on the notion that it is local actors who are best positioned to address many of the concerns of sustainable development (Marvin and Guy 1997).

The emergence of the agendas of global competitiveness and sustainable development over the past twenty years in part reflects the already remarked-upon growing porosity of national economies and improved communications technologies, plus awareness of global resource and pollution flows. The result is that discourses of 'globalisation' are used to legitimate the selective adoption of problems for the state to address at different levels, and also for a selective declaration of policy interventions no longer possible for national governments because of 'globalisation'. Interestingly, however, this can work both ways. So, for instance, global environmental concerns and European environmental legislation can be used to argue both for reducing the role of the state (e.g. water privatisation) and for increasing it (e.g. implementing higher water quality standards). In the English case in particular, it is fair to say that European debates have helped push forward environmental policy as a result of the strengthening of the environmental legislation required of member states of the EU.

The trend towards internationalisation is strongly evident in the changing approaches to rationalising and promoting regional economic development, where the agenda has shifted from *compensatory* policies for redressing imbalances within the national space economy to competitive 'catch-up' policies for promoting the international *competitiveness* of regions (see Chapters 1 and 7). Globalisation is best seen not as an unproblematic set of external (natural) market forces, then, but rather as a rhetorical device for 'post-national' states seeking to legitimate policies for lower business taxation and selective re-regulation. In regional policy, globalisation has become central to arguing that many forms of interventionism are no longer possible or desirable, and that the only viable approach available is supply-side policies which help build 'internationally competitive regions' able to compete in the global market-place for international investment.

One result of these shifts is that the terminologies associated with sustainable development and competitiveness have become central to recent planning debates, generating important controversies about how these concerns should be translated into policy. In particular, globalisation tendencies have served to re-emphasise the importance of place-making activities at local and regional scale, as policy-makers seek to build positive images in order to attract and retain both mobile investment and consumer spending within localities. Sustainable development likewise has become an important framing device for justifying particular approaches to place making, notably its attempts to improve quality-of-life conditions, from environmental standards through to supporting the provision of higher-quality housing.

The rise of multi-scalar governance

With responsibilities, funds and, to an extent, powers increasingly being reworked vertically to both supra-national and sub-national governance organisations, and horizontally to new institutional actors such as partnerships, nation-states have become decentred or 'hollowed out', though they have not necessarily become any weaker. Seen in this light, the current growth in regional institutions for economic development and planning in England represents a broader restructuring of the state which has to be analysed in the context of the wider scalar restructuring of state powers, from the local through to supra-national levels.

Jessop (1990, 2000a) argues that rather than losing power through recent 'hollowing out' tendencies, the 'strategic selectivity of the state' means that the state has retained a strong 'steering' capacity over the new governance arrangements (see also Jones 1997; Pierre and Peters 2000). This selectivity means that, though it is less directly involved in delivering policy, the state can retain much of its influence by virtue of deciding which bodies it will lend its powers, resources and legitimacy to, retaining the power to rescind its favours if the new arrangements are not to its liking. In this way, the state becomes involved in the government of governance, or meta-governance or meta-steering (Jessop 1999, 2000a). This approach has been extended to a concern with the spatial selectivity of the state; it is argued that in deciding which *scales* to favour in devolving responsibilities, nation-states remain important in shaping the emergent new rules of the game (Jones 1997; Jessop 2000a; Peck 2002). For the arguments in this book, the important implication is that the emergence of regional-scale policies is both a strategic and a political choice, and one that needs to be analysed as an issue of power struggles which range across scales.

Choices of policy scale, such as the current privileging of regional-scale organisations, represent wider struggles over social and power relations, which can privilege certain types of policy and policy actor over others (Jonas 1994; Smith 2003). There is a danger of over-reading arguments of the rescaling of goverance, particularly in the current context of major reworking of institutions at all scales, which suggests that a better way of thinking about this issue is multi-scalar governance. This phrase captures something of the complexity of how policies work out across scales. For instance, interest groups may work across scales in their activities, whereas different factions of, say, the business lobby group may also perceive and pursue their interests in very different ways at different scales (Cox and Mair 1991; Jonas 1994).

Despite the widespread view that planning remains dominated by central government (Cowell and Murdoch 1999; Healey 1999), it is possible to see evidence of multi-scalar governance in planning along these lines. For instance, there is the growing attention to regional planning as a mediating influence between the national and the regional planning systems, and also the increased attention to the ESDP. Arguably, then, in planning too there is evidence of a slowly emerging shift away from the dominant national institutional fix of a hierarchical, directive and top-down system towards more 'fluid, unstable and multiscalar regulatory configurations' (Peck 2002, p. 356). Yet it is unhelpful to take this line of argument too far, since in England planning remains a strong and relatively stable statutory framework, and retains its hierarchical shape. Planning, then, is becoming both more multi-layered and more porous, in the sense of being open to wider influences, while keeping its essentially hierarchical structure.

Where authors such as Offe (1975, 1984, 1985) stress how the state works selectively with those best positioned to help it pursue its goals, Jessop emphasises the state as a site of power dynamics, rather than an arbiter of power. In this sense, the power dynamics of a range of actors are mediated through state structures rather than simply by them. In this interpretation the state is a 'social relation', where the state apparatus is not driven by a single set of priorities, but rather is the site of a multitude of competing pressures and demands, which can involve a range of competing and contradictory regulatory and policy tendencies. Building local contingency and political struggle into the analysis helps highlight how particular state forms may be more or less amenable to given influences at different moments in time and in different places (Brenner 2000). Moreover, far from being passive, states seek to generate and take forward strategies, but in order to do this they need to negotiate and broker continuously between the interests of supportive, less supportive and oppositional forces, in the process becoming an institutional site of struggle, contradiction and tension (MacLeod and Goodwin 1999).

This relates to one of the themes of this book, which is how 'sustainability' discourses demonstrate the difficulties faced by the state in reconciling a host of competing demands, such as consolidating political legitimacy and ideological hegemony, regulatory pressures from the EU, and the demands of different locally dependent interests. Seeing the state as a social relation helps to conceptualise the state itself as a set of (potentially) competing and con-flictual priorities and interests. Regulatory changes, rescaling of state powers, and changes in state discourses all work towards providing better ways of resolving some of these conflicts, but in doing so open up the possibility for new areas of struggle, conflict and challenge. The outcome of such struggles is always contingent on multi-scalar political struggles which coalesce around key sites of regulation, including spatial planning. These struggles are in turn conditioned by the powers and resources of key interests within the context of the strategic and spatial selectivities of the state. At this moment of trans-ition in environmental, social and economic management, sustainability and globalisation have emerged as highly contested notions, as state and non-state actors alike search for a longer-term 'institutional fix' for helping to create localities and regions which are attractive to international investors and local stakeholders alike.

There are dangers in over-reading this type of state-centred analysis, in particular of underestimating the extent to which devolution and the opening up of systems of governance, though selective and conditional, can actually devolve levels of power which sub-national agencies, for instance, can use in their struggles with the state. These impacts may be evident not so much in terms of direct impact on negotiating powers, but in the more subtle ways in which the political negotiating climate between the state and other actors is influenced by the publicly stated intention to operate in a more devolved and consensual way.

Neoliberal experimentation, the lottery of policy formation and regional planning

The past quarter-century has witnessed constant and sometimes frenetic experimentation with ways of redrawing the boundaries between the state, civil society and the market, guided by an emerging understanding of the possibilities of and limits to the neoliberal approach to policy formation. Neoliberalism refers to the market-led approach to economic management, which involves a reduced role for the state, the promotion of international trade, and deregulated financial markets in an attempt to improve the mobil-ity of capital. Neoliberalism seeks to normalise 'free market' forces and prin-ciples as an economic ideal and as a political ideology.

Rolling back the frontiers of the state in order to reassert market primacy was a central part of this ideological agenda, with urban and regional policy high on the list of areas where less government was deemed to be better government, allowing the space for the market and civil society to expand. In its early manifestations, roll-back neoliberalism was marked by a strong hostil-ity to the interventionist state, tripartite corporatism and municipal socialism, leading to sweeping reforms to dismantle their organisational base (Peck and Tickell 2002). Where some form of government activity was still deemed necessary, new organisational forms emerged which reflected a more pro-market approach to policy making (Jessop 1999; Jones and Ward 2002). In English urban policy, for instance, funds were gradually shifted from the Urban Programme, with its approach involving partnership between central and local government, to urban development corporations, which were central government-appointed, private sector-led bodies with a strong emphasis on property and economic development (Haughton and Roberts 1990). Corporatist Regional Economic Planning Boards were abandoned in the early 1980s and not replaced. In these and many other ways, the institutional fabric was changed, but only temporarily so, as the limits of the new market-led institutional arrangements began to emerge (Jessop 1999; Peck and Tickell 2002). The narrow property and economic focus of urban development corporations lost favour as social and environmental issues rose up the political agenda, while their limited local accountability left them vulnerable to their critics (Haughton 1999a; Imrie and Thomas 1999). Regional planning re-emerged as businesses discovered the hard way the problems created by a lack of market coordination, particularly in housing (Breheny 1991).

Some of the early reformist zeal has been transformed in recent years, then, as governments have had to acknowledge the limits of the market-based approach, and the need for alternative systems of coordination (Jessop 1999). In urban and regional policy this has involved an enormous institutional turnover as discredited institutions and programmes have been revamped, renamed or simply replaced. This process was accelerated from the mid-1990s as neoliberalism proved adaptable to changing political circumstances, finding itself integrated into the so-called Third Way approach of Tony Blair and Bill Clinton (Fairclough 2000), neither pure capitalism nor command-and-control socialism. Though rhetorically cast as a new approach, for its critics the Third Way was essentially neoliberalism with a friendly face. International competitiveness remained the dominant theme, but became allied to a greater concern to integrate into economic development sensitivity to the views of 'stakeholders', especially on environmental and social issues.

The result is that it is possible to see not only how the neoliberal approach to economic management has altered since the late 1970s (Peck and Tickell 2002), but also how neoliberal approaches are mapping out rather differently from place to place. In this respect, it is valuable to consider Jessop's (2002) argument that the market-led approach of neoliberalism represents just one of four possible ideal-type strategies in the shift from KWNS approaches to SWPR approaches:

- neoliberalism – market primacy, with the state's main role being to regulate to support market forces;
- neostatism – market-conforming but state-sponsored strategies for economic and social restructuring;
- neocorporatism – developing agreements across a wide range of social actors, not simply the largest bodies; and

- neocommunitarianism − emphasising the role of the third sector and issues of social cohesion.

The four approaches are not seen as mutually exclusive, so that each might carry different weight in different contexts and at different scales. For example, whereas a neoliberal approach might dominate at the national level, in different sub-national contexts the weight of policy might shift more to neocorporatist or neocommunitarian approaches.

The value of this approach is that it helps to convey something of the alternative rationalities which are in effect competing for policy saliency with the more purely market-based approaches of neoliberalism. It also helps to explain something of the sheer variety and number of reformist experiments which have emerged in recent years. This is particularly evident at sub-national levels, as governments have sought to experiment with new ways of achieving their policy goals through devolved arrangements, ranging from contracting out, to new governance institutions. In a period of hyper-experimentation with different local–regional–national configurations of institutional architecture, new institutional forms find themselves being quickly judged, and depending on their perceived success they might be adapted, abandoned or appropriated for use elsewhere. Driving this process forward is a system of both externally audited and locally self-policed discipline, where institutions are aware of their temporary 'licence' to engage in policy formation, and fast policy transfer, a system which rewards those judged to be working well and punishes those which are not, or which fall out of political favour for other reasons (Peck 2002; Stoker 2002). Ideological projects in this way are presented as politically neutral, since what survives is 'whatever works', in a process which makes critical scrutiny of the selected policy goals and evaluation criteria ever more important.

The new institutional forms frequently involve experimental pilots, prototypes and pathfinders, from which new organisational forms may be rolled out on a wider basis, but always subject to constant monitoring, auditing and evaluation. Evidence-based policy becomes the means for ensuring that governance systems do what the government set them up to do, rather than go too far down the path of local freedom and experimentation. Moreover, in order to promote greater local coordination and reduce unnecessary duplication between the many new organisational forms, virtually all of them are required to operate as partnerships, creating interlocking local and regional governance systems which require all those institutional partners with a stake in a new initiative to have a further incentive in trying to make it succeed. Inevitably, all such governance experiments eventually come to be judged as failures, as part of the rationale for introducing new approaches (Jessop 1999). It is into this frenzied atmosphere that the new institutions of regional planning and regional economic development have been born and in due course must prove their worth, however that might be politically measured.

In summary, the version of state theory outlined here seeks to examine the social constitution of state powers, rather than simply assume its autonomy. Following on from this, the emphasis on the state as a site of power struggles rather than as an arbiter of power means that this framework has the potential to be used to examine resistance as well as the imposition of hegemonic approaches. In this sense, the approach is able to address 'bottom-up' issues, although to date it has mainly been used to examine how elite groups operate rather than how less powerful groups articulate their opposition. In addition, by emphasising multi-scalar governance, our approach explicitly seeks to move away from top-down versions of state theory by stressing how power and knowledges are continuously and selectively reworked across scales (Jones and MacLeod 1999; Brenner 2000; Jessop 2000b; Brenner and Theodore 2002).

Rather than seeing state power as a simple force of political will and economic might allied to regulatory sanction, the analysis here emphasises the way in which various groups can draw on selective values, ethical codes and scientific knowledges to seek to counter dominant tendencies. These counter-hegemonic tendencies have been potentially facilitated over recent years, albeit in highly conditional ways, by the ways in which the state has sought to bolster its legitimacy and its capacities by drawing in a wider range of policy actors. The state has sought to find new ways of enforcing its preferred approaches while also engaging in more transparent and meaningful ways with its 'stakeholders'. One result of this is that power-knowledge is increasingly less of a dominant assertion of political will and much more a process of mobilising and coordinating diffuse power relations and power-knowledges. In the case of planning, this has seen a still largely hierarchical system attempting to become more porous to outside influences in order to build its legitimacy and reinforce its credibility. This has allowed various groups in civil society and in business to develop further their capacity to influence, disrupt or derail planning processes, making planning more than ever a form of social relation rather than a simple form of state directive activity. This is not entirely new, of course, as some lobby groups have been working directly with senior government figures for many years (Hardy 1991); what is new is the range of different organisations which are now involved in such activities.

Institutions, networks, stakeholders and communicative planning

Reacting against the limits of totalising theoretical accounts of capitalism, postmodernist-inspired approaches represented a turn towards deconstruction, anti-foundational and pluralistic tendencies (McGuirk 2001). Cultural theory has likewise informed a growing interest in more decentred analyses of urban and regional change, developing accounts which foreground indeterminacy, complexity, struggles over meaning, and the construction, selection and utilisation of different knowledges.

These kinds of concerns have manifested themselves in a widening body of institutionalist approaches to regional development and planning, including communicative planning and work on associative democracy. The communicative turn in planning is strongly associated with the development of Habermas's ideas on communicative rationality by Healey (1997, 1998), Innes (1995), Hillier (2000), and others. Though we do not want to dwell too long on this work, a broad overview is helpful in developing an appreciation of how planning's role in place making is always an exercise in power, involving socially constructed and politically contested mediations over meanings, knowledge and political rationalities (see also Murdoch 2000; Painter 2002; and work on governmentality).

Communicative planning theory has emerged in part as a reaction against the instrumental rationality of modernist planning as it developed particularly in the post-war years, with its emphasis on forms of knowledge which privileged those able and willing to operate in systems dominated by appeal to techno-scientific knowledge and deductive logic (McGuirk 2001). The challenge to modernist planning can also be traced to growing concern about reflecting cultural diversity, awareness of gender issues, the strengthening of civil society, and the pluralisation of governance actors and institutional forms (Allmendinger 2001; McGuirk 2001). Some of the philosophical assumptions of modernism also came under scrutiny politically and philosophically, not least with postmodernism's deconstructive and anti-foundationalist emphasis on diversity, marginality and difference. The result was a growing dissatisfaction with the narrowness of the former welfarist goals and the means of achieving them – for instance, full employment for adult males, to be pursued by large institutions on behalf of the dominant interest groups in society. In the field of planning, modernist planning practices predicated on the dominance of male-centred, single-earner families and a relatively homogeneous society have likewise come to be heavily criticised, not least in relation to the design of some of the 1950s and 1960s new towns (Healey 1998).

Communicative planning has emerged as one of several related approaches which seek to ensure that the 'increasingly vociferous polity of active stakeholders in planning' (Healey 1998 p. 8; see also Friedmann 1998) have their voices heard more effectively within the planning system. Building from Habermas's ideas, communicative approaches emphasise processes of consensus building, involving rational argumentation being promoted through open and fair debates among equally empowered, equally resourced and equally respected protagonists. Opening up planning systems in this way to multiple stakeholders with different knowledges and rationalities represents a radical break from previous planning approaches, which might be caricatured as ones where experts mainly spoke among themselves in shared languages and with many shared assumptions. Where planning professionals and other experts once prepared technical plans which were then presented as much for public approval as for public consultation, collaborative planning suggests an alternative role for planners in mediating between diverse groups to ensure that their participation in the planning process respects and draws from different knowledges and value-systems. This strongly normative approach has come under increasing criticism for failing to capture fully the way in which unequal power relations infuse planning systems, involving a questioning of whether consensus is ever possible where participants have divergent aspirations and expectations of the planning system (Tewdwr-Jones and All-mendinger 1998, 2003; Phelps and Tewdwr-Jones 2000; McGuirk 2001).

Phelps and Tewdwr-Jones (2000) argue that there are similarities between planning theory's communicative turn, with its emphasis on building institutional forms which facilitate argumentative rationality, with the 'new institutionalism' approach being developed by geographers and others. In both bodies of work there is a concern with the remaking of institutions in response to the failings of previous approaches. For them, collaborative planning (Healey 1997), associative democracy (Amin and Thrift 1995; Amin and Hausner 1997) and 'new regionalist' networked forms of economic organization (Cooke and Morgan 1998) all represent institutional 'Third Way' approaches to sub-national governance, neither market led nor command-and-control in style. Each approach emphasises the importance of building local and regional social capital, in particular the importance of building trust relations around consensus and communication.

Amin and Thrift's (1995) account of the value of 'institutional thickness' in explaining regional success has been particularly influential in terms of shifting emphasis away from mainly economic factors towards consideration of institutional issues. Although institutional thickness is not of itself seen as an explanation for success, it helps to highlight the fact that social, cultural and institutional issues are essential to an improved understanding of processes of regional transformation. Four key themes emerge in this account: a strong institutional presence; high levels of interaction between institutions (networking, cooperation, information sharing); systems for exerting influence (e.g. coalition building, collective representation) to reduce conflict and rogue behaviour; and the development of a shared regional agenda for their individual and collective development. It is not the quantity of institutions which is being emphasised here but the quality of institutional capacity and interchange, together with the power relations within which they are embedded. For instance, there are real dangers in consensus building being used to impose narrow agendas, where one particular set of institutions or viewpoints are dominant or where a simple line of least resistance is pursued (Raco 1998; MacLeod and Goodwin 1999).

This concern with how to achieve effective and meaningful engagement with the widest possible range of stakeholders is a central theme in both communicative planning and work on associational democracy (Phelps and Tewdwr-Jones 2000). In the communicative planning literature there is a strong awareness of the asymmetries of resources, expertise, and both real and symbolic power among stakeholders. This approach suggests that a key challenge for planners is to identify and address these concerns in ways which promote greater fairness. Though methods for addressing such asymmetries are less of an issue in accounts of associational democracy, the literature does emphasise that not all networks operate in non-hierarchical ways, nor do they necessarily always pursue strategies for the collective good. This leads Amin and Hausner (1997) to highlight three alternative approaches: hegemony (structural dominance), leadership (formally constituted hierarchical leadership) and 'strategic direction'. Strategic direction, which in many ways is similar to the ideas of communicative planning, is presented as a relatively benign process of diffuse and reflexive governance, where key players seek to guide, arbitrate and facilitate, a form of 'power with' rather than 'power to' or 'power over' (Rabinow 1984; Bryant 2002).

Which leads us back to the issue of power in planning. McGuirk draws on an analysis of planning in Newcastle, Australia, to argue that key players may commit themselves to open systems, to respecting all voices and value systems, while working simultaneously in other ways to exert influence, through political lobbying, media campaigning, and so forth. While attempts to build successful communicative approaches are predicated on notions of truth, fairness and respect, it seems that political strategising through misinformation, disinformation, partial truths and downright lies is all but unavoidable, even when apparent agreement to open dialogue is the public basis for interaction between stakeholders in the planning process. The danger of assuming that power difference and unavoidable conflict are capable of resolution through a communicative approach is that it underestimates the fundamental tensions in building 'soft' bottom–up consensual processes in a system where hierarchical systems dominate. For McGuirk (2001) and others (Phelps and Tewdwr-Jones 2000), the theoretical challenge remains to consider what happens where conflict is pervasive and achieving consensus is not possible. The practical challenges facing those seeking consensual approaches are returned to throughout this book.

Environmental and planning narratives and discourses

Environmental and planning debates can be seen as arenas in which alternative sets of meanings and values are contested and developed as attempts are made to influence policy formation (Jackson 1991; Macnaghten and Urry 1998). These battles over meaning and values require attention to be paid to the production of culturally encoded discourses, including the language, signs and symbols deployed by different actors within the system. More than this, it is important to examine issues of power, in terms of hegemony, resistance and subordination, as groups set out either to establish or to contest hegemonic understandings of a problem and how best to address it. The contestability of discourses implies that they are dynamic articulations of evolving understandings, with competing discourses to an extent mutually constituted as particular views are presented as more 'natural', normal or acceptable than alternatives.

Discourses are important because of the ways in which they can 'normalise' particular ways of thinking and acting, creating a form of 'truth' which is embedded within particular social relations and their associated power-knowledge rationalities (Foucault 1991a, b). At the institutional level, successful discursive practices are important because they can 'consolidate a limited but widely accepted set of diagnoses and prescriptions' (Jessop 1997, p. 30), in effect normalising particular approaches within policy discourses, making them more difficult to refute or dislodge. In this reading, the seemingly dull world of planning debates and public inquiries becomes a critical site for battles over socially constructed and politically contested understandings of what constitutes the 'problems' which policy makers should address, and the preferred ways of addressing these problems. In particular, the discursive practices of policy making are important, as they can either open up or constrain the limits of our understanding of normal or acceptable policy approaches. In Foucault's 'strong' version of discourse analysis, individuals become situated within particular discourses, identifying themselves and thinking and acting accordingly (McGregor 2000).

In seeking to avoid the pitfalls of this kind of discursive determinism, it is helpful to emphasise the diversity and proliferation of discursive practices and their continuous and creative rearticulation, recognising human agency in shaping and resisting particular discourses (Harvey 1996; Fairclough 1998). In addition to human agency, however, it is helpful to examine the structural issues surrounding how discursive practices work. Of particular value here is critical discourse analysis (Fairclough 1998), which seeks to examine the interconnection of discursive practices with wider social and cultural practices. For Fairclough, this approach 'stresses the diversity and proliferation of discursive practices and generative processes in which they are articulated; but it sees these processes as limited by hegemonic relations and structures, and as a terrain of hegemonic struggle' (1998, p. 145). The importance of the approach is that the effectiveness of particular discourse practices frequently rests on how effectively they connect personal and collective narratives of events, institutional narratives, and from this how they link to wider institutional and cultural formations (Jessop 1997).

A key concern in discourse analysis of policy formation involves identifying the various discursive practices involved in creating particular 'storylines' or narratives, involving for instance the written word, public debates, protests, signs, symbols, metaphors, and so forth. Although alternative powerful storylines are not always evident, where a series of such storylines do exist, it may be possible to identify 'discourse coalitions' promulgating these in a variety of ways, coalitions which can change over time as debates move on (Hajer 1995; Vigar *et al.* 2000). Where powerful narratives or storylines are developed, they can become an important part of the policy process, as they are used to support particular policy approaches over others. With selective readings of events, past trends and future projections, narratives can be constructed which consolidate certain readings, while simultaneously rendering other accounts marginal, dysfunctional, overly politicised or otherwise undesirable (Jessop 1997).

Environmental discourses have been particularly subject to analysis in recent years, not least in relation to sustainable development and planning debates (Hajer 1995; Myerson and Rydin 1996; Macnaghten and Urry 1998). These analyses have focused on the selectivities involved in how the 'environment' is inserted into political debates. For instance, countryside nature tends to take a privileged position in such debates, backed by powerful interest groups. In this sense, how nature is represented needs to be seen as a form of tactics and social power, where it is inserted into debates in particular ways by particular groups. For this book, the key concern is with recent changes in policy discourses surrounding sustainable development, which have seen environment-led interpretations of sustainable development increasingly challenged by those who argue that these marginalise important social and economic considerations (see Chapter 3).

Because of their relative transparency, contemporary planning systems, particularly public inquiries and public examinations, can provide a particularly useful starting point for analysing debates on environmental issues (Vigar *et al.* 2000; see also Chapters 3 and 4). More than this, the study of discursive practices in planning is important for two key reasons. First, it helps to identify how certain planning issues are rendered visible and invisible, and how battles over meaning are mediated through the planning system. Second, it helps to emphasise how planning debates on international competitiveness and sustainable development are shaping the very practices of planning, directly and indirectly, through the ways in which individuals and institutions adapt to the dominant discourses in which they are embedded.

Spatial planning and sustainable development: social power and political strategy

Debates surrounding the development of spatial planning frameworks are important because of what they tell us about the aspirations of different groups in society for 'place-making' activities. With the shift towards more collaborative forms of planning, the processes of plan making reveal the tensions involved between differing conceptions of how places should change over the long term. Equally important, they reveal tensions over how to bring about change, notably which types of regulation should be used, and what mix of regulation, market adaptation, moral suasion and political exhortation. This book treats the processes of strategic regional planning as a form of social power and political strategy, creating opportunities for substantial power struggles over the differing underlying value systems and aspirations of protagonists. The resulting debates speak of what is hoped for as much as what is, which means it is important to examine not simply the surface conflicts but also the underpinning belief systems involved and how these are used in constructing alternative visions of future places.

The development plan-making system provides an 'an already existing arena where people can come together to work out strategic ideas and build sufficient consensus to pursue new initiatives in place making and place maintaining' (Healey 1998, p. 4). In the case of strategic regional planning, the debate is pitched less at the level of detailed aspirations for an area, more at the level of the general guiding principles and the suitability of differing planning techniques in moving towards agreed ends. Thus, it is important to see the process of plan making as providing an arena in which irreconcilable differences or unequal power relations may mean that differences are aired, in both formal and informal ways, but consensus does not emerge. In this sense, it is helpful to regard the process for preparing regional planning guidance as one which may build towards consensus without necessarily achieving it, with the final agreed documents essentially reflecting the socio-politics of plan production, with a resulting range of decisions, compromises, fudges and strategic silences.

Reflecting the erosion of public faith in the planning system since the 1960s, in recent years planning has sought to re-establish its legitimacy as a regulatory process, by building on a number of 'big ideas', of which sustainable development (Chapter 3) and urban renaissance (see Chapter 6) have been most to the fore in the United Kingdom. Sustainable development, however, is far from a neutral term, with the inherent ambiguities and tensions in its definition allowing it to be a battleground for people seeking to interpret it in different ways, for different purposes (Blowers 1993; Hajer 1995; Healey and Shaw 1993, 1994; Owens 1994; Owens and Cowell 2002). Environment-led interpretations of sustainable development, for instance, privileged the preferred policies of environmental groups, while making it more difficult for some business groups to use the term to legitimate their own preferred approach of using economic growth to promote environmental protection.

Rather than treat sustainable development as a fairly neutral term, we instead set out to analyse it as a politicised battleground for struggles over values, meanings and knowledges. In this sense, as we argue in Chapter 1, sustainable development is both a political strategy and a political resource, and one which is used by different groups to pursue often widely differing sets of interests. It is important to emphasise in this context that the widespread adoption of sustainable development discourses in British planning has exercised powerful disciplining effects on those who wish to present themselves as legitimate stakeholders in the planning system. Central government has been heavily involved in seeking to 'normalise' its preferred integrated approach to sustainable development, seeking to alter the terms on which debates take place and also seeking to insert tools that formalise the government's interpretation of sustainable development. It is not alone in this type of political strategising. Business lobbyists involved in planning for instance tend to be selective and strategic in how they adopt the terminologies and adapt the meanings of sustainable development, as part of their efforts to enhance their legitimacy in pursuing their interests (Eden 1996, 1999).

Conclusions

Drawing on insights from several bodies of separate yet interconnected theoretical work, an approach is developed here which suggests the need to examine regional policy and planning theoretically and empirically from both top-down and bottom-up perspectives.

At the theoretical level, the challenge is to meld an appreciation of the macro-dynamics of capitalism to an empirically informed account of how these changes map out in contingent ways in particular concrete circumstances. The framework used here draws principally on state theory in understanding the nature of 'top-down' selectivities within planning. But we would argue that there is considerable value in also drawing on institutionalist literatures to look at how decisions on the nature of planning practice are enacted, contested and resisted. In the example of the reformed governance arrangements for regional planning, for instance, it is certainly important to appreciate how the strong steer of central government is exercised. But this should not lead us to neglect an examination of the processes by which local and regional actors in this case sought to operate within the constraints not simply of the national system, but of locally contingent political tensions and tensions across different interest groups. It is for this reason that we attempt to meld state theory with a greater sensitivity to strategies of resistance, plus an awareness of the tensions and contradictions inherent within collaborative forms of planning.

The approach developed in this chapter also highlights the importance of analysing how changes at regional scale result from, and result in, tensions at other policy-making scales too. The importance of this is that both analytically and in policy terms, there are dangers in treating the region as a 'taken-for-granted' scale of analysis, coherent in its own terms. Indeed, since the mid-1970s, critical regional analysis has highlighted the importance of moving beyond analyses of purely regional economic problems, structures, institutions and strategies, to consider their place in wider economic and political processes (Lee 1977; Massey 1979). Rather than fetishise 'the region' as a scale for analysis, then, the approach here is to analyse regional issues in terms of wider contestations about the appropriate scales, methods and politics of governance, involving examining how changes at regional level link to local and national changes.

Our concern in this book is with examining the wider power dynamics set in motion by the increased policy attention to interventions at the regional scale, including the development of a deeper understanding of the political struggles which lie behind the adoption of the rhetorics of sustainable development. Whose interests are these changes serving, how, and why? The tactics of influencing power relations used by various political, professional and advocacy groups emerge as a central aspect of our analysis.

3 Spatial planning and sustainable development

> We are clearly beginning to see a new planning age in which sustainable
> development is accorded its proper place.
>
> (Jonathon Porritt, speaking at the Public Examination for Draft Regional
> Planning Guidance in the South West, 2000)

The emergence of environment-led approaches to sustainable development

The past four decades have seen a substantial fluctuation in the fortunes of
town and country planning in the United Kingdom, as many of the assumptions which underpinned it and the expectations of the system came under
growing scrutiny. Where in the 1950s and 1960s planning was centrally
involved in building the 'new Jerusalem', from the late 1970s through to the
early 1990s its scope was radically narrowed down towards more of a land use
function (Healey 1998), with its regulatory direction reoriented to a presumption in favour of development.

During the early 1990s, sustainable development emerged as the 'big idea'
which was to help resuscitate the jaded reputation and fading fortunes of
English planning (Bishop 1996; Selman 1996). This concern with sustainable
development developed partly out of the UK government's active involvement in and commitment to the Rio 'Earth Summit', the United Nations
Conference on Environment and Development in 1992, plus the government's acceptance of the scientific basis for concerns about global warming.
The UK government decided to respond quite rapidly to growing concerns
about global environmental issues, resulting in the publication of *This
Common Inheritance* (UK Government 1990), which committed it to a
strengthened environmental agenda (Healey and Shaw 1994).

Sustainable development became a useful covering term for this agenda,
following its rise to prominence with the World Commission on Environment and Development's report *Our Common Future* (WCED 1987). The
WCED definition of sustainable development – that is, development which
meets the needs of present and future generations – emphasised the import-

ance of economic growth and technology in addressing environmental and resource problems. This represented an important break from the dominant environmental debates of the 1970s, when environmental problems were often presented in ways which made their solution dependent on reducing economic growth. Shifting towards a view that growth was part of the solution rather than part of the problem was something which inevitably appealed to both business leaders and politicians, who would have had great difficulty in selling to their electorates anything which might suggest employment losses (Haughton and Hunter 1994).

Following the 1992 Rio Earth Summit, a growing number of UK strategies were published, including a national sustainable development strategy (DoE 1994a) plus thematic documents on biodiversity, climate change and forestry. There was also a growth of local environmental policy initiatives during this period, such as green audits and Local Agenda 21. These national and local initiatives marked the beginning of a new strand of national, regional and local policy for sustainable development, much of which occurred outside the regulatory constraints of town and country planning, allowing greater freedom for experimenting with a wider range of techniques. The sustainable development policy imperative consequently set in train some important debates and experiments in a whole series of areas, not just planning, leading to some interesting differences in approach to the subject (Table 3.1).

The early 1990s was also a formative time for European environmental policy, including the publication of the *Green Paper on the Urban Environment* (CEC, 1990). The Green Paper received a mixed reception in the United Kingdom, but nevertheless brought to prominence an important debate about urban settlement patterns (Haughton and Hunter 1994; Healey and Shaw 1994). It particularly promoted the idea of 'the compact city', an approach which was progressively incorporated into British planning policy with policies for higher residential densities, brownfield site reusage, promotion of mixed uses at the neighbourhood level, improved public transport and better urban design (see Chapter 6).

For planning, the rising concern for the environment was particularly remarkable in that it followed a decade in which the Thatcher government had placed economic growth and a faith in the market to the fore of national policy. The result had been a period in which, at the rhetorical level at least, the agenda was guided by largely deregulatory, anti-planning sentiments (Thornley 1993; Tewdwr-Jones 1996). In practice, though, the approach was always one dominated by re-regulation of the planning apparatus rather than its wholesale deregulation, as many people and businesses still supported a stable regulatory framework for development in order to control unwanted forms of development. By the late 1980s the 'deregulatory' stance had begun to weaken in key respects, not least as tensions emerged within the Conservative Party between business interests, generally promoting development, and traditional Conservative supporters in the shire counties, who

Table 3.1 Differences in approach to sustainable development between planning and other policy areas

	National	Regional	Local
Mainstream sustainable development policy			
Key institutions	• Since 2001, DEFRA. • Sustainable Development Round Table • Sustainability Commission • Conservation Agencies	• Regional chambers • Voluntary regional Sustainable Development Round Tables • Conservation agencies in regions e.g. Environment Agency	• County and district councils, unitary authorities • Local strategic partnerships • Local Agenda 21 partnerships
Main policy devices	Sustainable Development Strategies (1994, 1999).	Regional Sustainable Development Frameworks.	Local Agenda 21 and corporate sustainable development policy.
Key techniques	• Quality of life capital • Indicators and targets	• Indicators and targets • Scrutiny • Action plans • Advice manuals • Sustainability appraisal • Benchmarking • Compacts • Global footprints	• Indicators and targets • Action plans • Sustainability appraisal • Benchmarking • Compacts • Global footprints • Sustainability implications statements
Key aspects of planning's approach to sustainable development			
Key institutions	Since 2001, Office of the Deputy Prime Minister	Regional Planning Bodies	County and district councils, plus unitary authorities
Main policy devices	• Planning policy guidance notes (PPGs) • Good practice guidance	Regional planning guidance	• Structure plans • Local plans • Unitary development plans
Key techniques	• Environmental appraisal, later sustainability appraisal • Indicators and targets	• Sustainability appraisal • Regional indicators and targets	• Environmental capacity • Environmental capital • Environmental appraisal, later sustainability appraisal • Local indicators and targets

were more concerned with rural protection, house prices and quality of life (Thornley 1993; Allmendinger and Tewdwr-Jones 2000). Though there have been some notable changes in approach to planning (Table 3.2), it is perhaps important to reflect that there was always an element of evolution and experimentation, with some reversals in direction occurring.

Focusing on events since the early 1990s, the introduction of new national legislation, the Planning and Land Compensation Act 1991, was particularly important in signalling the reviving fortunes of the planning system, reversing some of the tendencies of the previous decade, in particular by emphasising the primacy of the development plan in local decision making – that is, plan-led development (Allmendinger and Tewdwr-Jones 2000). During the following six years a greater sensitivity to environmental concerns was written into a whole series of government documents on planning and related policy areas, including planning policy guidance notes. Emblematic of this changing focus was the use of environmental concerns to justify some important policy reversals, notably the move towards a sustainable transport policy and changes to advice on large out-of-town retail centres, which were recognised as contributing to car-borne traffic problems of congestion and pollution, among other things (DoE 1996a).

Integrated approaches

New Labour in 1997 adopted many aspects of the neoliberal agenda of the previous administration, including its reformist tendencies in moving away from 'roll-out' neoliberalism towards a more neocorporatist approach (Chapter 2 and Table 3.2; see also Allmendinger and Tewdwr-Jones 2000; Marshall, 2001). Not surprisingly, then, many of the new planning approaches introduced by New Labour have been broadly similar in terms of their rationalisation, in particular calls for greater speed and simplicity in planning as an aid to business decision making. Though there have been some claims that the new Labour government came into office in 1997 without any radical approaches to either the environment or planning (Allmendinger and Tewdwr-Jones 2000), it is fair to say that over time it became possible to see some distinctive elements emerging. In particular, the so-called 'Third Way' philosophy underpinning much of Tony Blair's thinking called for a consensual, partnership approach, emphasising the need to bring different interests together, seeking win–win situations for all, rather than conflict (Fairclough 2000). In addition, the government has placed great store on 'joined up' government and a more integrated approach to policy making.

The government's strong support for economic growth clearly influenced policy development in relation to sustainable development. After a consultation exercise in 1998, it published its sustainable development strategy with the title *A Better Quality of Life* (DETR, 1999a), defining sustainable development according to four objectives, which it argued should be met at the same time:

Table 3.2 Planning's changing circumstances, 1970–2003

	Planning under question, 1970s	Planning under siege, 1979–1989	Planning rediscovered, 1990–1997	Planning rehabilitated, 1997–
Era (see Chapter 2)	Late Fordism/ Keynesianism	Roll-back neo-liberalism	Neo-statism/neoliberalism	Third Way neoliberalism
Key changes	Questioning of the role of planners as experts, especially on social issues	Land use focus, supporting economic development	Growing concern with environment and 'sustainable development'	Integrated approaches to sustainable development
Dominant approaches to plan making	Plans based on detailed analysis with lengthy periods of preparation	Market-led – growing emphasis on speed and cutting red tape	Plan-led development. Tentative re-engagement with strategic planning.	Attempts to improve public participation and yet also speed up plan making
Civil society	Critiques of planning as a form of 'social engineering'	Individuals to be freed from 'tyranny of bureaucracy'	Consulting with 'the community'	Engaged with as part of a multiplicity of stakeholders
Local government role	Lead role in local planning	Part of the problem, being too anti-enterprise	Technical guidance and facilitator of development	Facilitator in widely based collaborative processes
Central government approach to regional planning	Dwindling enthusiasm	No enthusiasm	Useful role, if appropriately limited. Focused on new housing issue.	Key part of the new regional institutional architecture

- social progress which recognises the needs of everyone;
- effective protection of the environment;
- prudent use of natural resources; and
- maintenance of high and stable levels of economic growth and employment.

This new approach embodies two key changes: first, a decisive shift from an environment-led interpretation of sustainable development by explicitly requiring equal consideration of social and economic issues; and second, the implicit prioritisation of 'high' economic growth. Simply using the word 'high' imposes a powerful disciplining logic on all those required to adopt this definition, given that the other objectives all had less prescriptive words, such as 'progress', 'effective' and 'prudent.' For planners, the new definition was particularly significant, as it implied a shift from an emphasis on 'environmental limits' in favour of approaches more focused on reconciling environmental protection with economic growth.

The new approach to sustainable development was quickly absorbed into other areas of public policy, such as the RESs of the new RDAs (DETR 1998b) and RPG (DETR 2000a, b). In order to bring coherence across these strategies, and to ensure that sustainable development was taken seriously in all of them rather than treated as a separate policy issue, the government also required that each region produce an RSDF (see Chapter 1 and Box 3.1).

Particularly important in the new 'integrated approach' was the policy imperative to identify 'win–win' solutions as first-order policy preferences, rather than the traditional planning concern with balancing and trade-offs. 'Win–win' solutions are said to be those which encourage policy-makers to think creatively about ways in which policies might achieve *both* environmental protection *and* economic development objectives. Politically they are attractive because they offer the prospect of finding solutions where everyone is a winner, although reconciling these goals in practice was not to be quite so simple (Royal Commission on Environmental Pollution 2002; Rydin and Thornley 2002). By the early 2000s the preferred terminology had moved on slightly, with 'win–win–win' introduced to incorporate the social concerns of sustainable development alongside those of the economy and environment (Counsell *et al.* 2003). Addressing economic, social and environmental objectives at the same time, rather than giving priority to one over another, is at the heart of the Labour government's approach to sustainable development. More than this, integration of these objectives is a theme which the government has gradually pressed into the heart of its reforms of regional planning and regional economic development.

As part of its reforms, the new government issued a series of consultation papers from January 1998 (DETR 1998a, c), which consolidated many of the new directions already evident in planning while introducing some changes, such as the shift away from the 'predict and provide' approach for new housing towards 'plan, monitor and manage' (see Chapter 5). These proposals

Box 3.1 Regional Sustainable Development Frameworks (RSDFs)

In its official guidance on preparing RSDFs (DETR 2000b), the government argues that they should be seen as

> high level documents that set out a vision for sustainable development in each region, and the region's contribution to sustainable development at national level. In doing so frameworks should take a wide overview of regional activity and the regional impact of Government policy.
>
> (para. 1.2).

The Frameworks were to be drawn up by a range of local and regional partners in collaboration and had to be endorsed by the regional chambers. Their main role is to help integrate policy for sustainable development horizontally between different sectoral strategies and vertically with national and local policy. This policy integration is expected to be achieved by:

- providing an agreed 'sustainable development' vision for each region;
- providing a common set of objectives for sustainable development, which would be used in appraising regional and local policy; and
- providing a common set of indicators and targets for monitoring regional policy.

Although regional differences are encouraged, in practice most of the contents of the RSDFs were based on the four objectives of sustainable development in national policy, for pragmatic reasons. In most regions, RSDFs were in place by the end of 2000 and already being used in appraising regional strategies, e.g. regional planning guidance, Regional Economic Strategies, European Structural Programme documents.

and the government's new definition of sustainable development were eventually incorporated into planning policy guidance (PPG) notes, particularly into revisions to PPG3 *Housing* (DETR 2000c), PPG11 *Regional Planning* (DETR 2000a) and PPG12 *Development Plans* (DETR 1999b). In the latter document the pro-environmental sentiments in the previous version of PPG12 were rebalanced to give equal consideration to the other objectives of sustainable development. Quite explicitly, the government justified the changes by arguing that: 'Progress towards sustainable development can only be made if the various objectives are considered in a balanced way' (DETR

1999b, para. 4.3). For some groups this came to be seen as representing a worrying weakening of the government's environmental commitment, whereas others warmly embraced the new approach as representing a strengthening of the holistic approach towards sustainable development.

The adoption of the integrated approach to sustainable development represents an almost archetypal 'ecological modernisation' approach to sustainable development. 'Ecological modernisation' is a term which covers a range of policy approaches that embody an optimism about the ability of technology and better regulated markets to address environmental problems, frequently involving the invocation of 'win–win' rhetorics (Harvey 1996; Fairclough 2000). It is not a term likely to be familiar to many politicians, nor is it a uniform body of work: there are important differences between some of its proponents in terms of their levels of optimism about technology and markets (Gibbs 2002). The essence of the ecological modernisation approach is that environmental transformation is seen to be possible through technical and regulatory reforms under existing capitalist structures (see Blowers 1997; Davoudi 2000; Gibbs 2002). Indeed, in some readings, with appropriate forms of re-regulation the assumption is that the market can be redirected to address environmental problems, in the process creating new market opportunities and business efficiencies, for instance with waste management and measures to promote energy efficiency. Where business efficiency is improved by energy conservation measures, this can be discursively presented not only to argue the efficacy of 'win–win' approaches, but also to argue that the old approach of trading off economic growth with environmental loss is outmoded (Harvey 1996).

This lies in contrast to approaches such as Beck's risk society thesis, with its expectation that the changing scale, scope and nature of environmental risks is so substantial as to require profound societal transformations and political strategies which upset the status quo (Harvey 1996; Blowers 1997; Davoudi 2000). Work on political ecology has similarly taken a different route to understanding sustainable development, involving arguments that it is being used to rationalise the continuing exploitation of nature (O'Connor 1993). The critique here is that sustainable development debates serve to normalise market rationalities, which are then used to justify processes for commodifying nature, for instance the privatisation of water and its insertion into global circuits of capital. Simultaneously, market disciplines are invoked to justify cost-cutting programmes, which in turn can encourage a deregulatory race to the bottom in terms of environmental standards (O'Connor 1994).

There are other critiques of sustainable development, but this brief outline of some alternative approaches is sufficient to give a sense of the fact that the pursuit of an ecological modernisation agenda within planning reflected a particular choice, based on particular readings of the meaning and nature of sustainable development. In this reading, better policy making can be central to achieving 'sustainable development'. However, as Harvey (1996, p. 75) argues, there are not simply multiple definitions of sustainable development, there are also 'all sorts of rhetorical devices deployed by opponents to make the term meaningless or render it harmless – no one, after all, can be in favour of unsustainability'. The adoption of an integrated approach is not a simple apoliticial choice, then, but rather a decision which implicitly takes one reading of sustainable development as preferable to another. Thus the integrated approach embodies a particular viewpoint, and from this comes support for a set of policy approaches and policy tools which will alter power relations, for instance through challenging the legitimacy of those wishing to pursue an environment-led approach or a social equity-centred approach to 'sustainable development'.

The 'nature' of sustainable development

Both environmental and planning debates have involved a series of problem-atic dualisms which tend to work better as polemical devices than as analyti-cal tools. Environment versus economy, society versus nature, town versus country, sprawl versus compaction: the use of such binaries has become part and parcel of the discursive techniques of those seeking to alter the terms of debates around the role of sustainable development in planning.

Dualisms work by using the rhetorical device of creating two categories which can be portrayed as internally coherent and mutually exclusive. In doing this, they serve to create and perpetuate oversimplified accounts of complex concepts. Dualistic ways of thinking also tend to embody moralistic and emotional judgements, sometimes involving unexpected associations between different sets of dualisms, which can lead to problematic associations, fallacies even, and, with this, problematic polemical strategies for influencing policy. By drawing on Sayer's (1989) analysis of the tendency to conflate the binary opposites associated with Fordism and post-Fordism, it is possible to highlight the problematic nature of some of the dualisms used in sustainable urban development debates. Table 3.3 illustrates this concern, setting out some of the dualistic moral judgements found in some of the 'deep green' literature, which emphasises the importance of ecological values over anthro-pocentric concerns. The issue is that there is a tendency to rely on unhelpful dualistic antagonisms, while implying connections vertically down each column.

Such binary oppositions were particularly evident in some of the early-1990s policy debates around sustainable development, which tended to privilege 'environment'-centred understandings of problems and policies. To understand why this is problematic, it is useful to highlight recent critical social science perspectives on nature which have developed from a critique of dualistic modes of thinking that separate out nature and society (Macnaghten and Urry 1998; see also Braun and Castree 1998). According to such cri-tiques, rather than present society and nature as some form of opposites, it makes more sense to recognise that the two are mutually constituted – that is, interdependent. Instead of privileging pristine forms of 'nature', it is necessary

Table 3.3 Dubious dualisms in sustainable urban development debates

Society	Nature
City	Countryside
Globalisation	Localisation
Polluted	Pristine
Parasitic	Self-reliant
Self-harming	Self-repairing
Disequilibrium	Equilibrium

Source: Derived in part from Haughton (2003).

to understand that much of what is thought of as the 'natural' environment is in fact the result of complex sets of human decisions about how to exploit natural resources and manage environments. So, decisions to designate national parks or other forms of conservation area, for instance, are best seen as ways of seeking to preserve a landscape at a particular stage in its evolution, reflecting a particular form of nature–society relationship, rather than as attempts to preserve 'pristine' nature. In essence, this approach involves a recognition that debates about preserving 'the environment' requires the study of different environmental possibilities and a careful analysis of whose interests are being served by attempts to create particular notions of nature within policy debates (Whatmore and Boucher 1993; Harrison and Burgess 1994; Eden *et al.* 2000).

In similar vein, it is possible to argue that the tendency to talk of town and country, or urban and rural, as separate and meaningful categories is problematic. There are immediate problems here in accounting for the complexities of modern settlement patterns, suburbs and edge-city developments, expanding market towns, and the attempts to recreate substantial wildlife habitats in urban areas. More than this, towns and cities are ever more intimately interconnected by complex flows of commuters, tourists, day-trippers, food, goods and services, money, and so on. Yet in England still it is possible to discern in popular and media debates the influence of romanticised notions about what constitutes the countryside and a searching for a 'rural idyll', leading to a privileging of particular types of English landscape as a form of nature which merits conservation over others (Williams 1973; Evans 1991; Bunce 1994). The issue here is not so much the antiquated notions embodied in the town–country dualism, but the fact that it tends to be used to justify particular power strategies, often still rooted in class relations. In contemporary politics, for instance, there has been a growing politicisation of the rural lobby, not least as it has sought to portray the British Labour Party as dominated by a 'metropolitan' set of values.

It is helpful in the current study to highlight these kinds of binary tendencies in that they are frequently evident in the discourses of lobby groups as they seek to construct crisis narratives in pursuit of their goals. These approaches are sometimes evident in the discursive struggles over the meanings of 'sustainable development', as it is selectively interpreted to justify particular forms of regional planning policy. More than this, however, these debates over meanings and values in sustainable development are important because policies adopted within the regional planning sphere exercise a pervasive influence elsewhere in the system. Debates and decisions in regional planning can have impacts on local and national planning decisions, and on the activities of those other policy sectors reliant in some part on the planning system, for instance the work of RDAs on economic development (see Chapter 7).

Sustainable development's three pillars: society, economy, environment

With its statutory role and prospect of legal appeals against decisions, the search for definitional clarity in planning is always a strong theme. This has been one of the driving issues in the considerable effort to define more precisely what 'sustainable development' means for planning, and discussions on how to make it operational (Healey and Shaw 1993, 1994; Owens 1994; Counsell 1998; Owens and Cowell 2002). It was important in this context that the sustainable development visions adopted in regional planning should be carefully debated, hopefully leading to widespread acceptance as a result of the drafting process. In discussing these debates we draw heavily here on a three-year research project on regional planning guidance, whose methodology is outlined in the appendix to this book.

Though there were some interesting sources of variability in the draft RPG documents produced early on in each region, one of the disappointing features of the subsequent process is the extent to which the final visions for sustainable development tended towards a certain uniformity – conformity, even – as they focused on the government-approved definition. Rather than greater devolution to regional stakeholders resulting in distinctive visions, in practice the strongly prescriptive nature of planning coming from central government denied the opportunity for much variation to emerge in how sustainable development was defined and incorporated into planning guidance. This prescriptive element in part reflects planning's role as part of the statutory apparatus of land regulation, which has meant that the government has sought to foster distinctiveness but within certain centrally established parameters. These parameters in part at least reflect a concern to avoid legal challenge in future planning appeals by pointing to inconsistencies in different planning documents at different tiers of the system, or even between different parts of the country.

In terms of defining sustainable development, what has emerged through the recent round of regional planning guidance combines elements of both self-imposed and externally imposed pressures to conform to national expectations. The self-imposed pressures have come from a variety of sources, including a desire to minimise conflicts between the constituent local authorities responsible for producing draft RPG, and also attempts to anticipate the concerns of the wide variety of other stakeholders in planning, including both environment and development lobby groups. The externally imposed constraints have emerged as central government officials took over the final stages of preparation of RPG and have sought to ensure conformity to national guidelines, and also to ensure that the views of those who might have been marginalised through the regional policy formation process are given greater weight (Counsell and Haughton 2003).

Not surprisingly, there were many people who were disappointed with such constraints. According to Jonathon Porritt, the prominent national environmental campaigner, speaking at the South West public examination of its draft RPG in spring 2000, the government's increasing commitment to sustainable development in planning was an important step forward. There was a problem for planning, however, in that the central government definition of sustainable development was not all that helpful, he argued, since it was 'inherently confusing and inherently contradictory'.

Such sentiments were ones which kept emerging during the early 2000s, as those seeking to develop policies that reflected the political support for a broad-ranging definition of sustainable development struggled to cope with its consequent definitional ambiguities and slipperiness. Multiple sustainabilities emerged in the process, as groups sought to portray their policies as sustainable'. Terms such as 'sustainable economic development' and 'environmental sustainability' testified to the ways in which stakeholders sought to tie the concept down to a particular emphasis.

During the early 1990s in particular, environmental groups had achieved considerable impact on planning debates, advocating an environment-led interpretation of sustainable development and supporting the development of new techniques which might support this approach. Not surprisingly in this light some of the early draft RPGs, which had begun their preparations in the mid-1990s, also tended to interpret sustainable development as an environment-led concern, only to meet with opposition when it came to the processes of public and government scrutiny. Though opposition could have been expected anyway, the shift to an integrated approach to sustainable development in the new national strategy was particularly important in giving strength to those who argued against what they perceived to be too environmental an approach in some draft RPGs. The new integrated approach was 'policed' by the Government Offices of the Regions in particular, which were not slow in pointing out where RPGs no longer reflected government thinking on this issue. So, in one region a government official told us quite explicitly how draft RPG was seen as somewhat problematic, since 'They [the regional planning body] are effectively treating sustainable development as too environmental a concept rather than integrated thinking.'

This process worked the other way round too, in that in some regions the integrated approach was used to promote what was perceived by opponents as an agenda dominated by economic growth. Here, opponents were able to use the 'integrated' approach to sustainable development to argue that environmental considerations needed to be given at least equal weight in policy formation. Such concerns were particularly evident among many of the environmental groups we spoke to: 'It [draft RPG] was all about sustainability as far as the economy was concerned and not about sustainability as we understand it.... Sustaining jobs and industry... with no regard really to wider environmental concerns' (interview EM4).

The new integrated approach to sustainable development in planning was intended to focus on identifying solutions which achieved both economic and environmental gains, or at least solutions where neither economy nor environment experienced a net loss in standing, while at least one gained. This win–win approach is important because it represented a major shift away from planning's previous acceptance of notions such as 'balance' and the possibility of 'trading off' losses in one category against 'wins' in another. The new approach initially proved difficult for some planners to come to terms with, in part because their professional training had been largely based on notions of trade-off and balance, along with tools such as mitigation and compensation. As an example, the loss of an environmental site might have been compensated for under a planning obligation which required a developer to improve the condition of another site, perhaps developing a new wildlife park next door or even some distance away (Plate 3.1). For many planners, while integrated solutions were attractive, the practicalities seemed to suggest they would be the exception rather than the rule (see Chapter 4).

This was far from being a problem which only vexed professional planners, with environmental, housebuilding and economic development supporters all worrying that the adoption of an integrated approach might be simply distracting attention from making hard decisions about preferences and priorities. Those seeking to promote economic growth found the concept problematic where policies were devised which appeared to reject the possibility of negotiating trade-offs:

> The reference to exploiting opportunities which are in line with all four sustainable development objectives may imply that trade-offs will never be acceptable. This is unreasonable.... There will be circumstance in which economic and social objectives should have precedence. Equally there will be occasions when purely environmental projects... may have no appreciable economic impact but are nonetheless worthy of support.
>
> (North West Development Agency, in a written submission on draft RPG)

> We think 'win–win–win' is just about impossible.... The planning system is about creating a balance between social, economic and social issues. In some cases this balance has to be established by giving more priority to one aspect than another.
>
> (interview NW7: pro-development group)

Plate 3.1 Newly created nature reserve: Greenwich Millennium Village.

The other important aspect of the integrated approach was that it brought social issues directly into consideration in regional planning debates. For planning, this represented another important development, since for many years planners had tended to shy away from attempting to engage directly with social issues, following accusations of 'social engineering' during the 1960s and 1970s slum clearance programmes in particular. Even in the late 1990s, social issues still tended to be marginal in regional planning debates, despite government advice highlighting it as an area which needed to be considered. Instead, social issues tended to be raised mainly indirectly as a rhetorical device for bolstering support for economic development on the often implicit assumption that more jobs would benefit the poor (Vigar *et al.* 2000). For instance, those arguing for further allocations of employment land might seek to justify these in part as helping to providing jobs for those who need them, or for areas that need them. The lack of attention to social issues in these early debates may well reflect the fact that social issues were largely dealt with through localised agencies and sub-national government structures, including health, crime, social housing and educational issues. But in addition it is important to note that the shift to the regional scale of planning found some social bodies lacking a strong regional institutional infrastructure, which inhibited their effective involvement in regional planning debates (Haughton and Counsell 2002). By the early 2000s, however, the tenor of debates had changed, with strong concerns being expressed about the ability of public-sector and low-income workers to access affordable housing, particularly in the South East (see Chapter 5).

But at the end of it all, did these debates really matter very much? For many people, the niceties of definitions were a distraction from the fact that regional planning documents were seen to be using sustainable development as a logic for pursuing preconceived policy agendas, or for justifying policies in a particular way. During our interviews we came across a significant minority of actors who expressed deep-seated frustration, with some seeing ambiguities in the term 'sustainable development' as linked to ambiguities in the resulting planning polices. One interviewee, a government official, sought to characterise the approach to sustainable development in the draft RPG for their region as simply 'weasel words... pious phrases that don't mean anything' (interview YH5). In similar vein, there was some concern that the actual impact of sustainable development debates had been minimal, resulting in only superficial changes to policy. So, an environmental group representative in the South West felt that despite much debate, 'The main impact has been on the presentation of policies. I don't see policies as hugely influenced' (interview, SW5). Developers too expressed their frustration at spending considerable amounts of time on what they felt to be the niceties of definition rather than the practicalities of development: 'No one is yet clear what sustainable development means – it means all things to all men.... It has become a political slogan for something which is acceptable' (interview EM8).

It is difficult not to be reminded of the title of Wildavsky's famous article 'If planning is everything, maybe it is nothing' (1973). Maybe if sustainable development is everything, then perhaps it risks becoming nothing. When sustainable development is seen as a political resource rather than a neutral container, it can be seen as a useful political vehicle, for instance for business groups wishing to legitimate some of their strategic preferences (Eden 1996, 1999).

Sustainability appraisal's selectivities and the enforcement of the integrated approach

Finding ways of shaping the behaviour and expectations of those involved in planning is central to successful attempts to legitimate and embed particular approaches, something which can be achieved in part by inserting supportive techniques (see Chapter 2). In the case of the integrated approach to sustainable development, the key technique was 'sustainability appraisal'. This new approach was introduced with the new arrangements for RPG preparation in the late 1990s, immediately displacing the previously favoured approach for scrutinising the content of plans, environmental appraisal. Where environmental appraisal was an environment-led tool, sustainability appraisal set out to appraise policies in an integrated way which covered economic, environmental and social issues. The new approach involved appraising a particular strategy or plan against objectives. In the case of regional planning, this usually meant appraising them against the objectives of RSDFs, which largely reflected central government's sustainable development objectives (see Box 3.1, p. 54). This objectives-led approach became an important disciplinary technique for ensuring that the government's national sustainable development objectives were adopted and followed through in planning documents. The result was that sustainable development in planning became tightly constrained, interpreted in ways sympathetic to the national government's approach, oriented as it was to both ecological modernisation and growth.

Sustainability appraisal was first formally introduced in regional planning but quickly became used in assessing regional economic strategies, plus local and structure plans. In effect, it provided a mechanism for tying planning strategies at all scales, and both planning and economic strategies, into a single form of rationality based on central government's own integrated definition of what sustainable development means. The process to be followed in conducting sustainability appraisals is closely specified in central government guidance (DETR 2000d).

The recommended objectives-led approach involves identifying any compatibilities and tensions between the sustainable development objectives of the RSDF and the proposed options, spatial strategies and policies produced at various stages of the regional planning process. It is not a scientific process, then; rather, it is a checklist type of approach based on matrices using ticks and crosses, together with a number of other symbols, plus scope for a written commentary where appropriate. Sustainability appraisal is intended to be an iterative process beginning at the very start of the planning process and reporting at all the main stages – for example, looking at the initial 'strategic options' stage, the draft plan, and proposed changes to the draft plan. The recommended process is outlined in PPG11 *Regional Planning* (DETR 2000a) and given more substance in good practice guidance (DETR 2000d) (see Table 3.4).

Recent research on sustainability appraisal (Smith and Sheate 2001a, b; Counsell and Haughton 2002a, b) found that government advice had not always been followed; for example, alternative options for spatial strategies had rarely been appraised. Some of the concerns about the way sustainability appraisals were carried out stemmed from the fact that for many of the appraisals, government advice came too late to be of assistance. But for many stakeholders a more profound concern was with the perceived lack of scientific rigour, which in effect rendered the process into as much of a subjective as an objective approach:

> These appraisals are just tick boxes and lack critical rigour.
>
> (interview SE8)

Table 3.4 The main stages in sustainability appraisal

Development of the appraisal objectives and criteria	The initial stage provides the basis against which performance is measured. Government advice in England recommends the use of objectives based on the RSDF.
Testing the appraisal objectives	The framework is tested to ensure that is compatible with the central government policy and objectives for sustainable development.
Defining the baseline	A baseline assessment is carried out of the existing environmental, social and economic characteristics of the area being appraised.
Scoping the strategy (plan or proposal)	The content of the strategy is appraised: for breadth of coverage; for consistency with national and regional policies; for whether it addresses all of the appraisal objectives; and for internal consistency.
Appraisal of strategic options	The different strategic options are appraised against the objectives using an appraisal matrix.
Appraisal of policies and proposals	Each of the policies and proposals is appraised against the objectives.
Reporting	The results of the appraisal are reported.

Source: Adapted from CAG Consultants and University of Hull (2003).

Note
RSDF = Regional Sustainable Development Framework.

Quantification is the next step. At the moment sustainability appraisal still involves a finger-in-the-air approach.

(interview NW1)

It's a weak science . . . the science is still very crude and it needs a lot of refinement.

(interview SE11)

The underlying issue here is that in coping with emotional appeals on particular issues, planners have long found it helpful to argue that their judgements have some scientific basis which might be portrayed as rigorous, neutral or apolitical. That the choice of techniques was far from neutral or apolitical was of course not considered to be such an issue. In this sense, sustainability appraisal raised hopes of greater rigour and scrutiny which were not being met.

The approach adopted in sustainability appraisals frequently proved useful in highlighting where tensions might exist between the social, economic or environmental dimensions of the documents being scrutinised. However, very few sustainability appraisals appear to have led directly to the removal of these tensions. What they did do, though, was to help pinpoint and highlight these conflicts, with the results of sustainability appraisals sometimes helping to inform debates at public examinations of draft RPGs. Overall, sustainability appraisal to date has been a system which is good at highlighting potential problems at a fairly high level of generality, but which has tended not to make clear recommendations. It may be this lack of recommendations which in some cases allowed the drafting bodies to reword some of their policies without necessarily addressing the underlying conflicts of interest raised by the sustainability appraisal.

They did go through the process, but some of the key findings, which were real, were totally brushed aside.

(interview EM3)

It highlighted conflicts between policies in RPG but there is no attempt to take things forward and resolve those conflicts.

(interview NE12)

So far, it appears, then, that sustainability appraisal has not been used directly in moving towards win–win–win solutions in regional planning, although it has succeeded in ensuring that the effects of policies on all four of the government's objectives for sustainable development have been considered.

Perhaps surprisingly, as a technique it has gained acceptance from a broad spectrum of planning stakeholders, including many national environmental groups. This seems to have been because environmental groups, for instance, felt that the previous approach to balancing economic and environmental

considerations had in the majority of cases ended up with economic considerations taking precedence, and therefore environmental concerns were frequently 'traded off' against any anticipated future economic benefits. The
advantage of sustainability appraisal, and the 'win–win–win' approach which
it was policing, was seen to be in adopting as a first-order priority the search
for policy approaches where no environmental deterioration would result. By
laying out clearly what the potential losses might be, it was felt that sustainability appraisal was likely to play a key role in guiding planners away from
what environmental groups might consider unacceptable 'trade-off'
approaches.

Interestingly, then, whereas previous technical appraisal systems in planning tended to result in decisions being made on the recommendations of a
select group of 'technical' experts, one of the main effects of sustainability
appraisal process has been to open up to public view areas of conflict. In
effect, rather than depoliticise decision making, sustainability appraisal has
helped to repoliticise it, in the sense of opening up the underlying concerns
to public scrutiny and debate. This destabilised the control of professional
planners over certain aspects of planning debate, creating scope for more contestation rather than less, where debates could move beyond interpretations
of 'neutral' facts and professional judgements to debates over values, preferences and priorities. At one level, the new processes conformed to the expectation that environmental problems get translated into expert discourses
which bring them within the domain of state apparatus. Yet in another way,
sustainability appraisal may potentially prove to mark something of a shift
away from the purely bureaucratic-technocratic rationalities of the state
apparatus (Harvey 1996, p. 73), in so far as the new system opens up to
public view and wider debate the underlying values involved in the decision-
making process.

Introducing some key protagonists

It is useful to introduce at this stage some of the ways in which the arguments
of regional planning's main protagonists are based on different understandings
of sustainable development. These differences are sometimes implicit, but also
quite often widely acknowledged and commented on, since a common discourse device is to engage in a form of rhetoric which seeks to dismiss oppositional views to help legitimate one's own viewpoints (Potter and Wetherell
1994). This approach constantly emerged in our interviews, and also occa-
sionally during some of the public examination hearings which we attended.

For instance, business and pro-development groups sought to portray
environmental and rural groups as 'extremist' in their unwillingness to take
into account social or economic considerations. In terms of our binary oppositions, such tactics tended to portray opponents as obsessed with a one-
dimensional reading of sustainable development.

The environmental policies have been hijacked by green, as in country-side, issues.

(interview WM5)

We're saying if you're talking about people then you need to prioritise people first. Obviously some people will disagree.... They'll say, 'Oh no, you've got to put newts and bugs first.'

(interview SE7)

Though it is possible to identify broadly pro- and anti-development positions, in seeking to justify these kinds of positions most groups adopted more subtle arguments which interwove various aspects of the sustainable development debate. In seeking to counter the environmental lobby, pro-development groups sometimes found themselves claiming common cause with other groups, albeit motivated by different policy concerns. For instance, in the south-east of England, the scarcity of social housing drew into regional planning debates a number of social housing lobby groups which favoured a selective freeing up of planning constraints. The result was that housebuilding lobby groups seeking to loosen planning constraints on greenfield sites could use as evidence in their favour the cautious support for releasing more land for development from social housing providers. Adding further complexity to the case for releasing greenfield sites was the Town and Country Planning Association (TCPA), which argued the case for initiating selective new settlements as being preferable to either suburban sprawl or 'town cramming' in existing urban areas.

Ranged against these forces were environmental groups such as Friends of the Earth, the Royal Society for the Protection of Birds (RSPB), and various local wildlife trusts concerned about issues such as the impact of losing undeveloped land on biodiversity. Adopting a rather different approach was the Council for the Protection of Rural England (CPRE), which argued against the loss of rural land for further urban development. To counter accusations that it is seeking to cram people into towns, the CPRE emphasises the role of design in improving urban environments and the continuing importance of open space in cities. This is important, because it reflects something of the way in which the rhetorics of different groups are rarely one-dimensional; they frequently legitimate their particular concerns by reference to wider aspects of the sustainable development agenda. In this case, the CPRE used urban ideas and even urban planning techniques to defend rural land.

The CPRE is interesting as a leading lobby group whose role in planning has been much debated (Vigar *et al.* 2000; Murdoch and Norton 2001; Murdoch and Abram 2002). It has been an active player in planning debates at all levels of the planning system, from the local to the national, arguing against further rural land take and supporting polices which promote urban compaction. The group's influence attracted considerable comment during our discussions, often attracting wary admiration for the professionalism of the group's approach, but also some concern about its underlying agenda, with one interviewee forthrightly saying that 'CPRE are the kings of NIM-BYism' (WM4: commercial interest group). ('NIMBY' is the widely used acronym for 'Not in My Back Yard', a disparaging term used for those who object to any development close to their property and instead attempt to deflect it to other locations through their protests.)

These are far from being the only active lobby groups involved in promoting particular views on how future development should be managed through the planning system. Other key players include the government statutory and advisory bodies, such as the Countryside Agency (promoting rural issues), the Environment Agency (responsible for aspects of water regulation, flood control, certain aspects of pollution control, etc.), English Nature (responsible for promoting biodiversity and wildlife) and English Heritage (responsible for conserving the built environment), each with their own particular mandates. Others include large charitable bodies active in lobbying on planning issues, such as the National Trust, and local charities and community groups ranging from amenity societies to neighbourhood groups. The main professional bodies also lobbied hard, notably the Royal Town Planning Institute RTPI, but also at national level the Royal Institute of Chartered Surveyors (RICS) and the Royal Institute of British Architects (RIBA).

Commercial pro-development interests have tended to be promoted through bodies such as the House Builders Federation (HBF), chambers of commerce, the Confederation of British Industry (CBI), while various smaller consortia of property developers have often hired consultants to help make their cases to public examinations. Of these groups, the HBF occupies a key position in the planning process, as its members are relied on to implement development proposals for new housing, and they rely in turn on planning to release land for development (Marsden *et al.* 1993).

Finally, and not least, there are the local and national politicians, and their local and national planning officers. Local politicians and planners played a key role in the regional planning bodies which drew up draft RPG documents, from which the main public debates followed. They were given the sensitive task of seeking to develop strategic-level regional documents while also maintaining the support of local electorates who might disagree with some aspects of regional decisions, for instance in relation to the location of new housing, or decisions about where to favour the provision of land for future employment.

In the case of regional planning in the post-1997 era, most advocacy interests quickly came to realise the value of presenting their case in terms of the wider sustainable development debate. In particular, pro-development groups were quick to capitalise on the government's integrated approach to sustainable development and the opportunity this afforded them to argue that more growth, and therefore development, was very much what was required for sustainable development.

Governance and regional planning in practice

How these different actors came together to seek to shape the ideas within regional planning is at the core of the remainder of this book. Inevitably, this topic raises interesting questions about the governance of regional planning. In Chapter 1 we introduced the institutional framework for regional planning, and in Chapter 2 aspects of governance theory. Having introduced some of the key protagonists in the system, we now want to link these discussions by examining how the stakeholders of planning sought to engage with the revised regional planning system. In particular, we begin to unpick how actors within the system were subject to a variety of constraining influences, from both the top down and the bottom up.

Because of its critical legal role in deciding on land uses, the state has tended to retain a stronger grip on planning's functions than in many other areas of activity, leading some observers to argue that English planning is still dominated by government rather than governance systems (Cowell and Murdoch 1999; Healey 1999). The example of regional planning would initially seem to support this, with the government still retaining the final say in the form of RPG (see Chapter 1). Alternatively, however, it is possible to see signs of a shift towards a more 'governance' approach, for instance in the improved mechanisms for participation in preparing RPG. These trends reflect a broader shift within planning away from a system which did things 'to' or 'for' local communities or businesses, and towards one which seeks to work 'with' its stakeholders.

Responding to criticisms that the previous system for preparing RPG had been insufficiently collaborative and transparent, in 1998 the government introduced reforms which would change the balance of power in some important ways. Non-governmental stakeholders were brought more centrally into the system, sometimes even working as part of the regional planning bodies which produced draft RPG. In addition, a wide variety of interest groups were invited to provide formal commentaries on the draft RPG in advance of a public examination, which in itself provided a further forum in which objections and alternatives could be aired. The result was a 'a much more open process than previously... everyone has a finger in the pie' (interview WM1).

Though for most participants the new arrangements clearly represented a welcome advance, in practice many tensions remained as a result of central government retaining its final say. An environment lobby group in the South West, for instance, told us that 'I... got the impression that the hidden hand of Government Office was always there behind the scenes' (interview SW5). Adding some substance to such suspicions, two planners seconded to the South West regional planning body have written about their experiences of what they refer to as the 'policing' role of government office (Gobbett and Palmer 2002, p. 211). Though they praise the valuable advisory role and technical assistance offered by seconded staff from the Government Office, these officers expressed concerns that having government representatives at key debates sometimes had an inhibiting effect. They also note how the 'partnership' ceased once the panel's report had been issued, as the government went into 'legal' mode while it produced the final version of RPG.

As an interviewee from another regional government office told us, the relationship could similarly feel awkward for the officers involved: 'Government office is in a bit of an ambivalent position; we are both player and referee' (interview, pre-public examination).

For those outside central government there was also widespread concern that central government continued to exercise a centralising influence through its system of national planning policy guidance notes. For one development lobby group involved in RPG for the South East, 'RPG9 tends to merely put national policy guidances into the South East. It doesn't actually question whether national policy guidance is good, bad or indifferent for the South East' (interview SE7).

In many other regions too, a sense emerged that much of the regional distinctiveness present in the draft version of RPG documents tended to be 'blanded out' once government offices took over the process. So in the East Midlands, for instance, the disappointment of some of those involved in drafting RPG was palpable: 'We had regional ownership, but now it has been snatched away, almost' (interview EM9 post-Panel report).

A further striking theme within our interviews was a concern that the meta-governance system was not working effectively, with regional planning seeming too divorced from other strategic processes at the regional level, such as economic development: 'The government has allowed an organisation mess to develop, with strategies produced in silos, with resulting tensions between them' (interview WM12).

Interestingly enough, given Jessop's (2000b) change in terminology from meta-governance to meta-steering, a conservation agency official in Yorkshire and the Humber remarked that the government office at the public examination 'were trying to steer rather than come in with size 12 boots and step on people' (interview YH7). This quotation usefully gives a sense of how planning operates neither simply as a directive legal function imposed from the centre, nor as a purely collaborative venture, but increasingly as a system in which various actors seek to steer debate in particular directions. This happens sometimes overtly and prescriptively, sometimes through more open forms of dialogue. But it is a process which also operates across scales, as ownership moves from the group of local planning authorities which tended to lead in producing the first drafts of RPG, to the wider processes of regional collaboration which emerged during the consultation phases, and then the combination of regional and national government officials who work on the final drafting. More than this, however, we can already begin to see something of the processes of multi-scalar working and their associated tensions, as instanced by the ways in which central government officers are drawn into regional collaborative processes.

Viewing the process as simply a top-down imposition of power, however, misses some of the ways in which the opportunities provided by the reformed governance structures for regional planning were not fully realised. For this, we need to take a more detailed look at some of the local and regional tensions within the process. The first round of regional planning guidance documents had been widely criticised for producing rather bland documents, lacking strategic direction and tending simply to replicate national government guidance (Thomas and Kimberley 1995; Baker 1996; Roberts 1996). These types of criticism continued to be voiced during the recent round, despite efforts to promote greater spatial specificity in the new system. There was widespread concern among stakeholders that despite the gains made in greater collaborative working, the resulting documents failed to tackle some of the more difficult issues with which regions were faced. Sometimes this was attributed to local planning authorities preferring to avoid regional decisions which might have negative repercussions for their local areas:

> There has been some criticism that the guidance tends to veer towards what is called the lowest common denominator, getting agreement across all local authorities rather than tackling tough issues.
>
> (interview EM6)

> In order to keep everyone on board it was better to have a generalised document that everyone could sign up to than a more specific document that some members would walk away from.
>
> (interview SW4)

For others, the problems of lack of strategic content were seen to lie equally with the process of wide-ranging consultation itself, which one housebuilding representative told us 'has resulted in RPG being to an extent the lowest common denominator' (interview NW7).

Unequal power and effective exclusion were also concerns for many participants, given the differences which existed in terms of resourcing and access to expertise. In terms of unequal power, there was some concern about local and regional planners, who we were told by one development lobby group were 'paranoid about maintaining their control' (interview EE8).

In addition, it proved difficult for local groups to engage at regional level, while even some of the larger environmental and housing groups lacked an adequate regional infrastructure and the resourcing to participate fully in all regional planning debates (Haughton and Counsell 2002). In general, those who had been involved seemed to appreciate the relative openness of the new system, while being aware that not all those who might have been present at debates had been able to attend:

[On the public examination] 'I found it useful, but I could see we were only talking to ourselves, there was no public there! ... When you get down to it, it was just a wider bunch of experts sitting down debating something only they knew about.

(interview EM7)

As the debates on collaborative planning might have predicted, the revised system for regional planning did move towards more open and transparent forms of engagement with stakeholders, but this proved deeply problematic in many ways. In particular, as debates moved through the different stages of the plan-making process, some of the deep-seated asymmetries of power and resources between stakeholders were quickly revealed, not least the problematic relations between local-, regional- and national-level actors. Though levels of trust were built up through the new governance systems of regional planning, these were not in themselves sufficient to disguise or overcome some deep-seated differences in values and priorities for reshaping the future of regions.

Conclusions

The period since the early 1990s has proved to be one of substantial change in the context for, and scope of, British planning, notably in terms of:

- a broadening of scope, including taking a central role in central government policy for sustainable development;
- a greater emphasis on integrated policy approaches;
- a growing rediscovery of strategic planning, particularly in relation to finding locations for new housing;
- a growing commitment to regional-scale planning; and
- a revitalised role for planning in urban regeneration (Allmendinger and Tewdwr Jones 2000; Rydin and Thornley 2002).

At first glance it is difficult to square these changes with accounts of the retreat of the state (see Chapter 2), but in practice the powers devolved have been both conditional and instrumental to the government's own objectives. What is clear is that the state has not retreated in planning policy so much as reorganised and re-regulated the ways in which it pursues its distinctive policy agendas. Yet in reworking planning powers in this way, the government has sought to increase the legitimacy of the reforms by opening up the new arrangements to greater public consultation and stakeholder participation. With this has come the potential to contest central government approaches, which has required central government to find new ways of limiting this power to disrupt or dislodge its own preferred approaches.

We argued earlier that 'sustainable development' is a political strategy, a form of tactics where it is used in the discursive construction of particular understandings of the problems facing planners and the ways in which they should be addressed. Rather than focus on searching for a definitive meaning of 'sustainable development', the argument is that it is necessary to recognise the multiplicity of sustainabilities and to analyse the ways in which these are shaped and mobilised in political discourse. With its inherent definitional ambiguities and malleability, sustainable development needs to be seen less as a broadly accepted 'neutral' or 'feel-good' phrase and rather more as a profoundly problematic, highly politicised and deeply contentious issue around which major power and legitimacy struggles have emerged.

The growing concern with sustainable development can be found in both planning and other policy areas, not least economic development, transport, resource management and environmental protection. Each of these policy areas has its own sets of policy histories, stakeholders and professional knowledges, so even where they all agree ostensibly to pursue sustainable development, they can have very different understandings of what this might entail. These differences have played an important role in planning debates on sustainable development, as different groups have sought to mobilise the term 'sustainable development' in different ways. The result has been that the insertion of sustainable development as a core objective for the British planning system has not been smooth, nor has it been consistent, nor has it been entirely successful.

This chapter has introduced some of the rhetorical devices used by campaigners as they seek to adapt to central government guidance on sustainable development, sometimes using tactics of undermining other groups by claiming that they show one-sided extremism as part of portraying their own viewpoints as more balanced, less emotional or less money-grubbing. Having highlighted these differences, however, we have also sought to emphasise the convergences at work, as the government's integrated approach has required groups to accommodate themselves more readily to opposing viewpoints. In order to enforce its preferred interpretation of sustainable development, and hence to shift the terms of policy debates, the government has introduced a system of sustainability appraisal. In effect, this new system has served to enforce a form of both external and internal discipline which ensured that an integrated approach was constructed as acceptable and environment-led approaches were construed as problematic, in effect changing the terms of the debate and with this the possibilities for new policy formation. Finally, the new governance systems surrounding regional planning have certainly opened up debates to greater scrutiny, though as often as not, this seems to have highlighted areas of disagreement rather than creating consensus. If there is a consensus, it is that no one is totally happy with the power relations embedded within the revised arrangements.

4 Environmental quality and natural resources

From environmental protectionism towards an integrated approach to sustainable development

> The thresholds which determine environmental capacity may (in some cases) be informed by scientific understanding of nature's properties but they become determinants of decision making through political judgement and social choice.
>
> (Jacobs 1997, p. 67)

Contested concepts for environmental protection

Power relations have been subtly yet substantially reconfigured by the decisive shift away from an environment-centred interpretation of sustainable development. Environmental groups have had to present their arguments with much greater sensitivity to social and economic issues, while development groups have been able to draw on the legitimacy which derived from the government's interpretation of sustainable development including the 'high and stable economic growth' objective. As the case study of sustainability appraisal in Chapter 3 intimates, the shift towards an integrated approach to sustainable development has challenged the privileged role of environmental techniques. The key finding was that where environment-led approaches seemed to offer the potential to make seemingly 'objective' decisions, the need to integrate environmental, social and economic issues brings political choices back to the fore.

It is in this context that this chapter focuses on the development of environmental techniques in planning since the early 1990s, and the challenges which they encountered as a wider definition of sustainable development came to the policy foreground. The aim is to explore the ways in which regional planning in particular has provided a public forum for debates about some of these new approaches. The first part of the chapter looks at debates on how best to measure environmental assets in order to help justify protecting them, and then reviews some of the treatment of specific environmental issues in regional planning guidance preparation during the period 2000–2002.

One of the most interesting things about the experiments with new environmental and sustainability techniques over the past fifteen years has been their complex processes of diffusion. The new techniques have not simply cascaded downwards through the planning hierarchy, nor were they simply transferred upwards through some capillary processes of 'bottom-up' innovation. Rather, the processes tended to involve a rather messy set of policy pulses which continuously ranged across scales. An alternative sequence of events is that new concepts and techniques were championed by particular national advisory or campaigning groups, developed with the help of consultants and then experimented with through local planning authority application. Their underlying values and technical assumptions were then frequently challenged at local planning inquiries. For the planning profession, following these experiments through the professional planning press was an important way of keeping abreast of the techniques being experimented with in other local authorities, providing a source of new ideas about what was currently possible and what was not. Sometimes it took such local experiments and debates to clarify for central government its approach to these new concepts and techniques, which might then become translated into good-practice guidelines in national planning policy guidance, or else be rejected.

A key issue in debates about developing new environmental techniques has been how to capture the varying qualities of the countryside. This is particularly evident in the case of debates about protecting the green belts surrounding many metropolitan areas in England. Green belts are a formal planning designation to restrict development around certain metropolitan areas (Box 4.1). Some parts of the green belt, however, have only low levels of *intrinsic* value as habitat or landscape, which means that their value is mainly *instrumental*, that of containing urban sprawl. Despite the fact that much of the green belt lacks great ecological value, the popular attitude towards these areas remains highly protective, tied into wider notions of the need to protect 'the countryside', for which erosion of the green belt has become emblematic. Green belts have in effect become politically untouchable in the face of most development pressures, and so these pressures have been redirected towards more distant countryside and urban areas.

During the early 1990s the strengthening of national policy on the environment was reflected in a series of revisions to national PPG notes. Both PPG1 *General Policies and Principles* (DoE 1992a) and PPG12, *Development Plans and Regional Planning Guidance* (1992b) were substantially rewritten to give greater emphasis to environmental issues. The immediate driving concern was to encourage planning authorities to think more widely about their environmental responsibilities, taking into account the emerging debate on global climate change:

> Local planning authorities should take account of the environment in the widest sense in plan preparation. They are familiar with the traditional issues of Green Belt, concern for environmental quality and nature conservation, the built heritage and conservation areas. They are familiar too

with pollution control planning for healthier cities. The challenge is to ensure that newer environmental concerns such as global warming and the consumption of non-renewable resources are also reflected in the analysis of policies that form part of plan preparation.

(DoE 1992b, para. 6.3)

The combination of the increased importance given to development plans following the Planning and Land Compensation Act 1991 (see Chapter 3) and these PPG revisions encouraged local authorities to embark on a series of development plan reviews and revisions. These provided a critical opportunity for planners seeking to reconsider and expand their treatment of environmental issues (Healey and Shaw 1993, 1994; Owens 1994). Though some guidance was issued by central government on the new environmental

---

Box 4.1 Green belt policy

Green belts around urban areas are perhaps the most enduring of British planning policies, originating in early regional plans in the South East, and being formalised in central government advice in 1955. The original objectives of green belts were to manage urban growth and shape urban development (Elson *et al.* 1993). Though additional purposes have been added in subsequent policy guidance (see below), they have remained in essence tools for controlling the spread of urban development. Although periodically criticised for creating unintended consequences, such as housing leapfrogging over the green belt and generating even longer commuting trips, they remain popular with the public.

No government has managed to withstand the backlash of any sustained effort to undermine green belt policy. Since 1997 the Labour government has emphasised its commitment to safeguarding green belts, most recently including plans to extend green belt areas as part of its *Sustainable Communities* initiative (ODPM 2003a).

The official expectations of green belt policy have been added to incrementally over time:

- to check the unrestricted sprawl of large urban areas (1955);
- to prevent neighbouring towns from merging into one another (1955);
- to preserve the special character of towns (1955);
- to assist in urban regeneration (1984);
- to safeguard the surrounding countryside from further encroachment (1988); and
- to preserve the special character of *historic* towns (1988) (Elson *et al.* 1993).

agenda, for example *A Guide to the Environmental Appraisal of Development Plans* (DoE 1993a), more generally little central government advice was available on how this new agenda should be taken forward in planning (Healey and Shaw 1994). The result was that the focus of innovation passed to a small number of local authorities engaged in preparing strategic plans. These authorities engaged in a number of important experiments in defining and operationalising new environmental concepts and planning tools. The first half of this chapter examines some of the continuing debates about an inter-related set of ideas concerning how to identify different types of environmental capital, environmental thresholds and limits, and environmental capacity.

A key theme in environmental capital debates has been the search for a more scientific basis for assessing the 'real value' of nature. Central to this has been an attempt to distinguish between the *intrinsic* value of environmental features (value in their own right as natural capital) and their *instrumental* values (valuable because of the services provided) (Jacobs 1997; Lockwood 1999). This proved difficult to achieve, since the ways in which people value nature frequently contain some highly ambiguous and contradictory elements, with contestation occurring not just over whether to protect the environment but also about which environments are most worthy of protection (Urry 1995). A good example of the ambiguities in how nature is valued emerged at the West Midlands public examination, where the CBI representative commented:

> Not all development is bad for environmental capital.. . . CPRE describes the downhill slope of irreconcilable damage, but it is not always so. Mineral extraction has, for example, extended wetland assets.. . . Also housing can increase biodiversity by increasing tree cover, compared to agro-desert.

The key issue here is that it is dangerous to assume automatically that countryside nature (Plate 4.1) is somehow more valuable in ecological terms than disturbed or previously developed land (Plate 4.2). Particularly with the rise of large-scale, intensively farmed single crop fields, there is often little biodiversity evident in much of the farmed English countryside any more. Alternatively, there are often areas within cities which are quite rich in species by comparison, from derelict land to some suburban back gardens.

The new environmental tools tended to be first developed and applied by local planners in the most prosperous parts of the country. It was in these areas that local planning authorities were under most pressure to resist high levels of new development, with existing residents often concerned about the declining quality of the local environment, and local politicians fearing a political backlash. Though usually initiated with high hopes of diffusing political pressures, in practice the new techniques almost invariably proved problematic once they entered the political arena of public examination, as supporters of differ-

Plate 4.1 Agro-desert?

ent attitudes to development challenged the way in which environment was being treated (Counsell 1999a–c). Ultimately, attempts to use 'objective' techniques to avoid value judgements in deciding which features of the environment were most worth protecting against development proved difficult to implement, with planning debates serving to demonstrate that the value placed by humans on nature is in large part socially defined (Jacobs 1997).

Environmental limits and carrying capacity

Since the mid-1980s, local anti-development protests have been particularly evident in the growth pressure points in the south-east of England, creating a series of dilemmas for policy makers and politicians. As a group, anti-development lobbyists tend to be articulate and affluent, possessing considerable political clout in the shire counties, as the Conservative government found during the 1980s (Thornley 1993). The often ambiguous relationship between environmental stewardship and a concern to maintain local property values was at the heart of the pro-development case in debates throughout the 1990s, continuing when the focus of strategic planning shifted up a scale to RPG in the late 1990s.

The mid-1990s round of structure plan reviews for county councils was prepared in a climate of government projections of the need for substantial

Plate 4.2 Nature flourishing on a brownfield industrial site in Norwich designated for future housing.

new housing, some 4.4 million new homes by 2016, mainly in the growth areas of the South (DoE 1996b). In recognition of the political problems with allowing this much new development on greenfield sites, there was growing support in central government for locating as much development as possible on previously used land in towns (brownfield land), thus reducing the amount of greenfield land take required. It was during this period that the main debates on environmental capacity and capital took place, when a key issue driving experimentation with these approaches was the search for ways of challenging housing number allocations within strategic planning documents. The result was some highly charged political debates on housing numbers, which frequently spilt over from the local to the national political arena.

It is in this context that attempts to introduce new environmental concepts and measurement techniques need to be viewed. In a heavily politicised and highly emotionally charged policy environment, concepts such as environmental capacity afforded the opportunity to present arguments in less emotional ways than the usual 'don't concrete over our countryside' rhetoric of anti-development groups by appealing to seemingly neutral concepts and techniques. For that reason, seemingly esoteric or arcane concepts such as making a distinction between critical and non-critical capital stocks actually became the focus of considerable attention within the planning community. They raised the prospect of being able to argue that a particular policy approach was based on 'objective' methods, which provided clear-cut and unassailable assessments of which kinds of environment to protect, where and why. But it was not to turn out to be such an easy and ready solution to the vexed problems of where to locate new housing and employment land.

One of the most important environmental debates for the planning profession during the early 1990s concerned whether the environment should be balanced with other considerations through 'trade-offs' or managed within environmental limits and capacities (Healey and Shaw 1994; Owens 1994; Owens and Cowell 2002). The County Planning Officers' Society adopted a leading position in this debate, publishing the report *Planning for Sustainability* in 1993, which advocated the use of techniques and concepts such as carrying capacity, environmental capital, demand management and the precautionary principle to ensure that development took place within environmental limits.

Many of the concepts advocated in the County Planning Officers' Society report were tried out in practice during the early 1990s in counties such as Bedfordshire, Hertfordshire and West Sussex (Counsell 1998, 1999a, b, c). These counties are all in the south of England, the area subject to greatest development pressures, and consequently where views about how best to accommodate projected future housing needs tended to be most vigorously debated. The local politics of development tended to focus on efforts to resist new development proposals both at the level of strategic plan making and also when individual site proposals were put forward. Because of the contradictory local and national political pressures, respectively to restrict and to permit more housing development, these local planning authorities were perhaps more eager than those elsewhere to develop techniques which might support the local pressures for development restraint.

Environmental capacity, along with the associated issues of environmental limits and carrying capacities, was developed from the premise that the environment has a finite limit to the development which it can absorb without destroying its essential character. The approach became central to many of the early attempts to operationalise sustainable development in planning practice. However, problems quickly emerged because of difficulties in identifying with any clarity the actual limits, or thresholds at which development becomes unacceptable (Owens 1994; Jacobs 1997; Rydin 1998a). This proved difficult to determine at the technical level, perhaps because of a lack of scientific method but perhaps also because such thresholds simply did not exist in nature, as Jacobs intimated in research for the CPRE:

> This is why capacity is a metaphor. The environment's capacity limits do not exist simply in nature. They are products of an *argument* about how society should treat the natural world: the claim that human activity should be constrained within sustainability thresholds.
>
> (Jacobs 1997, p. 21)

However, it proved equally difficult to assess thresholds through social processes of consultation and participation, Jacobs went on to suggest, where it was often difficult to separate environmental concern from local self-interest.

Development lobby groups in particular tended to regard the use of techniques such as environmental capacity as a threat to the future availability of building land. A key rhetorical technique from the start was to seek to discredit work on environmental capacity by associating it with NIMBYism. The concern with technical method and social context is neatly encapsulated in the conclusions of research on this issue commissioned by the HBF:

> My contention is that 'capacity' is not too easily tied down and has real dangers. It is not simply that environmental capacity arguments can become a cloak for NIMBYism (and thus lose credibility). It is that in some situations the notion of capacity is just not valid.
>
> (Grigson 1995, p. 24)

Pejorative references to NIMBYism were a recurrent rhetorical theme in these debates. It is a problematic tactic, however, in that there are real difficulties in distinguishing between NIMBYism and a wider concern for environmental stewardship (Shucksmith 1990; Freudenberg and Pastor 1992; Burningham 2000). But it was precisely this lack of clarity which made it easy for the development industry to dismiss environmental objections, and the tools which might support them, as NIMBYism.

Identifying 'critical natural capital'

Another part of the environmental capital debate concerned efforts to identify 'criticial natural capital', something which became particularly important in relation to opposition to development in green belts. As indicated earlier, in many cases the main attributes of the green belt are *instrumental*, in that they were originally designated to fulfil a number of specific purposes such as containing urban development, safeguarding the countryside from encroachment, and preventing neighbouring towns from merging (Elson *et al.* 1993; RTPI 2000). New techniques of environmental assessment being developed in the 1990s (English Nature 1992) set out, in contrast, to assess the *intrinsic* value of the environment, dividing the natural environment into categories called 'critical natural capital' and 'constant assets'.

Critical natural capital was intended to cover those natural assets which should be treated as inviolable in the fact of development pressures, whereas constant assets would need to be maintained at constant levels through compensatory provision where losses occurred. The notion was that certain capital would be inviolable while other capital might be regarded as tradable, in the sense that losses could occur provided there was compensatory provision. Although the idea was a fairly simple one, difficulties were soon encountered in making it operational. The resulting debates fuelled a long-running sensitivity in planning circles to issues surrounding policy 'trade-offs', or attempts to achieve a balance between objectives, rather than working within environmental limits or achieving integrated approaches.

In addition to suffering from some of the conceptual problems associated with 'environmental capacity', the critical natural capital approach ran into particular difficulties when it came to dealing with green belt. Large areas of green belt consist of farmland with little landscape or ecological value, and as such would not normally be considered critical natural capital meriting strong conservation policies. In recent years there has been a growing lobby to consider de-designating the less ecologically valuable parts of the green belt to allow development, while making new extensions to the green belt in areas of greater ecological value. In effect, such proposals suggest that it might be desirable to 'trade off' within the 'environmental capital' category, substituting the loss of an area of green belt by designating another area as green belt. Concepts such as wildlife corridors and green wedges have also been put forward as more suitable ways of protecting areas of environmental value close to cities in ways which better respect their ecological conditions (Herington 1991; Elson 1999, 2002). The Regional Studies Association, the RTPI and the TCPA all issued reports calling for greater flexibility in attitudes to green belt designation rather than treating them as untouchable (Herington 1991; RTPI 2002; TCPA 2002a).

These issues emerge with some force in regional planning debates, where an underlying concern was that 'Green belts are not generally drawn up on the basis of sustainability criteria or such positive criteria as public accessibility to green space and may become an obstacle to developing more sustainable development patterns' (written evidence from the Countryside Agency, Yorkshire and Humber Public Examination, July 2000). Any attempt to devalue green belt resulted in a popular outcry, making it very difficult to do anything other than accept that areas covered by green belt designations were inviolable in assessing land for its development potential when producing strategic plans. This approach was vigorously supported by some key environmental groups:

> As pressure for new development mounts it is more important now than ever to protect Green Belts and make sure they continue what they do best. . . . Green Belts have been fulfilling these purposes for over 60 years. In meeting the Government's twin objectives of protecting the countryside and promoting urban renaissance, they need to be as central to the policies of the next century as they have to the last.
>
> ('Green belts – still working under threat', briefing, June, CPRE 2001a)

In government terms, green belts are seen to be of regional importance, while the possibility of designating green wedges is now recognised in planning guidance as covering areas of local importance (Elson 2003). Interestingly, in *Sustainable Communities* (ODPM 2003a) the government introduced policies to maintain and enhance the provision of green belt, while also introducing the prospect of improving protection for green wedges and green corridors. The mention of green corridors is intriguing, as it had not previously been clear how the government viewed them in terms of the hierarchy of planning protection (Elson 2003).

Case study: environmental capacity and the West Sussex structure plan

In producing its structure plan in 1996–1997, West Sussex County Council tried to develop the concept of environmental capacity into an operational planning tool. This was a bold move, given that a number of other local authorities had already unsuccessfully sought to develop the idea of environmental capacity in the hope that it would provide a technical solution to the amount of growth which could be accommodated in their localities.

Reflecting on this experience, West Sussex planners concluded that such a technique could never determine the precise amount of growth which the county could absorb, but they moved ahead with a detailed environmental capacity study on the grounds that it would nevertheless be useful in demonstrating the consequences of growth.

> With hindsight it is unfortunate that the appraisal was described as a study of 'environmental capacity', because this seems to have conveyed the wrong messages. There was no expectation that the study would show that West Sussex was 'full', or that any particular housing figure would be confirmed.... What it does show quite clearly is that the environment of West Sussex is declining.... Because of this 'a balancing of objectives' is considered necessary to select the least unsustainable ways of allowing development. Beyond the point of satisfying present needs, it is not a matter of balance: safeguarding environmental resources is imperative.
>
> (WSCC 1997, p. 2)

West Sussex's environmental capacity study in 1996 represented probably the most comprehensive attempt in England to explore systematically the constraints imposed by environmental features on development. It provided a detailed mapping of environmental characteristics of the county, bound in a large volume. The range of constraints, some fifty-eight in number, stretched from the normal planning considerations of protected landscapes and habitats and high-quality agricultural land to more intangible issues such as tranquillity, and practical considerations of accessibility to public transport. They also included local landscape designations, giving protection, for example, to 'strategic gaps' separating existing towns (Table 4.1). The conclusion of this substantial piece of work was that the environment of West Sussex, and in particular the 'countryside' environment, was deteriorating rapidly, to such

Table 4.1 Planning constraints in West Sussex

	Primary planning constraints		Other/potential planning constraints	
	Constraints at international or national level	*Constraints at strategic and local level*	*Areas where development may be wholly or partly constrained by policy or statute*	*Areas with potential to constrain development*
Land	• High-grade agricultural land • Areas of Outstanding Natural Beauty • Crown property • Natural Trust land • Common land • Land seriously affected by aircraft noise	• Land liable to flooding • Strategic gaps • Local gaps • Setting of Arundel/ Chichester, NE area • Undeveloped coast • Land outside built-up areas • Mineral land bank • Urban public open space • Contaminated/ unstable land	• Aquifer protection zones • Groundwater vulnerability areas • Airport and radar safeguarding areas	• Tranquil areas • Urban tranquil areas • Landscape character areas • Waste disposal sites with potential to gas • Land remote from public transport nodes and corridors • Valuable soils • Environmentally Sensitive Areas
Wildlife and geology	• Special Protection Areas • Special Areas of Conservation • Ramsar sites • Sites of Special Scientific Interest • National nature reserves • Local nature reserves • Tree Preservation Orders	• Sites of nature conservation importance • Other nature reserves • Ancient woodland • Wildlife corridors • Marine SNCIs		• Habitats defined as constant natural resources • Prime biodiversity areas

Category				
Buildings and urban areas	• Marine SACs • Conservation areas • Listed buildings	• Townscape protection areas • Other buildings and structures of architectural or historic interest		• Familiar and well-loved urban environments
Archaeology	• Scheduled Ancient Monuments (and setting) • Registered historic parks and gardens	• Non-registered historic parks and gardens	• Archaeologically Sensitive Areas	
Recreation	• Public rights of way network	• Country parks	• Individual rights of way • Strategic recreational routes	• Roadways and lanes of value • Facilities/areas of importance

Source: Based on West Sussex County Council (1996).

Note
SNCI = Site of Nature Conservation Importance; SAC = Special Area of Conservation.

an extent that levels of growth proposed in previous drafts of the structure plan would be unsustainable. The county council used these findings to justify adopting lower levels for future housing development than proposed in the 1994 RPG for the South East.

Because of the restrictions on future housing numbers and the strong approach to protecting a broad range of privileged environments, it was perhaps inevitable that the West Sussex structure plan would be challenged by the development industry. West Sussex is beyond the outer limits of the metropolitan green belt, so the debate focused not on green belt, but on the twenty-two 'strategic gaps' identified in the structure plan (DETR 2000e). These areas were a purely local designation, in effect a substitute for green belt, and as such were popular with local people (Figure 4.1). The strategic gaps were defined by the county council as forming part of the 'critical natural capital' – that is, they were considered so important that they should be subject to absolute protection from development pressures, in effect making them equivalent in status to green belt. Pro-development interests in particular challenged the privileged status given to strategic gaps. As most strategic gaps were located on the edge of urban areas, housebuilders argued that these areas were the most 'sustainable' locations for future growth.

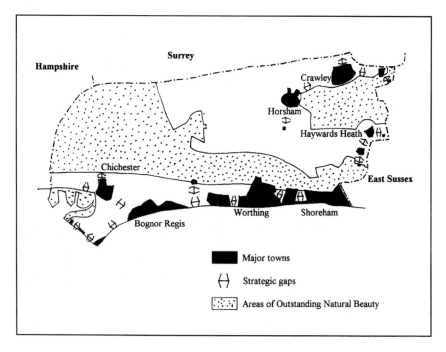

Figure 4.1 Strategic gaps in the West Sussex Structure Plan. (Source: Counsell (1999b).)

Strategic gaps therefore were portrayed as artificial environmental constraints, covering areas mostly lacking any intrinsic value (Counsell 1999b).

The examination in public (EiP) panel, in deliberating on the structure plan, accepted that the environmental constraints identified in the capacity study were not absolute and could be relaxed if the need was great enough. If this were the case, judgements would have to be made about relative priorities:

> No doubt the first priority would be to maintain those constraints whose relaxation would otherwise lead to irreversible environmental change in the natural environment, or those which are manifestly important national designations... We consider that if thresholds have to be crossed... to accommodate housing and employment growth, the strategic gaps could be considered less precious than other landscape constraints.
>
> (WSCC 1997, pp. 10, 30).

This conclusion removed the absolute protection proposed for strategic gaps, in effect downgrading their status from critical natural capital, also making a distinction between the locally designed strategic gaps and national green belt policy (DETR 2000e). The RTPI (2000) has subsequently argued in favour of abandoning such local designations, which it says confused the public and reduced confidence in designated green belts. Despite this weakening of the policy on strategic gaps, the panel in West Sussex did conclude that the ability of the county to accommodate further development was severely limited, supporting the case for a lower level of housing. This decision was subsequently challenged by central government, which directed the county council to increase its housing numbers to RPG levels, something which it was reluctantly forced to do after mounting an unsuccessful challenge in the courts.

Following the central government decision, West Sussex County Council shifted its position on environmental capacity, accepting that its approach was seen by many as an attempt to define absolute limits to development and that the approach led to a highly adversarial EiP (Connell 1999). It has instead opted to take its structure plan review forward using a more comprehensive technique which evolved out of the work on environmental capacity, involving a Strategic Development Options Study (SDOS). This is seen by West Sussex planners as a more joined up approach which aims to balance social, economic and environmental considerations in a similar way to the shift from environmental capital to quality of life capital in the work of the government conservation agencies, which we return to next.

From 'environmental capital' to 'quality of life capital'

As part of the move towards an integrated approach to sustainable development, environmental tools have tended to be subject to pressure to open up to consider economic and social issues. For instance, as Chapter 3 notes, environmental appraisal was reworked in favour of the more holistic approach of 'sustainability appraisal', which became the government's recommended method of policy appraisal in RPG.

In similar vein, the 'environmental capital' work led by the government conservation agencies has been reworked as 'quality of life' capital. During the mid-1990s, environmental capital techniques were strongly backed by the government conservation agencies (English Nature, English Heritage, the Countryside Agency and the Environment Agency), being seen as an approach which would help to define which aspects of the environment merited protection through the planning process. This in many ways represented a development of earlier attempts to make the concepts of critical natural capital and constant assets operational in planning (English Nature 1992). In turning away from this work as too simplistic, the agencies began to work jointly on a new technique which analysed the attributes of each piece of environmental capital and the services it provided for human well-being. It was proposed that in making decisions affecting environmental capital, issues such as scarcity, replaceability, substitutability and scale should be taken into account.

With the shift in the late 1990s towards a quality of life focus in the national policy on sustainable development, this technique was quickly relabelled 'quality of life capital', becoming reworked as a tool for maximising environmental, economic and social benefits. As in its previous guise as environmental capital, the technique considers the services and benefits which different pieces of capital provide for human well-being (English Nature *et al.* 2001). It is a technique which can be applied at different scales of planning, based on an appraisal of what is there; any piece of capital might provide different benefits depending on the scale at which it is being considered. The stages to be followed are described as follows:

- Decide purpose of study.
- Identify what is there.
- Identify the benefits and services potentially affected by the planning process.
- Evaluation.
- Decide who the services matter to and at what spatial scale.
- Decide how important they are.
- Establish whether we have enough of them.
- Consider what (if anything) could make up for any loss or damage to the service.
- Policy/management implications.
- Monitoring.

The essence of the approach is that decisions on development should not diminish the benefits and services provided by the capital, involving in the first instance planning solutions which maintain or enhance all three elements of capital: environmental, economic and social. Similar to win–win–win, this concept became known as 'no net loss' of quality of life capital.

This new approach attracted considerable interest among regional planning stakeholders, as it brought to the fore the issue of compensation – through 'planning agreements', for example, should a development result in a loss of any particular type of capital. However, there was some apparent confusion about whether 'win–win–win and 'no net loss' meant the same thing or were different. The government conservation agencies which had been central in developing and promoting the quality of life capital approach appeared to see win–win–win and no net loss as two parts of the same argument:

> In order to deliver sustainable development the Agencies consider it essential that priority is given to meeting economic, social and environmental objectives together (win–win–win) rather than balancing different interests. Specifically development should be required to show an overall net gain, or at minimum a neutral effect with no significant losses to any interests.
>
> (Joint Statutory Conservation Agencies: written evidence to the West Midlands public examination)

Although they were sometimes used interchangeably in regional planning debates about whether or not planning policy should promote trading between the objectives of sustainable development, in practice some stakeholders interpreted them differently, with 'no net loss' causing more concerns to pro-development lobbyists than 'win–win–win'.

Quality of life capital in regional planning, 2000–2002

Elements of the quality of life capital approach emerged in draft RPG for Yorkshire and the Humber (RAYH 1999). Though the core strategy was underpinned by the concept of natural and social capital, there was an acceptance that this approach would involve trade-offs between these resources. Where trade-off was necessary, the strategy proposed that sustainability appraisal should make the terms of this explicit, and seek to maintain or increase the total value of human and natural capital assets. In its report, the public examination panel (Swain and Rozee 2000) proposed that these two categories of capital be replaced by three: economic, social and environmental capital, to fit more closely with the central government approach to sustainable development.

References to 'trade-off' in draft RPG for Yorkshire and the Humber attracted considerable criticism during the public examination by those who felt that this could be used to give priority to the economic concerns, rather than meeting all objectives at the same time. Referring to objections from the RSPB and the RTPI about the idea of 'trade-off', the panel agreed that the aim should be to deliver an integrated approach which maximised the achievement of 'win–win–win' solutions. Irrespective of the panel's conclusions, in the final version of RPG for Yorkshire and the Humber (GOYH 2001b), central government steered away altogether from the 'capital approach', returning to a general policy on sustainable development and promoting an objectives-led approach to policy appraisal based on sustainability appraisal.

A similar debate took place in the East Midlands, where again the panel recommended removing any implication that trade-offs between the objectives of sustainable development might be acceptable (Parke and Travers 2000). The Secretary of State's 'proposed changes' to draft RPG, under a heading 'The overall aim of the guidance', included the statement 'all of the policies are mutually consistent and the purposes of one should not be achieved at the expense of another' (GOEM 2001, p. 22), a somewhat watered-down version of 'no net loss'. This reference was itself removed from the final version of RPG (GOEM 2002). In contrast to these debates, in the South West region the public examination panel reached the opposite decision on trade-offs. It concluded that 'win–win–win' situations would be the exception rather than the rule and that in most cases a degree of trade-off would be inevitable (Crowther and Bore 2000).

Case study: debating quality of life capital in the North West

The most comprehensive attempt to date in utilising the idea of quality of life capital at the regional scale emerged in draft RPG for the North West Region (NWRA 2000). The Countryside Agency, which had been particularly influential during the preparation of draft RPG in the North West, had helped develop a core policy promoting the enhancement of existing capital. This policy proposed that:

> The overall aim of sustainable development should be to enhance environmental, social and economic capital. Local authorities should carry out sustainability appraisals of development plans. ... to identify important elements of environmental, social and economic capital which might be affected. Development plans should contain policies which set out clearly:
>
> • those elements of capital where there is a presumption against any harm arising from development;
> • an expectation overall that there will be no net loss and clear benefits arising from development; and
> • the means, including planning obligations and conditions, the phasing or programming of development, or the use of bonds, by which any necessary compensation, mitigation or substitution is to be achieved.
>
> (NWRA 2000, p. 6)

This policy included a strong commitment to 'no net loss', which stimulated a lengthy and at times heated debate about quality of life capital at the public examination, where the policy was generally supported by environmental lobbyists, whereas strong misgivings were expressed by pro-development interests. The panel report (Acton *et al.* 2001) refers to the fact of this policy causing alarm to some participants because it would be too restrictive of development. The CBI is referred to as arguing that 'it would be dangerous to preclude a major economic development because of a small environmental effect' (Acton *et al.* 2001, p. 46).

The main concern of the pro-development lobby was that the existence of the 'no net loss of capital' policy would put the North West at a disadvantage when competing for investment with other regions. It is perhaps worth noting here how the rhetorics of globalisation and inter-regional competitiveness emerged as important in arguing against stronger environmental protection policies. The HBF went further and questioned what the 'no net loss of capital' policy actually meant, suggesting that the whole approach was too academic and moreover that it was premature to use it as a planning tool.

On the other hand, the Countryside Agency argued that

> People need to be aware of the potential loss of any type of capital, particularly where an economic gain will result in a loss of environmental capital. This is unsustainable and if people are to lose features that they value they need to be aware that this is happening so they can do something about it. At present there is no requirement to make good any losses.
>
> (oral evidence from the Countryside Agency, North West public examination 2001)

The public examination panel accepted the quality of life approach as an appraisal tool – 'armed with the results of the appraisal, the decision maker will be suitably informed to reach a conclusion' (Acton *et al.* 2001, p. 47). However, while accepting the overall approach, it also acknowledged the political nature of planning decisions, accepting that there were real difficulties in making objective decisions about whether a degree of harm to one element of capital is justified by benefit to another. The panel therefore proposed redrafting the policy so that it supported 'enhancing the quality of life without prohibiting a decision based on balance' (Acton *et al.* 2001, p. 48). This almost meaningless platitude effectively diluted the concept of 'no net loss' to a level where it had little remaining value.

Nonetheless, the policy on 'quality of life capital', together with the panel's amendments, was accepted both in central government's 'proposed changes' and in the final version of RPG12 (GONW 2003). This was important, as it was the first time a policy on quality of life capital had survived to this stage of the process. However, in the written explanation for the 'proposed changes' it is indicated that the government was still not convinced of its effectiveness as a planning tool:

> None of these techniques are sufficiently developed to provide local authorities with the tried and tested 'toolkit' to identify and evaluate which aspects of social, environmental and economic benefit matter for people's quality of life and how these assets might be enhanced, maintained or, where necessary, genuinely compensated for when accommodating development and change.
>
> (GONW 2002, p. 11)

Work is still continuing on developing this approach, with the conservation agencies still promoting quality of life capital as a planning tool, including developing a Web site dedicated to the technique (http://www.qualityoflife-capital.org.uk).

Is 'no net loss' preferable to 'win–win–win'?

These debates highlight the confusion among planners and others about what is meant by the terms 'win–win–win' and 'no net loss'. One national environmental campaign group, for example, was unconvinced by the quality of life capital approach because it brought to the fore the issue of compensation, which was seen as 'trading':

> The problem with the concept up until now is that every time it has been used everyone jumps in straight away with the tradeability aspects. . ... When you get into tradeability there are big questions about habitat replacement, and there are big questions with some habitats over whether it is possible to replace them.
>
> (interview SE9)

Along with other environmental groups, this group has been a strong supporter of the win–win–win approach, however. This is partly because of an aversion to trading between economic and environmental objectives, which many environmentalists believe had resulted previously mainly in economic gains. But more than this, the win–win–win approach was seen to be valuable as it provided greater credibility to the group's own case for environmental protection. The RSPB, for instance, has argued not simply for an environmental approach, but an integrated approach:

> We do not consider that the principles of sustainable development have been sufficiently integrated throughout the Guidance. For development to be truly sustainable it is essential that all three legs of sustainable development are fully integrated, not balanced.
>
> (RSPB, written submission: North East public examination)

Pro-development interests also appeared in many cases to have more concerns about the 'no net loss' concept than 'win–win–win', as the North West example illustrated. A possible reason for this is that 'win–win–win' is promoted as a first-order policy preference, and few would disagree that if solutions can be found which are mutually beneficial, then they should be adopted. If they cannot be found, though, this approach acknowledges that policy makers revert to achieving balanced decisions. Viewed in this light, 'no net loss' appears a much stronger concept, implying as it does that social, economic and environmental capital should at a minimum be maintained at current levels.

Treatment of the environment in regional planning guidance: inter-regional comparisons

There was a degree of similarity in the range of environmental issues covered in the various RPG documents after 1998. This is not too surprising, since central government guidance sets out in some detail the main environmental and natural resource topics which need to be addressed (DETR 2000a): rural development and countryside character, biodiversity and nature conservation, the coast, minerals, waste and energy.

In addressing environmental policy issues, recent regional planning documents have tended to draw heavily on national policy developed through the national sustainable development strategy, *A Better Quality of Life* (DETR 1999a). For example, on waste management, most regional planning documents adopted the national target of 30 per cent of household waste to be recycled by 2010 (see Table 4.2). Three regions also adopted the national target for 10 per cent of electricity generating capacity to be supplied from renewable sources by 2010, while the North East used a local study to suggest a slightly lower target. The national target for the reduction of greenhouse gas emissions (20 per cent) is also used in two RPG documents, though global warming, surprisingly, receives a fairly low profile generally in regional planning documents, where it tended to be subsumed into overall approaches to sustainable development.

The lack of attention to climate change as a central theme in RPG was raised by stakeholders in some regions. It was, for example, strongly criticised in the public examination of the West Midlands draft guidance, where the government conservation agencies indicated that it should be given much greater prominence and emphasis in the spatial strategy (see Chapter 7). They went on to suggest that treatment of climate change should cover both causes, such as reducing the greenhouse gas emissions, and effects, such as the greater risk of flooding. With the draft plan still under review, it remains to be seen what impact this debate will have on the final West Midlands RPG.

There were other environmental topics which generated more regionally distinct policies: targets for woodland cover, or the planting of new woodland, for example. Targets for woodland cover range from 6.5 per cent in

Table 4.2 Examples of environmental and resource efficiency targets in regional planning guidance (RPG) (derived from most recent versions of RPG documentation, as at October 2001)

	EM	NE	NW	SE	SW	WM	YH
Woodland (target coverage)	+65,000 ha, 2021	7%	+10%, 2010	15%		1,500 ha p.a.	6.5%
Recycled aggregate production (%)	+		20/25	+	+	10	
Waste recycling (2010)	30%	30%	30%+	30%	30%	30%	
Renewable energy capacity (2010)	400 MW (2005)	5–9%		10%	10%		10%
Greenhouse gas emissions (1990–2010)					20%		20%

Note
No targets were included in RPG for East Anglia.

Yorkshire and the Humber to 15 per cent in the South East, with planting targets of 1,500 hectares (3,700 acres) per annum in the West Midlands and 65,000 hectares (160,600 acres) by 2021 in the East Midlands. These targets, though, provide little comparative evidence of environmental performance, since much depends on the original extent of tree cover and on the existing initiatives in place.

In an attempt to analyse regional differences in approach towards the environment, the remainder of this chapter focuses on two topics on which central government is not especially prescriptive: biodiversity and water management/flood risk issues. Both topics had been debated in some detail at regional planning public examinations, despite the fact that PPG11 *Regional Planning* (DETR 2000a), does not specifically identify the latter topic.

Addressing biodiversity through regional planning

Maintaining biodiversity, now a widely used shorthand term for biological diversity or the diversity of life (DoE 1994b), is inextricably bound up with the use of land, with policies for conserving nature having traditionally had a clear spatial dimension (Owens and Cowell 2002). However, the main responsibility for protecting and managing biodiversity lies outside the land use planning system with English Nature, an agency of central government. English Nature adopted both advisory and adversarial roles during the preparation of RPG, working to promote stronger policies for the protection of nature. In consequence, on occasion English Nature frequently found itself aligned with voluntary-sector bodies such as the RSPB and the Wildlife Trusts in regional planning debates, rather than simply maintaining a governmental line.

In PPG11 (DETR 2000a) the government proposed that regional planners should incorporate objectives for biodiversity and nature conservation into regional development objectives, taking into account nationally or regionally significant species and habitats. Habitat and species conservation is traditionally linked to the protection of sites designated as having importance through international agreements and European and national law: Ramsar sites, international sites designated under the Ramsar Convention of 1973; Special Areas of Conservation and Special Protection Areas designated under the European Habitats and Species Directive; and National Nature Reserves, Local Nature Reserves and Sites of Special Scientific Interest (SSSIs) designated under British national legislation. Though these sites are important, they cover only a small part of the national land area and are isolated from each other. In consequence, it is widely recognised that nature conservation must also look to the wider environment, to protect other high-priority habitats (i.e. those which are scarce or declining) and rare or threatened species of plants and animals (English Nature 1992). As the regional planning debates were under way, these high-priority habitats and species were being identified by conservation bodies at the local level in Biodiversity Action Plans (BAPs). In some areas, biodiversity audits were undertaken to identify key habitats and species at the regional scale, but this was a voluntary activity which was not pursued during the RPG time-scale in every region. Biodiversity issues for land use planning (see PPG9, *Nature Conservation* [DoE 1994c]) also include habitat restoration and re-creation – that is, putting nature back into areas where it has been lost or damaged, mitigation to reduce the impacts of development on nature, and compensation measures where losses nevertheless occur (Eden *et al.* 2002).

A content assessment of RPG documents was made as part of our research, focusing on whether seven key aspects of biodiversity were specifically treated in the eight RPG processes. These criteria were identified from a review of the policy and academic literature (see Figure 4.2; for an earlier version see Counsell and Bruff 2001).

Overall, there was a levelling up and evening out of the treatment of biodiversity during the regional planning process in different regions (Figure 4.2). Nevertheless, biodiversity concern appeared to be less fully treated in some regions than others. For example, biodiversity was initially dealt with only at a very generalised level in the North East. Even after taking into account changes proposed by the public examination panel (Richardson and Simpson 2000), draft RPG still covered less of the biodiversity agenda than in any other region. It is not really clear why this should be the case, but it may in part be because considerable extents of protected areas already exist in the area, so biodiversity is seen to be less under threat than in some other areas.

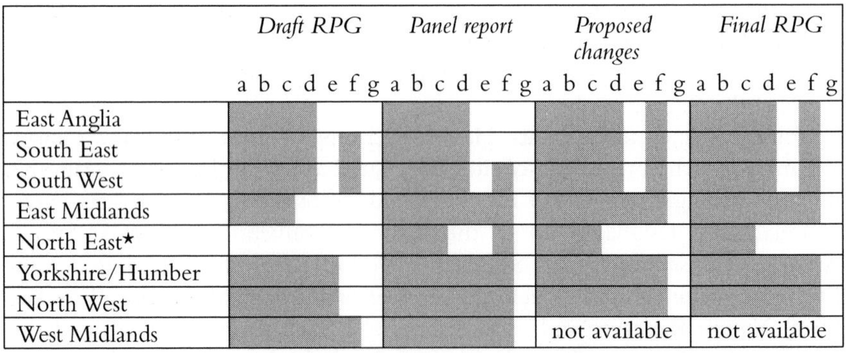

	Draft RPG	Panel report	Proposed changes	Final RPG
	a b c d e f g	a b c d e f g	a b c d e f g	a b c d e f g
East Anglia				
South East				
South West				
East Midlands				
North East*				
Yorkshire/Humber				
North West				
West Midlands			not available	not available

*Policies were not separately identified in the draft North East RPG.

The shading indicates coverage of the following criteria in RPG policies:
(a) maintenance and increase of biodiversity; (b) protection and enhancement of designated sites; (c) protection and enhancement of non-designated sites and species; (d) habitat re-creation, restoration and management; (e) compensation and mitigation; (f) habitats targets; and (g) species targets.

Figure 4.2 Comparison of regional planning guidance policies on biodiversity at different stages in the process.

This form of quantitative assessment represents only part of the story: when it is looked at qualitatively, a richer impression emerges of the treatment of biodiversity. The draft regional planning guidance for the South West (SWRPC 1999), for instance, featured a very detailed and comprehensive table setting out specific targets for protecting and restoring twenty different types of habitat, based on a biodiversity audit of the region (see Figure 4.3). In addition, as our case study of the East Midlands illustrates, interesting tensions sometimes emerged around the treatment of biodiversity.

Case study: biodiversity and the role of environmental groups in the East Midlands region

The East Midlands provides a useful example of how policies on biodiversity were improved substantially between the draft (EMRLGA 1999) and the final version (GOEM 2001). A key player in bringing about this change was the East Midlands Environmental Link (EMEL), a consortium of environmental groups set up specifically to address the regional planning agenda.

The East Midlands is relatively poor in its level of existing biodiversity assets: only 2 per cent of the region is safeguarded by statutory wildlife designations compared to the national average of 6 per cent, as is evident in Figure 4.4. Environmental groups which had come together in 1999 to form EMEL expressed disappointment that biodiversity had not been given stronger treatment in draft RPG. Their concerns centred on the fact that the region had relatively little of its area covered by statutory protection, which itself reflected the fact that biodiversity was at a low level in the region. In consequence, EMEL partners argued that biodiversity should be given as much attention as economic development.

> [T]he unique situation with this region is that we have planned it so badly that there is virtually no biodiversity left. It's a virtual blank throughout. . . so the key issue is putting it back, not just protecting what we have got!
>
> (interview EM3)

This topic had initially been addressed through a single overarching policy which also covered landscape conservation:

> Habitats and species of importance for nature conservation should be identified in local biodiversity action plans and species surveys, and given the appropriate level of protection. Action to protect and enhance the region's character and the natural diversity of the countryside and urban areas should be supported by appropriate levels of resources, and by giving guidance on their conservation, enhancement or regeneration through all the policy instruments available, including development plans. Management of habitats and landscapes should:

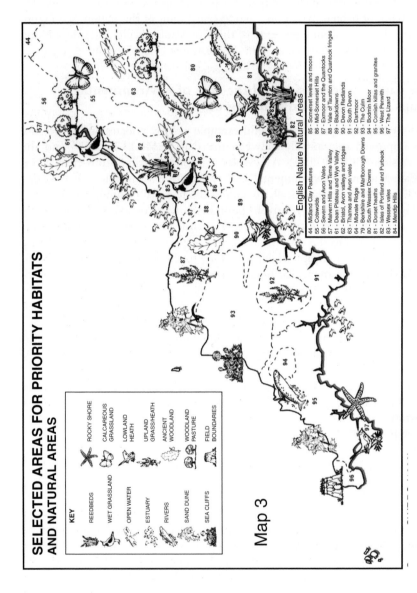

Figure 4.3 Nature conservation map for the South West. (Source: SWRPC 1999 reproduced with the permission of the South West Regional Assembly.)

- maintain and enhance the ecological and landscape value;
- optimise access for education and recreation;
- protect them from detrimental visitor impact and insensitive change and exploitation; and
- enable the rural economy to adapt and regenerate.

(EMRLGA 1999, p. 53)

Responding to criticism from EMEL, East Midlands Regional Local Government Association (EMRLGA) submitted additional material prior to the public examination, including an appendix showing priority habitats and regional biodiversity targets. These changes, however, were still not sufficient to satisfy EMEL, which felt that draft RPG continued to have too much of an economic bias.

At the public examination, therefore, EMEL submitted a paper on the environmental capacity of the East Midlands, which, taking into account issues such as biodiversity, landscape and tranquillity, suggested that the region was approaching the 'limits of acceptable change'. Notions of 'tranquillity' had been developed to measure the freedom of rural areas from urban or traffic intrusion, either visually or in terms of noise. Tranquil-area maps of England had been produced jointly by the CPRE and the Countryside Agency in 1995, though they were not much used or referred to in regional planning debates.

In adjudicating on these debates, the public examination panel accepted that the EMRLGA appendix showing key habitats and targets provided a better focus for biodiversity conservation than the draft RPG, but also suggested other changes to give greater prominence to the topic (Parke and Travers 2000). These included rewording the explanatory text and including a new policy covering species and habitat protection and enhancement (both in designated sites and elsewhere), restoration and management. The panel report also identified the need for wildlife corridors and for inter-regional cooperation, considerably strengthening the approach to biodiversity compared to the draft RPG.

The resulting policy on biodiversity in the final version of RPG is consequently more strongly worded and more clearly focused than the original policy:

Local authorities, developers and other agencies should retain, manage and enhance the region's biodiversity. Development plans should recognise the relative significance of international, national, local and informal designations in considering the weight to be attached to nature conservation interests. They should give priority to the protection and enhancement of specific species and habitats of international, national and sub-regional importance, as identified in Biodiversity Action Plans (BAPs), in order to:

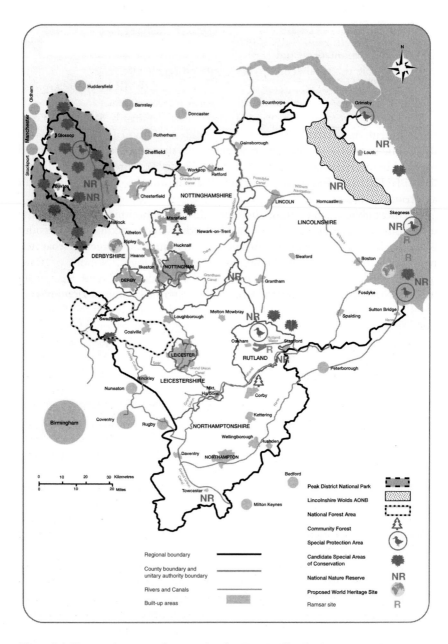

Figure 4.4 Key environmental assests in the East Midlands. (Source: GOEM 2002. Crown copyright material reproduced with the permission of the Controller of HMSO and the Queen's Printer for Scotland (licence number C02W0002008).)

- conserve and enhance sites of nature conservation value; and
- identify locations for habitat management, restoration and creation schemes, especially where a connected series of sites and buffer zones can be achieved.

Where development would be likely to affect nature conservation account should be taken of the advice in PPG9.

(GOEM 2002, p. 50)

Improvements in the treatment of biodiversity in RPG can also be linked to other drafting changes which addressed some of the concerns expressed by EMEL about its perception of an economic bias in draft RPG. This shift in emphasis during the regional planning process suggested to members of EMEL that presenting a coordinated case on the environment had resulted in their obtaining greater influence over the planning process. As a government conservation agency official commented, 'East Midlands Environment Network [referring to EMEL] was fundamental in getting the message across; if we hadn't done that, we wouldn't have got anywhere. We were presenting the alternative to jobs and growth are all that matters' (interview EM5).

The treatment of water conservation and management in regional planning

Water management is another issue which lies outside the direct control of the regional planning process. The environmental aspects of water regulation lie principally with the Environment Agency, an agency of central government, while provision of water is the responsibility of the water companies created in the 1989 privatisation of water.

Nonetheless, water is an important consideration in strategic planning because it exerts a strong influence on the development process: new developments need an adequate water supply and need to be located in areas where run-off will not make flooding a recurring problem. The issue of development on floodplains was selected as a criterion for comparing the performance of regional planning on water management. This was debated at several regional planning public examinations and, although they were not included in many original drafts, maps showing areas liable to flooding were included in the final versions of RPG in most regions. This issue moved further up the planning agenda following major floods in the autumn of 2000, when several newly built housing estates were flooded, for example in the Selby/York area in Yorkshire and the Humber, raising public and media concern about planners having allowed development to occur on floodplains. These floods were perhaps also instrumental in the timing and content of PPG25 *Development and Flood Risk* (DTLR 2001a), which gave an enhanced role to regional planning guidance in preventing development in areas of flood risk and managing run-off in a sustainable way.

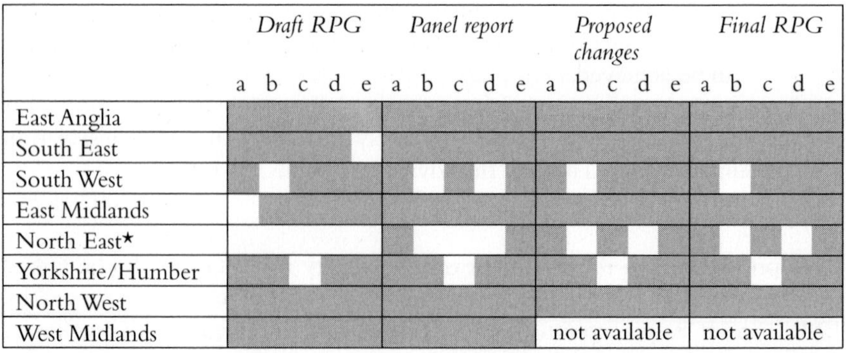

	Draft RPG					Panel report					Proposed changes					Final RPG				
	a	b	c	d	e	a	b	c	d	e	a	b	c	d	e	a	b	c	d	e
East Anglia	■	■	■	■	■	■	■	■	■	■	■	■	■	■	■	■	■	■	■	■
South East	■	■	■	□	■	■	■	■	■	■	■	■	■	■	■	■	■	■	■	■
South West	□	■	■	■	■	■	□	□	■	■	■	■	□	■	■	■	■	□	■	■
East Midlands	□	■	■	■	■	■	■	■	■	■	■	■	■	■	■	■	■	■	■	■
North East★	■	■	■	■	■	■	□	■	■	■	■	■	□	□	■	■	■	□	□	■
Yorkshire/Humber	■	■	□	■	■	■	■	□	■	■	■	■	□	■	■	■	■	□	■	■
North West	■	■	■	■	■	■	■	■	■	■	■	■	■	■	■	■	■	■	■	■
West Midlands	■	■	■	■	■	■	■	■	■	■	not available					not available				

★Policies were not separately identified in the draft North East RPG.

The shading indicates coverage of the following criteria in RPG policies:
(a) development of floodplains; (b) development where abstraction would damage river flows or wetlands; (c) effect of development on water quality; (d) development which would create water supply problems; and (e) greater efficiency/sustainability in water use.

Figure 4.5 Comparison of regional planning guidance policies on water conservation and management at different stages in the process.

Development on floodplains was one of five criteria selected to evaluate the thematic coverage of RPG documents. Figure 4.5 suggests that the coverage of water management issues in regional planning tended to be most comprehensive in the drier east of England, reflecting some localised water supply problems. In East Anglia, for example, a region of relatively low rainfall and one where water resources are already under pressure, the issue of water management was treated fairly comprehensively in draft RPG (SCEALA 1998), with a separate chapter devoted to water supply and quality. The public examination panel report (Acton and Brookes 1999) acknowledged that serious concerns had been expressed about the effects of abstraction on watercourses and wetland habitats. Additionally, there is a strong economic imperative to protect water in this region, because its wetlands are an important tourism asset, especially in areas such as the Norfolk Broads.

The final version of RPG for East Anglia (GOEE 2000) deals with water issues comprehensively in a suite of policies relating to development in areas of flood risk, liaison on water issues, protection of water resources, inter-regional water issues, and water efficiency and recycling. Coverage of these issues was also comprehensive in the East Midlands and South East, both of which have depleted groundwater resources and important recreational waterways.

Water management issues were dealt with least comprehensively in the North East, a region with a current over-capacity for water supply, largely because of the Kielder reservoir, built during the 1970s. There was some discussion of water resources at the public examination in the North East, and the panel proposed to strengthen RPG by including a policy which addressed the issue of flood risk and another on the conservation of natural resources (Richardson and Simpson 2000). As with biodiversity, though, treatment of this issue remained relatively superficial, with only three out of our five criteria covered. In essence, development is less likely to be subject to constraint due to water management concerns in the North East than in other regions, yet this is not really linked into wider issues such as the availability of water for economic development activities, say. More than this, the absence of a national spatial plan means that no connection is made between the fact that water is more readily available in the North East than most regions, whereas there are severe water availability problems in parts of the South East and the South West. The assumption, as we will see, is that water should follow development, rather than the other way round.

Case study: water supply – a constraint on development or an obstacle to be overcome?

In the context of growing concern about water scarcity in parts of the south of the country, water supply constraints proved a key issue in debates about future development in the Swindon area. Swindon, located in the South West region but lying adjacent to the South East, is a major population and employment growth centre. Draft regional planning guidance (SWRPC 1999) had indicated that water supply problems were likely to occur in this area after 2015–2016 if development were to continue at past rates. Thames Water Utilities Limited (the water supply company) had advocated the provision of a new strategic water resource, a reservoir, to satisfy the demand. However, the Environment Agency resisted this proposal, as it did not consider the need to be proven, instead asking Thames Water to deal with the issue by demand management, including the constraining of future development. The relevant policy in draft RPG emphasised demand management:

> To achieve the long term sustainable use of water the demand on water resources and supply infrastructure, together with the need for new water resources, should be minimised through:
>
> •   maximising demand management
> •   appropriate location, scale and programming of development across the region.
>
> (SWRPC 1999, p. 29)

There was a lively debate about the relationship between water supply and development at the public examination, with housebuilding interests arguing that the provision of infrastructure should follow strategic planning decisions on new development. They pointed to the statutory duty of water companies to supply water, arguing that if the need for development was proven, then water must be provided. Environmental groups such as Friends of the Earth and CPRE, on the other hand, argued that difficulties in providing infrastructure *should* act as a constraint on development, using the argument if they did not, the environmental capacity of the region would be exceeded.

The regional debate focused in particular on the Swindon area, where a new reservoir would be needed to supply water in the longer term. Thames Water had first proposed a new reservoir in 1990 in south-west Oxfordshire to satisfy regional demands, including those from Swindon (Hunter *et al.* 1996). While supporting the need for more attention to be paid to demand management measures, the South West public examination panel felt that this would only delay rather than eliminate the need for a new reservoir (Crowther and Bore 2000). The panel therefore concluded that RPG should recognise the need for a new strategic resource for water supply which would serve this area, while also serving parts of the South East region. More generally the panel considered that the policy in draft RPG was inappropriate in suggesting that the distribution and scale of development would be determined by water supply issues: '[I]t is the regional strategy that should determine the location and scale of development and decisions about infrastructure investment should follow the strategy and not the other way round' (Crowther and Bore 2000, p. 124). This basic approach was accepted by central government in the final version of RPG10, which includes the following policy:

> To achieve the long term sustainable use of water, water resources need to be used more efficiently. At the same time, water resources and water treatment infrastructure must be made available in the right location and at the right time to support development planned for the period covered by regional guidance. . . . Local authorities, the Environment Agency, water companies and other agencies should seek to:
>
> • plan their water infrastructure and water treatment investment programmes in accordance with the regional spatial strategy;
> • aim to conserve water through demand management.
>
> (GOSW 2001, p. 99)

Having seemed to accede to pressures to accommodate more development through addressing water supply, RPG10 goes on to say in a potentially contradictory manner that development plans should 'seek to avoid sites where water supply and/or drainage provision is likely to be unsustainable' (ibid., p. 99).

The regional planning debates in the South West brought to the fore significant differences in the attitudes of public bodies over whether water supply should be seen as a constraining factor on development or a difficulty to be overcome by expenditure on infrastructure. This goes to the core of the 'efficient use of resources' objective of national sustainable development policy: should development be located to 'use up' spare capacity in current infrastructure and constrained where infrastructure would be environmentally damaging to provide, or not?

In terms of the final version of regional planning guidance for the South West it remains unclear how to interpret the clause 'avoid[ing] sites where water supply. . . provision is likely to be unsustainable'. What appears to be being said is that infrastructural capacity, one of the components of the environmental capacity debate, is of less importance in achieving sustainable development than allowing the continued expansion of the built environment in areas of high demand.

The Swindon case study illustrates some of the difficulties in achieving 'win–win–win' solutions in planning. Development of a major new reservoir in southern England would inevitably involve some localised environmental and social costs in order to achieve wider regional economic benefits. Admittedly, it is difficult to assess the total costs and benefits of this sort of development at the regional scale, because of the lack of detail available to the public examination. Without knowing the detailed circumstances, for example, it is not possible to judge the claims of those who supported the reservoir that it could result in significant environmental benefits which would offset the losses. But this raises another problem, that of assessing the value of the lost environmental features compared to those which will be gained. As noted earlier, different groups have different views on what values should be attributed to environmental assets: in this instance the gains would most benefit urban interests, while most of the losses would be borne by rural interests. The debate serves to reinforce the view that a simplistic approach to 'win–win–win' solutions in planning glosses over what are in effect complex decisions, in which the inevitable winners and losers emerge only when the details of a development proposal are considered. What appears to be 'win–win–win' in a regional overview may well not seem so clear-cut once all local interests are considered.

Towards more effective environmental protection?

This discussion illustrates how the new environmental concepts and techniques have largely failed to deliver socially acceptable ways of making decisions on which aspects of nature should be preserved and for whom. In the end, the search for a valid independent scientific technique proved politically unsustainable, as the very basis of scientific assumptions about how to value environmental assets came under scrutiny, not least when it came to assessing environmental values against either economic or social concerns.

Environmental techniques tended to be welcomed initially by environmental and countryside groups in so far as they seemed to offer the potential for justifying protecting the countryside against urban threats. By contrast, they have been contested by development groups, which have tended to argue that the new techniques are unscientific and unworkable. The considerable efforts of the HBF in developing a critique of the concept of carrying capacity suggests that its members did indeed see this renewed fascination with planning techniques as a threat to the finding of land for future development. But planners were already concluding that many of these techniques were unworkable, recognising that planning remains at heart overtly political, involving processes which are imbued in many different ways by both the explicit and the implicit values of those involved in the process (Blowers 1980; Healey 1990).

Though the recent political commitment to integrated approaches to sustainable development has again suggested that it is possible to identify rational solutions which are universally beneficial, circumstances in which all the objectives of sustainable development can gain equally through planning processes are likely to be in a small minority. Indeed, even where such solutions are claimed to have been identified, it is always likely that these claims will be dismissed by those who value things differently. In its report on environmental planning, the Royal Commission on Environmental Pollution argued that 'there are substantial practical difficulties in achieving economic, social and economic goals simultaneously' (RCEP 2002, p. 38). The report goes on to suggest that: 'achieving environmental sustainability means achieving legitimate economic and social goals in ways that safeguard and where appropriate enhance the quality of the environment' (ibid.).

One of the underexplored issues in developing new planning techniques has been the importance of the opening up of planning processes to public engagement. This has offered new opportunities to challenge the underlying assumptions of these techniques early on in their formation, leading to changes and in some cases rapid abandonment of particular concepts and techniques. In addition, the detailed case studies have revealed something of the way in which the processes of dissemination, critique and validation work across the different scales of the planning system. Particularly intriguing is the role of central government, key lobby groups and also mediating agents such as consultants, in acting as key pulses in the transmission of knowledge within the system. This is important in the case of regional planning guidance, where in a short period a number of planning examinations took place around the country which involved crucial critiques and decisions that were to shape the ways in which debates elsewhere were conducted.

5 Finding places for new housing

The role of regional planning

> The level of housing provision is probably the most contentious part of RPG, at least in the southern part of England. The tensions between those who believe that trend growth should form the basis of housing provision, and those who oppose such an approach for environmental and NIMBY reasons have increased substantially in recent years. The concept of sustainable development appears to have added a good deal of confusion to the debate. Both sides hijacked it to substantiate their cases.
>
> (Gobbett and Palmer 2002, p. 216)

Housing's central role in regional planning, and regional planning's central role in new housing

In the popular imagination Britain is a small, overcrowded island, with London and the south-east of England seen as particularly congested (Evans 1991). Housing developers and others have sought to challenge this view, pointing to the relatively small proportion of land which is currently taken for urban usage, around 19 per cent in the South East (Evans 1991; HBF 2002). The problem facing those seeking to promote further housing development is that for many existing residents the prospect of further new housing in their areas can be anathema, potentially changing the character of a village, town or suburb, taking away valued countryside, and holding back property prices. In consequence, planning constraint policies, such as green belts, are often highly valued by local residents, who see them as helping fend off unwanted developments. This can prove particularly problematic in regions experiencing strong pressures for new housing, where the effect of one area fending off new development may simply be to increase pressures in neighbouring areas. Efforts to limit new development can also contribute to housing scarcity and, with this, rising land values and spiralling housing prices and rentals, putting pressure particularly on those with low incomes while also creating wage inflation pressures.

In stark contrast to the experience of such growth areas, there has been the growing phenomenon in recent years of wholesale abandonment and dereliction in parts of many northern cities. The scale of this problem only became really apparent in the late 1990s as it became clear that the problems stretched across the industrial towns and cities of northern England. Large numbers of public-sector housing estates appeared to be experiencing unprecedented massive net outward movement, while owner occupiers and private landlords in some areas found themselves 'trapped' by falling prices. Though there have been successes in rejuvenating problem housing areas, elsewhere the problems seemed to persist even after substantial refurbishment of the housing stock and improvements to the local environment. More positively, there has been growing success in attracting people back into city centres across much of England, with major developments on former industrial, hospital and school sites, and some conversion of former commercial properties into residential apartments in city centres. We return to these themes in Chapter 6, 'Towards an urban renaissance'.

The result of such varying pressures has been that housing has continued to rise up the political agenda in the past decade, with regional planning emerging as a key forum for some of these debates. Regional planning's role since the early 1990s has principally revolved around allocating figures for new housing development across the country. The issue was already growing in importance by the early 1990s, but the release of government projections for new household formation in 1995 added urgency to the debate, as these suggested that around 4.4 million new households would be created by 2016 (Breheny 1999). The rapid growth in household numbers was only partly driven by population growth and inter-regional migration, with much of the anticipated growth in new households resulting from social trends such as people marrying later, divorcing more often and living longer (Breheny 1997, 1999; Murdoch 2000; Vigar *et al.* 2000). The household formation projections suggested a need for new housing to be built at well above the existing rates of new housing development, in particular around London and the South East.

The planning system essentially sought to allocate the projected growth figures through the planning hierarchy, from the national level to regional planning guidance and then down to local plans. Because of the strong anti-new development sentiments in some areas, particularly in the shire counties and in the home counties in the south of England, attempts simply to centrally impose housing allocations frequently met with local resistance. Not only have resident groups objected to plans, but local councils have been prepared to challenge the government, as we see in Chapter 4 in relation to the discussion on environmental capacity in West Sussex. The combination of regional planning guidance allocating housing figures to the strategic planning authorities within regions and the opening up of the system to greater public engagement during the late 1990s meant that regional planning quickly emerged as the arena in which these debates reached public prominence.

Regional planning techniques and new housing development

This chapter examines recent housing debates across England, focusing on debates around new and existing planning techniques for controlling where new housing is located, from the long-standing green belt policy (see Chapter 4) to new techniques such as the sequential test, brownfield targets and urban capacity studies (Table 5.1). These techniques have been centrally involved in debates about how best to guide urban development, and the balance between urban and rural development, providing both a focus for debate and a way of legitimising certain approaches rather than others.

Since the early 1990s the cornerstone of successive governments' approaches towards new housing has been a desire to concentrate as much development as possible on brownfield sites, especially in existing urban areas. An initial target of 50 per cent of new development being on previously used land was already under pressure for upward revision when the Conservative government published its Green Paper *Household Growth: Where Shall We Live?* (DoE 1996b). The incoming Labour government quickly introduced a higher national brownfield development target of 60 per cent, which remains in place despite pressures from some environmental groups to increase it further to 75 per cent.

Other policy devices introduced in pursuit of this approach included the sequential test for considering development options, which is now widely used for both housing and employment development, with development on greenfield sites to be permitted only where all other options had been considered and ruled out (Table 5.1). In order to ensure local planning authorities did not simply ignore these other options, a parallel process of urban capacity studies introduced a new requirement to examine the existing stock of brownfield sites which might be reused for development. In addition to existing sites, efforts had to be made to predict future 'windfall' sites, such as possible closures of factories, warehouses, schools, hospitals, and so forth, or the release of other land such as the sites of disused railway sidings.

It is possible to see these various techniques as representing particular ways in which the government seeks to enforce its preferred rationality for planning. This is a theme which has already been explored with some success in relation to the system for allocating housing numbers through regional plans (Murdoch 2000; Murdoch and Abram 2002). Drawing on a governmentality approach (e.g. Foucault 1991a, b; Dean 1999), Murdoch (2000; see also Murdoch and Abram 2002) argues that the housing numbers allocation system is a technique which represents a particular form of rationality based on the use of statistics and numerical targets to govern behaviour. The allocations of housing numbers at different scales of planning serve to draw actors together into a shared set of behaviour patterns, enforced through the discipline of targets. In effect, the cascade of numbers down to the level of local planning authorities, via the regional planning system, is a way of enforcing

Table 5.1 Brownfield land targets, the sequential test and urban capacity studies

What is it?	*Origins and scales of application*
Brownfield land targets 'The British Government has set a national target that by 2008 60% of additional housing should be provided on previously-developed land and through conversions of existing buildings. Each RPB should propose a recycling target and, if appropriate, sub-regional targets in RPG which should contribute to achieving the national target. . . . 　　RPBs should draw on urban housing capacity studies in proposing the recycling target for their region'. (DETR 2000c, paras 5-12, 5-13)	First suggested in the mid-1990s, when the target was 50%. This was formally increased to 60% by the New Labour government in PPG3 (DETR 2000c). Overall targets are set at the regional scale in RPG. Development plan authorities are asked to adopt their own local land recycling targets which contribute to attaining the regional or sub-regional targets.
Sequential test In identifying sites to be allocated for housing a search sequence should be followed starting with the reuse of previously developed land and buildings (brownfield land) within urban areas identified by urban housing capacity studies. Only when brownfield sites have been exhausted should the sequence move on to consider urban extensions, and finally new development around nodes in good public transport corridors (DETR 2000a).	Applied to retail development from 1996 and to housing from the publication of the revised PPG3 in 2000. Relevant at all scales of planning
Urban capacity studies 'In order to establish how much additional housing can be accommodated within urban areas and therefore how much greenfield land may be needed for development, all local planning authorities should undertake urban housing capacity studies. These should consider various options in relation to density of development, levels of parking provision, different residential layouts and the mix of housing types' (DETR 2000c, para. 24)	Proposed in PPG 3 and subject to good practice guidance (DETR 2000f) Applied at the local scale, but providing the basis for regional brownfield targets

the central government's policies. Drawing on a case study of the South East, Murdoch also suggests that opponents to the numbers system sought to undermine this approach, using discourses of sustainable development to provide an alternative rationality (Murdoch 2000).

Plate 5.1 Urban infill: high-density residential development on brownfield land in Leeds.

The approach in this chapter emphasises how this debate has tended to vary regionally, with sustainable development being co-opted in rather different ways in different regions. More than this, the approach here suggests that these processes of contestation do not always work in simple hierarchical fashion; rather, they involve some complex iterations which work recursively across scales and between various sets of actors. To achieve a broader understanding of regional housing debates, the analysis here also moves beyond debates on housing numbers to examine the broader array of techniques developed by governments in the past fifteen years, as they have sought to enforce particular approaches to planning through the various scales of the system.

It is worth noting that a 'shadow' effect is exerted when the underlying rationalities of some of the tools enter the mainstream, as alternative rationalities are marginalised which might, for instance, help justify thinking about whether new settlements might be viable. As an example, once techniques such as the sequential test have been adopted, planning for large-scale development on land outside the existing urban fabric becomes all but unthinkable, other than in exceptional cases such as Cambridge and some of the recently announced growth areas in the South East, which are discussed later in this chapter.

The figures don't add up: regional housing allocations

'Predict and provide' is the term used to described the traditional approach to planning for new housing and new transport infrastructure. In the case of housing, central government produced household projections based on the most recent population projections in order to calculate future levels of housing demand. As we noted earlier, the national projections cascaded down into the other tiers in the planning hierarchy, first into structure plans, then local plans. In the first round of RPGs and in structure plan reviews during the 1990s, housing allocations were rigidly applied by central government, particularly in the South East, giving little scope for reluctant county councils in the Home Counties, for example, to justify lower housing numbers because of local environmental constraints on development (Counsell 1998, 1999a).

Soon after coming to office in 1997, the Labour government announced its intention of moving away from the 'predict and provide' approach to housing numbers to one based on 'plan, monitor and manage'. This shift represented an attempt to take some of the rigidity out of the 'predict and provide' system, giving regional plans greater scope to take account of factors other than the household projections, such as inter-regional migration (Gobbett and Palmer 2002). The new approach was incorporated into national planning guidance in PPG3, where it was suggested that

> In planning the provision of new housing, factors to be taken into account should include the Government's latest published household projections, the needs of the regional economy, the capacity of urban areas to accommodate more housing, the environmental implications, and the capacity of the existing or planned infrastructure.
>
> (DETR 2000c, para. 5)

The 'monitor and manage' aspects of the new approach required regional planning bodies to monitor housing provision, publishing the results in an annual report and formally reviewing allocations at least every five years 'for signs of either under or over-provision of housing land' (DETR 2000c, para. 8). The new approach was accompanied by a switch to publishing annual building rates rather than housing demand projections for a twenty-year period. These changes were largely welcomed by the conservation lobby, while planners tended to be concerned that they might lead to short-termism in planning for new housing (Gobbett and Palmer 2002).

Perhaps inadvertently, the new approach to housing numbers resulted in increasing tensions between stakeholders in the regions. When the numbers were established and allocated centrally, there was a fair degree of certainty about them and their ability to meet housing need projections. By contrast, bringing new factors into consideration and giving regions scope to adjust their figures introduced an element of uncertainty. Through their role in the regional planning bodies, local authorities now had the opportunity to imprint their preferences on to housing allocation figures much more clearly. The resulting draft RPGs in the South tended to demonstrate caution and constraint, reducing their housing allocations below the government's projections. Alternatively, in some regions in the Midlands and North, allocations were made for levels of new housing above the figures suggested by the national figures, which raised the prospect of an oversupply of housing, and avoidable incursions on to greenfield land.

Central government found itself in the position of arbiter of these housing figures, just as it had under the 'predict and provide' arrangements, attempting to steer a middle ground between meeting the projections of housing need while retaining some scope for regional differences to emerge. Following some highly contentious debates during the preparation of the most recent round of regional planning guidance, the housing numbers changed in all regions between the draft produced by the regional planning body and the final version issued by central government (see Table 5.2). More specifically, the numbers were increased in the three regions experiencing strong growth (the South East, East Anglia and the South West) and reduced in two of the three more disadvantaged northern regions.

Rather than provide a summary of the debates in all eight regions, we have selected the following two case studies to provide a flavour of the differing types of debate which emerged in regions where the dominant approach was to resist growth, represented here by the South West, and a region where pro-growth sentiments dominated, represented by the North East.

Table 5.2 Changing housing numbers between draft and final regional planning guidance (RPG)

	Draft RPG	Panel report	Proposed changes	Final RPG
North East (RPG1)	5,950	5,500	5,000–6,000	5,050–6,000
East Anglia (RPG6)	9,738	11,624	9,650	**9,900**[a]
East Midlands (RPG 8)	14,000	13,600	13,900	13,700
South East (RPG9)	33,300	55,000	43,000	**39,000**
South West (RPG10)	18,650	20,350	20,350	**20,200**
West Midlands (RPG11)	15,680	15,375	n.a.	n.a.
Yorkshire and the Humber (RPG12)	13,983	14,611	14,650	**14,765**
North West (RPG13)	15,035	15,035	12,790	12,790

Note

Figures given are average annual building rates. Figures in bold are those where the final number has increased from the draft.

a Subject to the results of the Cambridge sub-regional study.

Contesting housing constraint in the South West

For some years now, the economically more buoyant areas in the east of the South West region have been experiencing strong pressures for further housing development. However, as we were told by one local authority planner, in most of these areas an underlying tension was that most of 'the local authorities are keen to attract jobs, but nobody wants housing' (interview SW12). The result was political pressure for draft RPG to produce housing allocations below those which central government projections suggested were needed.

The draft RPG (SWRPC 1999) was strongly criticised by pro-development groups for exactly this reason. Rather than accept the proposed draft RPG housing allocations, these groups pushed hard at the public examination for much higher levels of housing to be allocated, in the range of 480,000 –506,850, as against the 367,000 figure put forward by the regional planning body.

In its report, the public examination panel accepted the argument that the draft RPG figures had been set too low, proposing an increase in total housing numbers of up to 407,000, still well short of levels suggested by developers. The panel's conclusions were accepted by the Secretary of State in issuing the 'proposed changes', which converted the housing numbers to an annual building rate of 20,350 per year. The local authority-led planning conference then objected to the higher housing figures on the basis that they were not justified and did not sit easily with the national policy on urban renaissance. The numbers were subsequently marginally reduced to 404,000 (20,200 per annum) in the final document, RPG10.

The proposed distribution of these new houses was particularly contentious. The public examination panel recommended that much of the increase in housing should be borne by Gloucestershire, Wiltshire and the former county of Avon (in the eastern part of the region), to meet the expected increases in the number of jobs in these areas. However, anti-growth sentiments were strongest in exactly these areas, with one local authority, South Gloucestershire, seeking to disassociate itself from the level of housing in the draft RPG on the grounds of its being too high, and therefore 'unsustainable' (interview SW12).

The way in which RPG policy cascades into local plans is particularly interesting in this case. Following from the previous 'old' RPG document of 1994, South Gloucestershire, along with the other local authorities in the former county of Avon, was already in dispute with the Secretary of State about the level of proposed housing in the draft joint replacement structure plan (Joint Strategic Planning and Transportation Unit 1998). The local authorities in the Avon area had been directed by central government to increase the amount of housing from a proposed 43,600 dwellings in the structure plan to the figure suggested in the first RPG of 54,300 (for the period through to 2011). After lengthy deliberations, and with some reluctance, the local authorities eventually indicated that they considered the area to have a maximum capacity for 50,200 new housing units. These protracted deliberations caused considerable concern to both central government and the housebuilding industry, since the lack of an approved structure plan was holding up the approval of local plans and particular development proposals:

> The proposed modification. . . . not only falls short of the [Secretary of State's] direction but falls far short of the new RPG. They are basically delaying difficult decisions about greenfield land release. They say they will deal with this through monitoring but we argue that monitoring should not be used as justification for under-provision.
>
> (interview SW11)

The result was that the position on planning for housing in Avon from the 'old' RPG remained unresolved while the 'new' RPG was being deliberated. In the final version of the new RPG10 it was proposed that 74,000 additional dwellings would be needed in Avon (3,700 per annum) up to 2016 (Table 5.3). This figure once again proved contentious locally, as it suggested many more new dwellings than the structure plan had identified capacity for. On behalf of central government, the Secretary of State eventually accepted the figure of 50,200 new homes in the proposed modifications to the Avon structure plan, in effect deferring the resolution of differences with the new RPG to the next review of the structure plan.

New housebuilding as an antidote to outward migration from the North East

Where proposals to increase housing numbers caused considerable public outcry in the South West, in the North East the debate was muted. There appeared to be considerable support for the argument from political leaders and planners that there was a need to diversify and up-grade the region's housing stock by looking for higher allocations for new-build housing, specifically to increase the stock of executive-style housing. The existing

Table 5.3 Comparison of housing numbers for Avon, as suggested in RPG10 and the Avon area structure plan

'Old' RPG10	Draft structure plan	Proposed modifications to structure plan	Draft 'new' RPG	Final RPG10
54,300[a]	43,600[a]	50,200[a]	69,000[b]	74,000[b]

Notes
a To 2011. [b] To 2016.
   RPG = regional planning guidance.

housing stock was argued to be too concentrated on low-income housing, not matching the aspirations of many people for better-quality housing. Without improvement at the top end of the housing market, the fear was that the outward drift of people from the region would continue, and efforts to encourage inward investment be undermined.

Despite the widespread political support in the region for this position, draft RPG for the North East (ANEC 1999) was criticised by environmental groups such as Friends of the Earth and the CPRE. The essential concern was that the proposed levels of new-build housing were much higher than indicated in government predictions as being necessary, involving proposals for 119,000 additional houses as against the predicted demand of 74,000. In justifying its proposals, ANEC pointed to the need to support aspirations in the North East Regional Economic Strategy to turn round the North East's economy. The HBF invoked sustainable development in the cause of permitting new development in its written submission to the public examination: 'Sustainable development must imply that the North East region provides for a secure economic future for its people, stemming environmentally wasteful out-migration to other regions and providing the sufficient number of homes required.'

Interestingly, despite the widespread support in the region for the proposals, in the final version of RPG1 the government decided to trim regional aspirations back to something closer to national policy. The overall allocations of new housing were cut back, while there were increases in the proportion of development to be accommodated in the conurbations and in the target for development on previously used land. More than this, in its *Sustainable Communities* (ODPM 2003a) document some time later, the government used its actions as a demonstration of its willingness to intervene in order to ensure that urban regeneration was supported in northern conurbations by such measures (see Chapter 6).

In terms of the policy cascade, again some local planning authorities held out against the imposition of housing allocations from the centre, via the RPG process. In the case of the Tees Valley structure plan preparation, for instance, planners challenged the use of the original government household growth projections, using later figures to argue successfully for an increase in housing allocations within the structure plan. These were nearly 20 per cent above those proposed in the draft RPG (Counsell and Haughton 2002c). In other words, the planners tactically opted to adopt the government's rationality, using the opportunity of revisions to the data to argue for more housing than the government seemed originally prepared to countenance.

An interesting contrast emerges between the South West and North East experiences. In the more economically buoyant areas of the South West, which had arguably been the main beneficiaries of national economic deregulation policies, planners contested national housing allocations and argued for stronger use of land use regulation to constrain housing growth. On the other hand, in the industrial areas of the North East, which had perhaps suffered more than most from national policies of economic deregulation, planners argued for a relaxation of land use zoning in order to allow more development on greenfield sites. Even more bizarrely, perhaps, it was national government which stepped in to argue against the regional aspiration for less land being allocated for new development in the South West region, while to a degree over-riding the North East region's stated preference for being allowed to provide more land to encourage extra new development.

Sustainable development as a multi-faceted and highly contested planning rationality

If we take a wider look at housing debates, sustainable development proved to be a key rationalising logic for all those involved in promoting alternative approaches to housing development, particularly in terms of attitudes to development on greenfield land, creating a distinctive geography to regional housing debates. In the North West and North East, local planners promoted approaches which involved *releasing* new greenfield sites, particularly for executive housing. The argument here was that this was 'sustainable' as it emphasised the social and economic needs of the two regions, with creating jobs being seen as more important than protecting the environment in the context of limited economic opportunities. Although the media were largely quiescent about the approach, making it difficult for environmental groups to garner substantial media coverage and public support, nonetheless in both cases the government stepped in to reduce the scale of residential greenfield incursions. By contrast, in the South East region the draft regional planning document produced by local planners emphasised *protecting* greenfield sites from development proposals, with environmental concerns often being used to provide a form of rationale.

Taking up positions: the role of lobby groups

Chapter 3 argues that influential lobby groups had inserted themselves powerfully within planning debates by seeking to adopt and shape the terminologies of sustainable development to support their different positions on managing growth. Nowhere is this more evident than in planning for housing since the early 1990s.

One of the main shaping forces in creating a distinctive housing 'storyline' within regional planning has been the CPRE. For many years now, the group has promoted policies which minimise development in rural areas, lobbying hard against 'urban sprawl' and in favour of policies which seek to contain development within urban areas (e.g. CPRE 2002a). It has in particular set itself against any relaxation of green belt designations. However, far from simply arguing for 'town cramming', the CPRE has also emphasised the limits to urban intensification and the need to set about this in ways which emphasise high-quality urban design. For instance, in its promotional leaflet *Urban Footprints* (CPRE 1994) there is a clear argument set out that 'Open spaces are vital to the urban environment. Parks, playing fields and fragments of woodland in our cities need not be sacrificed for new building' (p. 6). In more recent years, adopting the government's own preference for 'urban renaissance' and for 'win–win–win' solutions, the CPRE has continued to argue that supporting the rural environment need not be at the expense of the urban environment.

Other environmental groups at all levels, from the local to the national, have been active in lobbying for the retention of planning tools such as the green belt in order to protect 'nature' in these areas. Typically, the twin tactics of opponents are to claim that developers are 'concreting the country-side' and to accuse developers of avoiding hard-to-tackle urban redevelopment sites, instead preferring to buy up undesignated rural land and wait for it to be designated for housing. In such readings, it is the development lobby which is the villain, sometimes assisted by a weak government resolve to enforce local will through planning policies. The lobby group Corporate Watch, for instance, in its editorial 'Take action for social housing and defend the green belt', was worried that the government was about to relax its approach to green belt policy:

> Developers, who have been buying up cheap agricultural land for many years, are rubbing their hands in excited anticipation at the long-awaited cash bonanza. The noise of corporate snouts in troughs has been deafening. . ..
>
> Campaigners in Stevenage have been working round the clock to defeat their scheme [a green belt development proposal]. They are being supported by CPRE, FoE [Friends of the Earth] and that merry bunch of eco warriors, the Tory party – led by William Hague [then Conservative Party leader], complete with green wellies and banners. . . .
>
> . . . if the developers have their way we shall see over the next twenty years the most appalling corporate rampage over what is left of this beautiful land.
>
> (Deluce 1998)

Language is used in deliberately unsubtle, emotive ways here, leaving little scope for alternative readings of the situation, instead appealing to a traditionalist view of 'this beautiful land' and a vilification of developers who 'rampage' and have 'snouts in troughs'. The quotation also highlights rather effectively that there were some unusual 'discourse coalitions' emerging during this period.

In direct opposition to such views, the HBF, an industry-sponsored lobbying body, has maintained a high public and professional profile. It has presented its case at public examinations of draft plans, in the media and elsewhere for allowing more development on greenfield sites, arguing that constraint policies reduce consumer choice and potentially lead to higher house prices and homelessness. In this reading, housing problems are nothing to do with the development industry and everything to do with various protest groups and government inertia:

> The stark reality is that the 30-year campaign by the anti-housebuilding lobby coupled with a collapse of public investment in housing has resulted in a society unable to house itself. Far from 'concreting over the countryside', urban expansion takes up just one percent of England's land area every 50 years.
>
> (HBF 2002)

Like the CPRE, the HBF took care to embrace central government's 'win–win–win' philosophy and the language of urban renaissance and sustainable development. However, for the HBF the key argument was that its opponents tended to neglect the economic aspects of sustainable development. In other words, the argument is presented less in terms of simplistic 'negatives' about environmental protection, and more in terms of the 'positives' of developing a higher proportion of development on out-of-town greenfield sites where, it argued, most people wanted to buy.

Environmental groups and others, including political parties, which sought to argue against greenfield development tended to be portrayed by their opponents as extremists. A frequent refrain during our interviews concerned the hidden social agendas of those resisting development, most eloquently expressed not by a developer, but someone from a government conservation agency, who argued that the shire counties were opposed to development outside the conurbations essentially because 'They don't want the urban poor messing up their green fields' (interview EM7).

Of the other voices which have emerged to promote alternative approaches to guiding future housing development, perhaps the most distinctive has been the TCPA, another powerful group actively engaged in directly lobbying national government (Hardy 1991), presenting at RPG public examinations and conducting press campaigns. With its roots in the Garden City movement, the TCPA has long argued the case for selective new settlements being allowed where proposals can be demonstrated to be creating what are often referred to as 'sustainable communities' – that is, 'in centres which are big enough to sustain jobs, services and amenities in a balanced social mix, but which are small enough to create a sense of community and proximity to open countryside' (TCPA 2002b). Its views until recently seemed unlikely to prevail, given the forces ranged against it. Recent government announcements on new housing in the South East suggest that this situation may be changing, however (see chapter 6).

National debates on managing growth: the special role of the South East

Debates on greenfield and brownfield site development have not so much oscillated between national, regional and local scales, as been conducted across scales in complex ways. It is important, therefore, to emphasise that revisions to the main piece of government advice on these issues, PPG3 *Housing* (DETR 2000c), were being made at a time of considerable media attention to housing numbers as a result of the draft RPG for the South East and the report of the public examination panel.

The South East Regional Planning Conference (SERPLAN), the consortium of local authorities which published draft RPG for the South East in December 1998, proposed housing allocations substantially less than official government projections of household growth suggested would be needed (Williams 2002). This in part drew from a 'regional capability study' which attempted an assessment of the region's environmental and land resources with a view to clarifying the impacts of alternative levels of development (Murdoch and Tewdwr-Jones 1999; Murdoch 2000; Murdoch and Abrams 2002). This study, taken together with a challenge to some of the technical assumptions of the housing projection figures, provided SERPLAN with its main technical ammunition in arguing against higher levels of housing development. It is perhaps worth noting that the politics of SERPLAN changed over time (it was disbanded in 2000), but in general it was dominated by the shire county councils, whose political constituency tended to be predominantly anti-development (Allen *et al.* 1998). Within SERPLAN, tensions existed between the London-based authorities and those in the Rest of the South East (ROSE), with London authorities, for instance, seeking to promote higher levels of development in the ROSE area than the majority of ROSE authorities themselves (Willams 2002).

Rejecting SERPLAN's proposed housing numbers, the public examination panel report suggested that much more housing would be needed and that the figures should be revised upwards (see Table 5.2, p. 113). The panel made other recommendations, including a reduction in the target for development on brownfield land from 60 per cent to 50 per cent, which its opponents also saw as potentially threatening to greenfield sites. Unusually, planning hit both national and local headlines, with the backlash to the panel's report producing media headlines such as:

- 'All party revolt at homes betrayal' (*Daily Telegraph* 1999a);
- 'Mutiny in Middle England' (*Independent* 1999);
- 'New homes gobble up green belt' (*Evening Standard* 1999); and
- 'Concrete is for ever' (*The Times* 2000).

The media reports tended to draw directly on the press releases of the various lobby groups and political parties which were supporting alternative views in their attempts to make public their case for protecting certain types of green space rather than others, and certain balances between urban and rural development over others. The Conservative politician John Redwood (then Shadow Environment Secretary) is quoted as describing the proposals as a 'massacre of green field sites' (*Daily Telegraph* 1999b), while an environment spokeswoman for Surrey County Council is quoted as saying that the panel's proposals heralded 'the end of the green belt' (*Evening Standard* 1999). Tony Burton, then assistant director of the CPRE, is cited as arguing that the report presented 'a nightmare future of urban decay, traffic congestion and sprawling development' (*Evening Standard* 1999).

Television news programmes were aired which similarly allowed the different protagonists to present their views, while also drawing on the personal experiences of people alternatively looking for affordable houses or seeking to resist new houses being built in their areas. In addition to fears over green fields and green belt, the key storylines included arguments that the government should seek to bolster the northern regions by restricting housing growth in the South East, a case argued by the then Conservative Party spokesperson on the environment and the SERPLAN director among others.

It was environmental considerations which dominated the debate however. A Friends of the Earth press release (1999a) gives a sense of the vehemence of some of the environmental protests:

> Almost 200,000 extra homes could be built on greenfield sites in the South East over the next 16 years, if Deputy Prime Minister John Prescott forces local councils to accept his Inspectors' recommendations. This represents two new cities the size of Southampton.
>
> Councils could be forced to designate Green Belt land, Areas of Outstanding Natural Beauty and even major wildlife sites for housing if the plan goes ahead. This could become an electoral nightmare for the Labour Government.
>
> Tony Bosworth, Friends of the Earth's Housing Campaigner, said: 'If John Prescott forces councils to plan for over one million new homes, almost 200,000 more will have to be built in the countryside. This will wreck some of Britain's most beautiful areas, generate huge amounts of traffic and cause more congestion and pollution, in an already overcrowded area. It will provoke huge opposition from suburban communities in marginal constituencies.'

Note the political calculations being provided here for Ministers and the media, lest they could not work them out for themselves. Note too the strategic use of 'could' in relation to the possible impact on certain types of protected environments as a result of the new housing proposals. The result is a storyline which emphasises hypothetical risks to such areas, even though the proposals as they stood affected only green belt boundaries and not other protected areas.

The tone of most press reports was antagonistic towards the scale of development proposed by the public examination panel and in favour of constraint policies and greater urban compaction as the best ways of addressing future housing in the region. This is not to say that there were not counter-arguments, just that these did not tend to make the headlines at that time. The TCPA, for instance, developed a strong defence of the panel's report, while the HBF and the development industry also sought to provide support for aspects of the report. A consultant for housebuilding groups is quoted in *Planning* (15 October 1999, p. 7), for instance, as saying that 'This report has shone the light on the inadequacies of SERPLAN's dishonest approach. The planning profession should unite around it and stop acting as agents for "nimby"ist areas.'

In March 2000 the government issued proposed changes to RPG which reduced the housing figures for the South East to a level between those proposed by SERPLAN and by the panel, figures which were further modified downwards by the time of the final RPG in 2001 (Table 5.2; Howes 2002; Williams 2002). Three things are important to emphasise here. First, the resulting figures on housing in the South East were far from the process of deliberative argumentation which is aspired to in visions of communicative or collaborative planning. This was a highly politicised process of media campaigning involving some bodies engaging in public vilification of those holding alternative views, with the public examination panel especially subject to attack:

> [T]he RPG process for the South East. . . hit a wall. The selfish home counties that want to avoid their share of immigration, and to export their children, divorcees, and elderly folk somewhere else (anywhere else), shamelessly campaigned against the South East Panel Report. The Panel members were outrageously vilified personally and professionally, and the Secretary of State was cowardly enough to accede to the baying mob and disown the Panel Report. He has been unable to broker a practicable RPG himself for the South East ever since.
>
> (Lock 2002, p. 155; at that time, David Lock was chair of the TCPA).

Second, the resulting compromised figures failed to win over the housebuilding lobby, whose efforts were essential if new housing was to be developed. Though it was not clear to all at the time, developers held the powerful veto of simply keeping hold of land they had bought in anticipation of its being rezoned as housing land rather than accept government directives to build elsewhere. They were bolstered in this by the fact that the market tended to favour firms with large land banks in terms of share prices (Hutton 2002).

Third, the South East RPG process had more than a regional significance, with the debates very much influencing national planning policy formation.

It is in this context that the revised PPG3 *Housing* (DETR 2000c) argued that future housing development should be concentrated in urban areas, reducing the need for development in the green belt and on greenfield sites more generally. Among its recommendations was the introduction of the sequential test for identifying sites to be allocated for housing in development plans, giving priority to brownfield land, higher densities and mixed-use developments as well as confirming the national target of 60 per cent of new housing being on previously developed land (see Table 5.1, p. 110).

In effect, those campaigning against urban incursion into rural areas had made some major gains, influencing policy in ways which safeguarded the rural environment first and foremost, leaving undeveloped urban land under pressure to be used for housing rather than as open spaces. In pursuit of these ends, some new techniques of planning were formalised and introduced into the state apparatus – not just the sequential test but also urban capacity studies and the use of brownfield site targets. The retention of strong support for greenfield and green belt constraint policies meant that the strong, well-organised rural lobby had in effect gained much of what it sought. On the other hand, and perhaps surprisingly, the well-resourced development lobby failed to achieve much of what it wanted, possibly leading it to be even more active in local and regional planning debates as it argued in favour of greater flexibility in relation to greenfield sites, relaxation of green belt policy, more houses being built, and lower brownfield targets.

Local growth management in action: west of Stevenage in Hertfordshire

Background

Stevenage is an interesting case study both because of its emblematic status as the very first new town in the country to be designated, in November 1946, and also because it has been the scene of major tensions over proposals for expansion throughout the past ten years. Stevenage is located in Hertford-shire, which is one of the three county areas which found themselves reas-signed from the South East to the East of England region during 2001. In planning terms, local strategic planning is undertaken at the county level. There are ten district councils, including Stevenage, which are responsible for producing local plans and taking local planning decisions.

Stevenage was put forward for consideration as a new town to relieve the pressures on London by Patrick Abercrombie (1945) in his Greater London Plan. For Abercrombie, the 'small old established agricultural and residential town on the Great North Road' (p. 161) would be ideal as a new satellite town for London, being located 30 miles (50 kilometres) from London, and not least being 'excellently located for transport' (p. 161). Though many of Abercrombie's suggested locations were not adopted, Stevenage certainly was.

Before designation as a new town, Stevenage had a population of 7,000, which the proposals suggested should be increased to 60,000. The proposals generated considerable local opposition at the time. At a public meeting in the town to explain them, Lewis Silkin, the government minister of the time,

> was greeted with cries of 'Gestapo!' 'Dictator!' The tyres of his car were let down and sand put in the petrol tank of his car. The name boards on the local station were replaced with ones marked 'Silkingrad.' A residents' 'protection association' conducted a vigorous and prolonged opposition campaign.
>
> (Schaffer 1970, p. 28)

Approval came after a heated local inquiry, only to be challenged through the courts, during which one of Silkin's comments at the previous heated meeting was apparently much referred to: ' "Stevenage" said Mr. Silkin, "will become world famous" (laughter). "People from all over the world will come to see how we here in this country are building the new way of life" ' (Shaffer 1970, p. 29).

And indeed they did come to Stevenage, keen to see, talk about and photograph Europe's first pedestrian-only shopping centre, among other things (ibid.). In this classic creation of the post-war state, development had been largely in the hands of the state-appointed and resourced Stevenage Development Corporation. This was disbanded in the 1990s, by which time Stevenage had emerged as a relatively prosperous town of some 75,000 people.

Since the early 1990s, proposals for a major extension on a site to the west of the Stevenage have dominated planning debates for Hertfordshire County Council and the district councils involved. It is worth noting, perhaps, that politically the town has frequently been at odds with other districts in the county, reflecting its particular origins as a large urban settlement. The proposals had originally been included as a 'reserve site' in an earlier draft of the county structure plan, intended to be brought forward only should the need arise as a result of monitoring. The initial intention had been to provide most of the 21,000 additional houses required by the government for the period to 2011 through development within existing urban areas. However, following the public examination, the panel report on the structure plan recommended in favour of including the development as a firm proposal. The approved plan in 1998 incorporated this proposal for a new development west of Stevenage. An initial phase of 5,000 dwellings was expected to be completed by 2011, with an additional possible second phase to provide a further 5,000 houses. As the chosen site straddled the boundaries of two local authorities, the rural North Hertfordshire District and the urban Stevenage Borough, the detailed dwelling split between these administrations was left to the relevant local plans (Hertfordshire County Council 1998).

These seemingly firm plans were to unravel very quickly, as the Hertfordshire County Structure Plan was subsequently reviewed to roll it forward to

2016, a process which saw the Stevenage development once again emerge as the dominant issue of contention. The future of this site became such a key focus for the structure plan review that one county council officer told us that 'there has only been one main issue in the structure plan review and that is housing, particularly the proposed development west of Stevenage'. For this officer, the main objectives of the review could be reduced to just two aspects: 'One is to keep the area of greenfield development to the absolute and unavoidable minimum. The other is to promote town renaissance' (interview EE10).

Revisions to the structure plan had to take into account the RPG for the South East published in 2001, which had proposed an annual building rate of 3,280 housing units for Hertfordshire, amounting to 49,200 new homes over the fifteen-year period between 2001 and 2016. This building rate was about the same as that included in the approved Hertfordshire structure planning, so on the face of it what was being proposed was simply a continuation of previously agreed building rates. Critically, however, the regional plan guidance was not specific about identifying where the new houses in Hertfordshire should be located, with that task being delegated to the county structure plan.

The centrepiece of work to bring forward the structure plan review was a comprehensive urban capacity study (see Table 5.1, p. 110), linked to a town renaissance campaign giving a wider dimension to the debate. The preliminary results of the Hertfordshire capacity study suggested that there was an overall potential to provide up to 62,000 houses in the existing built-up areas of Hertfordshire through to 2016. Since this amounted to 12,800 more than the 49,200 houses allocated to Hertfordshire in the RPG, in effect it meant that the county could now expect to accommodate its growth through urban compaction, *without* the need for the west of Stevenage proposal.

However, and of critical importance to the ensuing debates, the Stevenage extension proposal was supported by the urban Stevenage Borough, within which part of the site lies, while being strongly opposed by the rural North Hertfordshire District in which the remainder of the site is located. North Hertfordshire had originally reluctantly included the proposal in its local plan. Perhaps buoyed by the strength of publicly vented anti-development feeling, it then caused consternation within the development industry by changing its mind, and with it any lingering prospect of acceptance of the development proposal. Where Stevenage Borough Council questioned the interim urban capacity study, North Hertfordshire supported the findings. Interestingly, North Hertfordshire used the urban capacity study to argue that the development west of Stevenage did not conform with revised government policy in PPG3 *Housing,* namely that greenfield sites should be considered for development only if insufficient brownfield land was available. Critically, PPG3 allowed for existing greenfield designations to be reconsidered and overturned.

Local opposition to the Stevenage extension proposal had been carefully orchestrated by the anti-development group CASE (Case Against Stevenage Expansion), which brought together a number of local amenity groups and environmental campaigning groups. Its Web site (www.case.org.uk) includes evidence of widespread support for its case from the national and local press and national environmental groups. Quotations reproduced on the Web site include 'the settlement, if it goes ahead, will result in a seamless urban sprawl between Stevenage and Hitchen' (*Observer*, 23 July 2002) and 'This is a devastating and unjustified blow to green belt policy. It will give the go-ahead to applications to build all over the county' (*Welwyn and Hatfield Times*, 12 June 1998). For many of those involved, the Stevenage case was of more than simply local importance because of its timing and the sensitivity about how the new national government might treat green belt land.

Housebuilders, by contrast, felt particularly aggrieved that the proposal was being reopened for debate, because they had already invested heavily in the site on the basis of the existing structure plan allocation; two planning applications had been submitted. As one development lobby representative told us,

> Despite the lengthy process which led to the proposal being included in the 1998 structure plan there is still uncertainty, and the consortium set up to develop the site feels it has wasted its time. What point is there having a plan-led system if it falls down at the end?
>
> (interview EE13)

Referring to the renewed local emphasis on urban renaissance and town regeneration, the representative went on: 'We must be coming to the end of what we can squeeze out of urban areas, it's a diminishing supply.'

The strengthening social pillar of sustainable development

Regional planning has not traditionally played a strong role in the provision of social (sometimes referred to as affordable) housing. Regional planning guidance documents included estimates of the need for affordable housing, but government advice suggested that these should be considered simply as indicative, since assessments of need are matters for local authorities (DETR 2000c). Local authority and voluntary-sector housing associations come together with the Government Office in each region to produce Regional Housing Statements, which identify policies for social housing provision. These have not been well integrated with regional planning, though the introduction of a new system of Regional Housing Strategies should change this (ODPM 2003a).

In the early phase of RPG production under the post-1998 system, debates tended to focus on the tensions between environment and 'development' in a broad sense. Very quickly, however, things started to change, with social housing rising up the agenda, involving an unusual mix of groups. These have included housebuilders using social arguments to pursue their case for a more liberal approach to designating land for development, plus lobby groups concerned with homelessness and social housing, such as Shelter, the National Housing Federation and the Joseph Rowntree Foundation. The Joseph Rowntree Foundation published a particularly influential report in April 2002 which stressed the housing problems facing low-income public-sector workers and the need for planning policies to be changed to expedite more housing development. Engaging at the rhetorical level with those perceived to be the source of the problem, the government was encouraged not to be timid in the face of opposition: 'We have collectively allowed people who are anti-development to take control of the argument and achieve a position where anyone who opposes them is seen as wanting to concrete over the South East' (Ken Bartlett, Joseph Rowntree Foundation, quoted in *Planning*, 5 July 2002). This report attracted considerable media coverage, generating a debate which was to gather considerable momentum in the following few months. The issue went beyond just planning and housing concerns, as attention was focused on the impact on key public services, given problems in attracting and retaining sufficient new teachers for schools, nursing staff, police and firefighters in the context of the overheated housing market of the South East.

The regional dimension was important here, as previous debates on 'environment versus development' conflicts appeared to have produced a compromised South East RPG document, which as far as developers were concerned was failing to release sufficient land for development. In effect, private housebuilders were not developing the levels of housing expected by RPG, they argued, because not enough land was designated in the types of location which buyers preferred – that is, on greenfield sites. These debates were again conducted in part through the media.

Drawing on its own commissioned research, the HBF (2001a) declared in a press release that 'Excluding the war years of 1940–46, less new homes were built in 2000 than in any year since 1924.' In a press release a year later, the message was still being reinforced and linked to the emerging coverage of problems in the South East: 'By 2000 there were 4.2 per cent fewer homes than households in London and 1.4 per cent fewer homes than households in the South East' (HBF 2002).

For the housebuilders, the problems lay firmly at the door of central government, local planners and anti-development pressure groups. Opponents took to the media to present different viewpoints. Responding to the debate raised by HBF press releases, Friends of the Earth for instance attracted media coverage for its counter-argument that in fact it was the developers who were to blame, hoarding land and playing the planning system in pursuit of higher profits (*Observer*, 12 May 2002), a view supported by influential commentators such as Will Hutton (2002).

The government again found itself in the unenviable position of arbiter between seemingly irreconcilable views on future housing, coupled with the prospect of alienating two sets of supporters: middle-class homeowners

Plate 5.2 New greenfield site on the edge of Norwich. The site says that the developer is looking for more land with or without planning permission.

fearing greenfield development, and low-income workers needing affordable housing. In July 2002 the Deputy Prime Minister, John Prescott, reacted to the growing public concern about housing problems in the South East region, declaring that 200,000 new homes would be provided in four growth areas for the region: Milton Keynes, Stansted in Essex, Ashford in Kent, and the Thames Gateway area to the east of London. If councils did not respond

Plate 5.3 Greenfield housing development, East Yorkshire.

positively to this initiative, they were warned that they would face severe consequences, although what these might be was not spelt out. In addition, a package of subsidies was announced to assist in housing low-income workers, targeted particularly at the south-east of the country (ODPM 2002b).

Reflecting some of the complex scalar reworkings of power relations which were emerging, Shelter responded to the government's proposals in 2002 to push for more social housing through regional planning: 'Intervention from central Government on planning at a regional level is particularly welcome. This will ensure that local councils fulfil their obligation to build new homes, regardless of campaigns from nimbyist lobbies' (Shelter 2002). This call for greater regional and national intervention, as a response to local blockages, is also frequently found in HBF documents, reflecting a perhaps unexpected concern for *more* centralised intervention. More predictably, perhaps, the HBF's underlying aim is to prompt a deregulation of land controls by over-riding local resistance to change.

In a by now familiar pattern, environmental campaigners accused the government of wanting to concrete over the countryside. This accusation was backed by the Shadow Minister for Environment and Rural Affairs, the Conservative Eric Pickles, who was quoted in the media as saying that the government plans would concrete over the 'green fields of Kent and Essex' (BBC 2002).

Plate 5.4 New social housing in Regeneration area, Norwich.

Interestingly, in contrast to Shelter's welcoming of central intervention in its press statement, Mr Pickles said the government's approach was a 'tribute to central planning' and likened the responsible minister, John Prescott, to Stalin. This was part of a recurrent theme in the Conservative opposition's critiques of planning under Labour. At the launch of its greenfield campaign bus during the 2001 election campaign, for instance,

> Tim Loughton, shadow minister for regeneration, accused Labour and Liberal Democrats of conspiring to ruin rural areas. He said: 'Across the country, Labour with their Lib Dem cronies, are planning to concrete over the countryside and bulldoze the greenbelt. John Prescott is issuing Soviet-style diktats to local councils forcing them to construct millions of buildings on greenfield land.'
>
> (BBC 2001)

Again, the language is interesting, as it attempts to link government policy to discredited Soviet-era planning techniques. Central government is accused by its main political opponents of being both centralist and authoritarian. This is essentially the political price which is paid for the contradictory aspects of only partially devolving aspects of regional planning, aiming to develop regional consensus through this, yet retaining tight central control over the final documents.

Brownfield targets

Finding ways to encourage housing development on brownfield sites has emerged as a major theme in recent regional planning debates, as it offers the potential to stem the outflow of urban population while reducing the pressures to release greenfield sites (Plate 5.5). Despite such attractions, there have been some substantial barriers, from the costs of cleaning up any site contamination to the anomalous position of the government levying a sales tax (VAT, currently at 17.5 per cent) on brownfield sites but not on greenfield sites (Urban Task Force 1999). In addition to being often more difficult and costly to develop, brownfield developments also tended to be less popular with housebuyers than those on greenfield sites.

The government's targets for development on brownfield sites proved almost as contentious as housing numbers in regional planning debates. Nevertheless, its strong allegiance to brownfield development was confirmed in a string of ministerial statements during the period when these debates were taking place (2001–2002) The following pronouncement by Lord Falconer, then Planning Minister, was perhaps typical:

Plate 5.5 Recent high-density residential development on a former factory site near Leeds, including Sustrans Cycle Route 66, Leeds–Liverpool Canal.

We know we can do better. Over the last decade land was squandered, particularly for housing. Greenfields were developed when brownfield sites stood idle. And when land was taken out of countryside it was wasted. . . . Make no mistake. We mean business on development of brownfield sites before greenfield sites.

(DTLR 2001c)

Not unexpectedly, development and housebuilding lobby groups usually took the opportunity presented by regional planning consultations and public examinations to seek to increase the proportion of development allocated to greenfield rather than brownfield sites. Alternatively, countryside and environmental groups such as the CPRE generally considered the initial brownfield targets set in draft RPG documents to be insufficiently challenging, later supporting the government in increasing these.

Although a key aim of increased brownfield site development was to reduce the tensions associated with using greenfield sites, the issue was frequently presented in terms of its also being the most 'sustainable' approach. Questioning this approach were some who argued that the targets issue was a means for circumscribing debates around alternatives for promoting sustainable urban form. For instance, a representative for pro-development groups at the Yorkshire and Humber panel examination complained of the 'danger that we equate sustainability with brownfield allocation'.

In the South West, brownfield targets generated an interesting public debate, as demonstrated in a Friends of the Earth national press release in 1999 (Friends of the Earth 1999b).

'If the House Builders' Federation (HBF) gets its way, almost 300,000 new homes could be built on greenfield sites in the South West by 2016, according to figures released today by Friends of the Earth. . . only 35% would be on brownfield sites, leaving 65% (a total of 299,000) to be built on greenfield sites. The HBF is a rich and powerful lobby group, with close links to New Labour.

Mike Birkin, Friends of the Earth's South West Regional Campaigns Coordinator, said: *'If the House Builders' Federation has its way, thousands of acres of greenfields in the South West will be concreted over for housing. . . .'*

Some house builders have suggested an even higher level of housing. One consortium has called for the building of a total of 536,000 new homes, a level 44% higher than that proposed by South West councils, and has rejected any regional target for the use of brownfield land. . . .

Tony Bosworth, Friends of the Earth's Housing Campaigner, said: *'These figures show that the threat to green fields from housing isn't confined to the South East. The House Builders' Federation seems only to be interested in the profits of its members and won't let the British countryside stand in the way of this selfish objective.'*

Again, the language and tactics here are interesting. Higher brownfield targets are justified by the threat of green fields being 'concreted over'. Developers are portrayed as powerful, rich and politically influential, putting profits before the countryside, while, as we have seen, the HBF prefers to present itself as the friend of those seeking affordable homes located in the areas where they want to live. Interestingly too, the quotation is quite similar to the Friends of the Earth press release on greenfield sites in the South East quoted earlier in this chapter (p. 121), suggesting the conveyor belt-like nature of the objections to regional planning proposals which were resorted to in this period.

A lively debate also took place on brownfield targets in the North West, where the regional planning body had set an initial target of 65 per cent. The public examination panel accepted the target, but the Secretary of State appears to have paid heed to the strong pressure from environmental groups such as the CPRE, whose regional policy officer was quoted in *Planning* following publication of the panel report as saying, '[T]his is a sorry day for those of us who wanted a boost for urban regeneration in Merseyside. To allow one third of new homes to be built on greenfield sites would be unforgivable' (*Planning*, 17 August 2001, p. 6). The target was increased to 70 per cent in the 'proposed changes'.

On the other hand, some environmental groups had reservations about high targets for brownfield sites. The Wildlife Trust, for instance, has argued against the automatic assumption that brownfield development is good and greenfield bad, pointing out that many brownfield sites have high value to nature and are located close to where people live (Shirley 1998). An officer from a prominent national environmental group also expressed this concern to us: 'With the pressure to achieve 60% development or better [on brownfield sites], I am concerned that we could lose sites with high social and environmental value' (interview SE9).

The result of these intensive negotiations during the recent process of regional planning in England has been that targets for development on brownfield land were increased in six out of the eight regions. Overall, there was a narrowing of the boundaries of regional discretion in setting brownfield targets, as central government assumed responsibility for the later stages of RPG production, and also a clustering of targets to a band within 10 per cent either side of the national target (Table 5.4). In other words, this new technique within the planning repertoire, though a rather blunt one, has been used to force forward urban compaction. Brownfield targets provided a means of shifting debates away from the emotional arguments, such as developing on urban wildlife sites, to a more technocratic-focus debate on whether one target level was preferable to another, in effect neutralising the terms of the debate and normalising 'targets' as the main concern.

Plate 5.6 Eco-park on former industrial land at Middlesbrough.

Table 5.4 Regional planning guidance (RPG) targets for development on 'brown-field' land

	Draft RPG	*Panel report*	*Proposed changes*	*Final RPG*
East Anglia	40	40+	50	50
South East	60	50	60	60
South West	36[a]	44	50	50
East Midlands	45	60	60	60
North East	60	60+	65	65[b]
Yorkshire and the Humber	60	60	60	60
North West	65	65	70	70
West Midlands	65	70[c]	n/a	n/a

Notes
a Shortly before the Public Examination SWRPC proposed that this target should be raised to 44%.
b Post-2016.
c Post–2011.

Greenfield development options

By contrast with the prominent debates about brownfield land, strategic options for developing greenfield sites were rarely openly discussed in any detail during the eight regional planning processes (Counsell 2001). This was despite the government's own national target of 60 per cent brownfield development, which implied that it expected 40 per cent of new development would need to occur on greenfield sites. One of the few places in which this was pointed out was the sustainability appraisal of RPG for the North East:

> Thirty five percent of the housing requirement may be met by development beyond the existing boundaries of settlements and/or on greenfield land therefore, and RPG1 is silent on the way this land is to be identified, or on the performance to be sought from this development. The way this development takes place will be an important determinant of the contribution new development makes to more sustainable development.
>
> (Baker Associates 2001, p. 30)

The way in which greenfield issues were generally tackled was through considering the sequential test (see Table 5.1, p. 110). National guidelines (DETR 2000c) favour urban extensions in public transport corridors over free-standing new settlements.

In the South West, draft RPG included policies for concentrating most development into larger towns, identified as the Principal Urban Areas (PUAs). The aim was to promote development in the PUAs, on brownfield land and on land close to transport networks and employment opportunities. This approach was backed up by an early version of the sequential test, yielding an interesting set of debates at the public examination. In its report, the public examination panel noted its concerns about the sequential test, which it argued was not useful in testing which land uses might be most appropriate for a piece of land, not least since it excluded issues such as 'social exclusion, the need to provide for all land use requirements and creating balanced development' (Gobbett and Palmer 2002, p. 219). In addition, the panel argued that the limited opportunities for brownfield development in the region meant that more attention might be needed to promoting higher densities, mixed land uses and regeneration. In an article covering these debates, two of those working for the regional planning body acknowledge that housing was not necessarily always the best use for brownfield sites, while admitting that, with hindsight, the regional planning body 'allowed itself to be influenced by the GOSW [Government Office for the South West] view that the sequential approach was the panacea to ensuring sustainable development' (Gobbett and Palmer 2002, p. 220).

The importance of this debate for us is that it illustrates both the ways in which this new tool was inserted into the regional planning process, and also something of the way in which it was contested and consequently reshaped.

Returning to the issue of how best to guide greenfield development, the West Midlands was the only draft RPG in which the possibility of allowing urban extensions was specifically excluded. This was justified on the grounds that 'on the basis of past experience such urban edge provision would encourage an outward movement of people and this would be against the interests of urban regeneration' (WMLGA 2001a, p. 10). While not excluding urban extensions from being considered, none of the other draft RPG documents identified specific proposals for them, leaving pro-development lobbyists to try to make the case for greater guidance on how to plan for new greenfield development.

Nationally, it is fair to say that those seeking more relaxed approaches to greenfield development failed to make much headway against the combined forces of the countryside, green and local protest groups. Indeed, it is still not clear in most cases how the 40 per cent of development expected nationally to be developed on greenfield sites will be managed, since most firm proposals in draft RPG documents have been either rejected or deferred for consideration in sub-regional studies or in local development plans (see the Cambridge case study below). In effect, the government appeared to be simply deferring or sidestepping some difficult decisions.

Case study: the Cambridge new settlement proposal

Whereas Stevenage represents an example of new developments being aborted through the new planning system, Cambridge in the East of England provides the only English example of where there was a serious debate about the contribution a new settlement might make towards meeting future housing needs. At the time that regional planning guidance was produced for the area, Cambridgeshire formed part of the East Anglia region, whose draft RPG (SCEALA 1998) raised the possibility of a new development in Greater Cambridge, where there were both strong development pressures and severe constraints due to a tightly drawn green belt. Because Cambridge is not an old industrial town, the lack of easily identifiable brownfield sites raised concerns about possible effects of 'town cramming' on the character of the historic City of Cambridge should urban compaction policies be pursued.

The new settlement remained as nothing more than a rather vague proposal through the regional planning process. No specific site was identified for the proposal, with detailed consideration of this instead deferred to be considered at the local scale in the Cambridge and Peterborough Structure Plan:

> Proposals for a new settlement with the potential for construction to start by 2006 should be brought forward through the Cambridgeshire and Peterborough Structure Plan. The plan should define the role of such a settlement within the sub-region, its initial site and broad location, and

provide guidance on its early implementation. It should be designed with the potential for longer term expansion, if needed.

(GOEE 2001, pp. 34–35)

In a sub-regional study commissioned by SCEALA, various options for the new settlement were appraised before the structure plan was completed (Colin Buchanan 2001). This study examined the feasibility of three development options, each of which involved an initial settlement of 6,000 new homes:

- A 'Cambridge centred' option, which maximises urban concentration in the City and surrounding areas including the inner Green Belt
- A 'Mixed strategy' option with part of the City and Green Belt housing distributed to the market towns. . ..
- A Market Towns/Corridor option a much greater proportion of growth allocated to these areas.

(p. iii)

Subsequent studies were commissioned by local authorities affected by these proposals. There was a distinct tension between the city and county councils, on the one hand, which favoured concentrated development in the green belt to the east of Cambridge, and South Cambridge District Council on the other, which was opposed to all development in the green belt. These studies confirmed what the commissioning local authorities already believed. First, that around 10,200 homes could be built on the site of the Cambridge airport, with further development around nearby villages, and second, that development there would cause significant damage to the green belt and to the setting of Cambridge.

The Cambridgeshire structure plan opted for development to the east of Cambridge, focused on the airport and villages, though it was vigorously opposed by South Cambridge District, with the support of local amenity groups. Not surprisingly, the proposals were debated at length in the six-week-long examination in public (EiP), which took place from October to December 2002. The EiP agreed with the use of land at Cambridge Airport and the county council's proposals for several other incursions into the green belt, although not to the full extent that was originally proposed.

The Cambridge growth debate brings out many of the storylines and alliances found in other localised struggles over the location of new housing. Claims were made that new development would be the sustainable option, needed to solve housing shortages and high prices. Counter-claims argued that new developments would totally destroy the character of the green belt and the city. The main difference was that in Cambridge the pro-development case was put forward by two of the affected local authorities, allowing the development lobby to take a back seat, whereas in many other high-growth regions housebuilding organisations have been much more active in putting forward the case for new greenfield housing.

Conclusions

Housing has been a central issue in regional planning guidance over the past decade, providing its most publicly contentious debates and the testing ground for some of the most important changes to planning techniques. In concluding this chapter, we want to focus on four central issues, which we return to in other parts of this book.

First, there are clear tensions in the ways in which housing policies map out across the different scales of planning. Most accounts rightly emphasise the controlling and policing role of central government in forcing through its policies, involving selectivities in choice of planning techniques (Murdoch 2000), retention of the responsibility for issuing the final document (Baker 2002; Williams 2002), and also the policing role of central government officers as RPG was prepared. This latter point emerges from the commentary of some of those involved in the process, who point to the great value of having government officials working side by side with them, in terms of advice and technical speed, but of the nagging suspicion that this was also acting as a way of 'policing' their behaviour (Gobbett and Palmer 2002, pp. 211, 221). But though centralism was the dominant tendency, it is important not to lose sight of the many and diffuse local, regional and national resistances to central government policy. Many of the debates in regional planning did appear to influence the government, not least in setting parameters within which it was possible for the government to revise regional planning guidance documents without large-scale opposition. In this sense, it becomes important to examine these debates in ways which go beyond the simplistic dialectics of (malign) 'top-down' controlling or (benign) 'bottom-up' resistances. Instead, it is necessary to examine the multi-scalar nature of governance, including the ways in which debates and pressures work recursively across scales. At a theoretical level, this suggests the need to adapt theories of state selectivity to look at how central government policy is influenced by the ways in which it necessarily intersects with the policy processes set in train at other levels of governance.

Second, many of the problems which regional planning has been confronted with reflect the lack of a national spatial strategy. In the absence of such a national strategy, the considerable body of government guidance becomes a way of embedding introspective practices of policy formation within regions rather than policies which seek to balance regional and national interests. This becomes particularly problematic when it comes to arguments about whether it is possible or desirable to deflect housing growth in pressure areas to other regions. So while there was some interchange between neighbouring regional planning bodies, this was limited in scope and content. Regional planning in this way remains a rather inward-looking process which finds it difficult to grapple with the big issues, such as the national settlement pattern and national patterns of housing and economic growth.

Third, there has to be a concern with the way in which policies such as brownfield targets and the sequential test have been inserted as a central logic for future planning. Not only is it still unclear whether these approaches represent the most effective way of addressing many sustainability concerns, but it remains to be seen whether they can help in creating better-quality urban environments (see Chapter 6). By developing a set of inter-related techniques (housing allocations, urban capacity studies, brownfield targets, the sequential test), the government has in effect short-circuited such arguments, while at the same time seeming to open up the planning system for greater public debate. The related concern raised with us by some housebuilding representatives is that eventually the supply of urban brownfield sites will start to diminish, yet there remained a lack of guidance about how and where any future large-scale greenfield development might emerge.

Finally, it is worth pointing again to the way in which environmental concerns emerged in regional housing debates, being worked into them selectively according to region, issue, and lobby group focus. But rather than despair at sustainable development being 'hijacked' by different lobby groups (Gobbett and Palmer 2002), we may find it useful to see how the concept might be helping to open up and clarify some of the key debates in planning. In particular, the requirement to examine all policies against social, economic and environmental criteria is potentially helpful in moving away from simplistic 'development versus environment' debates, to a much greater concern to examining the multiple ways in which housing development might impact for good or bad, or both good and bad, in different places.

6 Towards an urban renaissance?

> One of the key political challenges of the new century is to make Britain's towns and cities not just fit to live in, but thriving centres of human activity.
>
> (John Prescott, Deputy Prime Minister, in Preface, *Towards an Urban Renaissance*, Urban Task Force 1999, p. 3).

Reshaping cities

Promoting sustainable urban form has been a central part of planning's contribution to sustainable development debates. This chapter specifically examines regional planning's role in seeking to guide the broader settlement patterns of regions as well its attention to improving urban environments through better urban design. In terms of settlement patterns, there have long been major debates about how best to capitalise on the momentum of growth areas: whether to seek to spread their growth to less buoyant areas through constraint policies, or instead to encourage growth wherever it emerges and hope for a beneficial 'spread' effect. Though in the short term encouraging growth areas might seem the obvious solution, the longer-term dangers are that this can lead to negative consequences which can undermine the very basis of success, such as wage, land and housing price spirals, traffic congestion, urban sprawl and longer trips to work, social polarisation and a deteriorating quality of life. To put it another way, unregulated growth runs the risk of undermining the very basis of a region's success.

Looking for a win–win approach, the current preferred approach is to avoid constraint policies, but to manage growth in a 'smarter' way (Box 6.1). It is in this context that debates have arisen about how best to improve the quality of life within cities and also how best to address urban development in its wider regional context.

In the United States such debates are generally associated with movements such as 'the new urbanism' or 'new regionalism', where concepts from sustainable development debates are used to provide a normative framework for planning, setting out key principles for regional settlement patterns and urban form (Wheeler 2002). The Smart Growth movement has sought to promote

---

Box 6.1 Smart Growth in the United States

Reacting to concern about urban sprawl and flight from the inner cities, in cities such as Portland there has been a growing questioning of whether it makes sense to abandon infrastructure such as schools in the inner parts of cities at the same time as having to build new infrastructure on the edge of cities. Likewise, there is widespread concern about the social and environmental costs associated with the growing separation of places where people live from where they work. Much as in British planning, there is a concern about leaving brownfield sites undeveloped at the same time as new development is moving on to greenfield sites.

The result has been a move towards 'smart' policies to help concentrate developments into suitable areas whilst protecting sensitive areas. With smart growth, development tends to be focused on existing rural and urban settlements, while resource areas are protected. Economic growth is favoured as a means of achieving these aims. In addition, designs are favoured which support public transport and pedestrian access, and which provide a mix of residential, commercial and retail uses. Open spaces and other environmental amenities are actively created and nurtured.

Sources: Based on Burchell and Shad (1998) and International City/County Management Association with Anderson (1998)

---

a return to compact forms of development as an alternative to sprawl (see Box 6.1).

Since the early 1990s, federal and state governments in Australia have likewise sought to respond to the dangers of low-density suburban sprawl, using 'Ecologically Sustainable Urban Development' as the uniting theme. Federal government policies sought to encourage innovation in this area through the government's 'Building Better Cities' programme, which involved a wide range of experiments with encouraging local governments to plan for higher density, more mixed-use inner and outer suburban developments (see Haughton 1999b). This agenda was driven by a number of concerns: not simply a commitment to sustainable development, but also a growing realisation of the extent of state subsidy for standard low-density sprawl, as the state was required to build new roads, clinics, schools, and so forth. Thus a large part of the Australian agenda was based on improving the cost recovery of suburban development, while seeking to reduce the extent of rural land take.

Underpinning these international debates has been a concern that low-density residential urban sprawl was in many ways a key feature of unsustainable behaviour patterns, as it represented an urban form which in most respects was land inefficient and energy inefficient. In particular, urban sprawl was linked to increasing car dependence, and with this, car pollution. The typical housing form – detached and semi-detached family houses – was also seen as energy inefficient relative to other housing forms, in terms of heat loss and consumption of building materials. More than this, the growing spatial separation of the different functions of the city and the related tendency towards large-scale service infrastructure (shopping malls and superstores, schools, hospitals), in a context of limited public transport provision, was having the effect of creating mono-functional residential areas and driving the trend towards greater car dependency. For planners, these debates suggested the importance of promoting higher residential densities, more mixed-use zoning of areas and better provision of public transport.

It was out of such concerns that debates on Sustainable Cities, Sustainable Communities and Sustainable Settlements first emerged (Owens 1986; Breheny 1992; Haughton and Hunter 1994; Barton *et al.* 1995; Roseland 1998), involving a growing critique of the claims and counter-claims of the relative environmental friendliness of alternative urban settlement patterns. From an early stage, however, it was clear that it would be necessary to look beyond environmental concerns at the economic and social functioning of cities, and also the relationship between cities and their wider regional and global hinterlands (Haughton and Hunter 1994; Rees 1995; Satterthwaite 1997). More than this, however, it is important to recognise the political ecology of debates around sustainable urban form, involving attention to why certain forms of city are being promoted, and which kinds of alternative settlement patterns – new settlements, for example – are largely being scripted out of policy (Chapter 5), by whom, and in whose interests.

Linking outer urban sprawl and inner urban decline

One of the strongest arguments for sub-regional- and regional-scale planning has been the concern that competitive localism in both planning and local economic development has contributed to processes of outer urban sprawl. Particularly with the more *laissez-faire* approaches which emerged during the 1980s, the national government's insistence on a presumption in favour of development made it difficult for local planning authorities to resist developer pressures to build new out-of-town facilities. This was particularly apparent with the rapid growth of large retail and leisure developments such as Meadowhall in Sheffield, but it was also evident in most substantial towns, where increasing numbers of large-scale commercial developments started to appear outside the existing city centres. In many areas a form of lowest common denominator approach seemed to exist, which saw local planning authorities providing permission for such developments even where they anticipated negative impacts on existing inner urban facilities.

Symptomatic of this approach was that around the country some of the planning authorities which had allowed large out-of-town retail centres simultaneously found themselves trying to devise policies to regenerate existing retail centres which were having investment, spending and jobs sucked out of them. Those individuals without ready access to the new out-of-town facilities found themselves faced with fewer and often more expensive local shops, a problem that affected the carless and the elderly in particular. The alternative, however, of refusing planning permission raised concerns that car-borne shoppers might simply take their spending outside the locality anyway, to new developments elsewhere. Moreover, for people able to access the edge-of-town facilities, the benefits were often substantial, in terms of lower prices and the ability to park close to where they shopped.

For that reason, it should be stressed that out-of-town sprawl was not universally regarded as a negative outcome of the national *laissez-faire* political climate. Indeed, some local authorities saw the development of new out-of-town sites as a way of bringing much-needed jobs and investments into their areas. In effect, the 1980s acceleration of out-of-town development was the result of a complex interplay of local authorities fearing the costs of central government's overturning any refused planning permissions at appeal, plus local competitive bidding for investment. In a world not simply of hyper-mobile investment, but of highly mobile consumers and workers, local authorities making planning decisions had to bear in mind that if they refused permission for a development, then a neighbouring authority might in any case allow a similar development. The result was that competitive localism undermined efforts by planners to impose conditions on planning applications to improve the quality of a development. Some built-up areas suffered from this more than others, particularly those along motorways, where in the absence of a regional planning framework a local authority seeking to resist development might find its efforts undermined by a local authority either on the other side of a motorway junction or one junction up – West Yorkshire and the M62 corridor is a classic example, where retail and warehousing development has been substantial for some years now. In addition, it must be stressed that some local authorities managed this difficult balancing act better than others, sometimes because they were in relatively prosperous areas and better able to resist low-quality development schemes.

With the call for greater spatial specificity in the post-1998 round of RPG documents, the possibility existed for local planning authorities to collaborate in addressing these concerns, buoyed by the official recognition that inner-urban decline might be associated with a relaxed approach to allowing out-of-town development (DoE 1996a; DETR 2000g, p. 43).

Case study: proposals for the 'Southern Crescent' in the North West

The potential for the new regional arrangements to deal with such tensions is well illustrated by the proposals to create a new economic growth area focused on what came to be called the Southern Crescent. The RES produced for the North West Development Agency (NWDA 1999) introduced

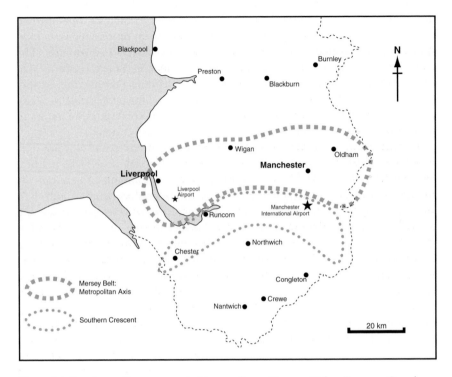

Figure 6.1 Southern Crescent and Metropolitan Mersey Belt. (Source: Based on NWDA 1999.)

the concept of the Southern Crescent into the regional debate, involving an area centred on north Cheshire which was already showing signs of strong economic buoyancy (Figure 6.1). Importantly, however, it was an area which lay outside the main urbanised area between Manchester and Liverpool, the so-called metropolitan 'Mersey Belt' (Figure 6.1).

Those drafting regional economic strategy took care in wording their justification to argue for selective new development in order 'to release potential creatively without compromising on the principles of sustainable development' (NWDA 1999, p. 42). The proposal was somewhat sketchy at this stage, although some other elements were flagged up, including the need for transport improvements and the consolidating of urban form. In this sketchy shape the proposal was inserted into the RES without substantial resistance.

In an attempt to show complementarity with the RES, the draft RPG for the North West (NWRA 2000) ended up adopting a somewhat anomalous approach towards the Southern Crescent. In the 'spatial development framework' section it was suggested that demand for development in Cheshire should be *resisted*, in order to support regeneration in the major existing urban areas and to minimise traffic congestion. In the economic policies, however, it was indicated that 'within areas of economic opportunity, including the Southern Crescent, development plans and local economic strategies should target those key sectors... that add value, raise regional competitiveness and attract investment which would otherwise locate outside the North West' (ibid., p. 18). Such internal inconsistencies probably reflect the fact that the North West draft RPG was produced through a series of topic groups, often consisting of different mixes of stakeholders developing somewhat different agendas.

During the regional planning process the Southern Crescent concept was strongly supported by commercial development interests, which argued that footloose investors would be relocating in relation to other locations in Europe, not simply in competition with the North West's conurbations. It was widely opposed, however, by local authority planners (in north Cheshire as well as the conurbation areas) and by environmental groups, who both argued that growth constraint policies in north Cheshire represented a powerful weapon in the promotion of regeneration in the urban areas. The key argument was that there would be no point in defining the Southern Crescent unless the intention was to encourage major development in the area. The public examination panel agreed with these sentiments, concluding that 'in our opinion no useful purpose would be achieved if RPG identified a southern crescent outside the Mersey Belt' (Acton et al. 2001, p. 67). Likewise, there was no mention of the Southern Crescent in the Secretary of State's 'proposed changes' to RPG for the North West, where the overall policy towards north Cheshire was retained as one of strong constraint. Local authorities were instructed to review immediately their existing housing land allocations to ensure

> that they are fully justified having regard to the core development principles... only those allocations which are sustainable and which will add significant value to the development of the national economy or which are greater than regional significance should be retained.
>
> (GONW 2002, p. 20)

Interestingly, subsequent to these debates, the second version of the RES for the North West (NWDA 2003) opted to avoid all mention of the Southern Crescent concept, which had in effect been killed off during the regional planning process.

The intriguing issue here is that constraining out-of-town development in order to support urban regeneration in the existing urban core emerged as the government's preferred approach in the North West, yet different decisions were taken in other parts of the country. In East Anglia, for example, the regional strategy favoured supporting growth in areas of economic buoyancy over dispersing it to communities in need of regeneration (see Chapter 7).

Urban migration and urban renaissance

It is important to stress that the pressure for new out-of-town housing not only results from recent household formation rates, but also reflects a long-standing drift of the population away from the inner urban areas. Growing personal mobility, associated particularly with car ownership, increased personal wealth, plus a combination of dissatisfaction with urban living and a search for something approximating to the 'rural idyll' all made a contribution to this population drift. It is difficult to summarise adequately the many factors at work here. Sometimes it was simply a long-standing life-cycle pattern, of young families seeking out suburban houses with gardens, but often it was linked to wider issues such as the quality of schools in urban areas and differences in house price trajectories, which in some cases were enmeshed in wider issues of racial stereotyping and discrimination. Again, competitive local planning sometimes played a part, as local authorities in some areas felt compelled to provide planning permission for new housing on their peripheries, for fear that people would simply move out to adjacent areas and commute back into their jobs. Moreover, the continuing voluntary outward drift of people from the cities is used by some of those seeking to justify alternatives to compact city solutions, from edge-of-town development to new settlements. For instance, the TCPA argued that 'the fact that counter-urbanisation has been occurring in the UK in recent years displays people's preferences for non-city living' (TCPA in written evidence to the South West public examination, 2000).

Plate 6.1 Abandoned housing in Hull.

By the mid-1990s it had become clear that there was something more deep-rooted and problematic at work than the desire for a new house on a new suburban or out-of-town residential development, with areas of housing abandonment emerging in many northern cities. At first these were seen as isolated examples, but by the late 1990s it had become clear that whole areas of abandoned or semi-derelict older private rental housing and public-sector housing stock were emerging, often despite substantial public-sector 'regeneration' investments. Quite simply, increasing numbers of people appeared to be unprepared to live in certain areas of some cities, areas which had become dilapidated in terms of their housing stock, local environmental conditions, educational and medical facilities, and social fabric. Stigmatised and residualised, they came to be perceived as poor places for either individuals or institutions to invest in, because of the danger that there would be little return on investment. Perhaps equally important, these areas became perceived as poor areas to live in, even by those who had lived there for years, as fears grew of crime, often associated with drug abuse and gangs of youths preying on the vulnerable. The perception was as important as the reality, as local media sought to convey complex messages of huge problems and the positive aspects of resistance to these from local communities. But in residential investment, the prevailing mantra remains 'location, location, location', and those in 'poor' locations found it increasingly difficult to operate as part of a fully functional housing market. The result was that in cities such as Hull and Leeds in Yorkshire it became possible to have areas of massive dereliction and downward house price movements within two miles (three kilometres) of areas experiencing substantial housing booms.

The outward flow of investment, jobs and people was not a simple unidirectional and universal phenomenon, however. A substantial return to inner-urban living has emerged in the past twenty years or so, in part stimulated by experiments such as Salford Quays and London Docklands, which revealed the extent of the market for 'lifestyle' apartments. The back-to-the-city trend also responded to a series of demographic and labour market trends, the increased gap before childraising and the rise of dual-income households with no children, but keen to be close to cultural facilities. The convergence of these issues is closely linked to the emergence of 'post-industrial chic', with its penchant for warehouse conversions and the associated gentrification of some former industrial buildings and neighbourhoods. The selectivities at work are important. Larger and more prosperous cities benefited first from this trend, for instance parts of London, plus parts of regional capitals such as Birmingham, Manchester and Leeds. Sympathetic local authorities helped by removing planning restrictions in former industrial areas which they had previously zoned as 'employment use' only, and also by encouraging the nightlife of these areas through their attitudes to licensing laws. The Leeds '24 Hour City' initiative, for instance, though something of a misnomer, certainly helped in turning round the image of the city, as did the growing café and bar culture of Manchester's Canal Street area.

Plate 6.2 Bringing people into the city: The Deep, Hull.

It is worth emphasising the importance of these urban issues to the regional agenda. The rise of regionalism is in part predicated on the belief that the decline of some urban areas is linked to wider regional issues, in the sense that it is competitive localism in the absence of strategic regionalism which has set the scene for so much investment being diverted away from inner-urban areas to out-of-town areas.

Urban compaction, urban renaissance and sustainable communities

Urban compaction policies have increasingly come to play a central role in English planning. At the regional scale the current mainstream view is that it is better policy to support further development in existing towns and cities which have a range of employment opportunities and a better-developed infrastructure, rather than imposing substantial new development on smaller settlements. New settlements have generally been out of favour politically, especially following the abortive private sector-led initiatives in the South East during the 1980s (see Chapter 1). At the urban level, the dominant theme is to counter urban sprawl while seeking to make existing urban areas more attractive. This has typically involved a series of inter-related policies to promote planning for mixed uses rather than the rigid zoning of the past (Plate 6.4), higher residential densities (Plate 6.4), improved design of buildings and public spaces, and measures to improve the attractiveness of public

Plate 6.3 High-density mixed-use development in Leeds.

transport over the car. These policies reflected the dominant view that weak planning in the past had contributed to the worst of both worlds, with urban sprawl eating into the countryside, together with growing social segregation as investment and jobs were sucked out of some inner-city areas. This point of view is summed up by the national environmental group the CPRE in a press release:

> Housing sprawl is continuing to blight the countryside and undermine the urban renaissance despite new Government planning policies intended to put an end to wasteful development. Tony Burton, CPRE's Assistant Director, said 'The government's flagship policies are being thwarted by a combination of inertia and weak delivery by local authorities and its own regional offices.'
>
> (CPRE 2001b)

Despite the broad support which has emerged for urban compaction policies, there are two major problems with the arguments promoting them. The first is that there appears to be doubt about whether the resulting homes and neighbourhoods are sufficiently attractive to encourage people to live in the city (Breheny 1997). The second is that the available evidence is far from uniformly supportive that compaction policies make much of a contribution

Plate 6.4 Greenwich Millennium Village: high-density development.

to the desired policy goals. The issue is not that there is no research to support the compaction policies (see the useful review by Stead 2000), but rather that policy-makers seem to undervalue some of the concerns which exist, many of them long-standing, about whether the approach is leading to the desired effects and whether it might be having some unanticipated negat-

Plate 6.5 Greenwich Millennium Village.

ive effects (Evans 1991; Breheny 1992; Haughton and Hunter 1994; Williams *et al.* 2000). For instance, it is far from clear whether higher residential densities of themselves are enough to move people away from cars (Plate 6.5)

However, for recent UK governments, compaction policies have had considerable appeal, representing a means of satisfying both those seeking to preserve the countryside and those wishing to stimulate urban regeneration. In particular, the compaction approach appears to offer a way of reducing the conflicts which arise from addressing the national need for more housing development. By emphasising good urban design, policy-makers have been able to argue that it is possible to attract people to return to living in inner-urban areas, occupying brownfield land without sacrificing the quality of the urban environment. The attempted win–win solution here is that pressure to develop rural land is reduced, yet new houses are provided and city environments continue to be improved.

Planning for compaction

The emergence of compact-city policies in England can be traced through the growing body of planning advice to promote higher residential densities, greater attention to mixed-use developments, and increasing the proportion of new development on 'brownfield' rather than new ('greenfield') sites. The Conservative government signalled its intention to move policy in this direction with increasing determination during the mid-1990s. A particularly clear statement of its rationale was provided in *Sustainable Development: The UK Strategy* (HMSO 1994, p. 161, para. 24.20):

> Urban growth should be encouraged in the most sustainable settlement form. The density of towns is important. More compact urban development uses less land. It also enables lower energy consumption through efficient generation technologies such as district heating and through the reduced need to travel, for example, from homes to schools, to shops, and to work. . . . The scope for reducing travel, especially by car, is dependent on the size, density of development and range of services on offer at centres well served by public transport as well as local centres within walking distance.

This policy direction was given teeth through policy guidance which required local authorities to address these issues in their development plans.

With the election of a New Labour government in 1997 this policy direction was not simply confirmed but strengthened in many ways. The revised national strategy for sustainable development helps pinpoint the new government's view of how it would set about this (DTLR 1999a, pp. 61–62, para. 7.56):

> In order to create more sustainable patterns of development we need to:
>
> • concentrate the majority of new development within existing urban areas;
> • reduce the need to travel in planning the location of new development;

- reuse previously developed land, bring empty homes back into use and convert buildings to new uses;
- extend existing urban areas rather than building isolated new settlements; and
- encourage a high quality environment with the provision of green spaces.

The same section of this strategy also commits the government to encouraging high-density development near existing transport corridors and town centres, and to promoting more mixed-use development for all types of housing (including social housing), retail and work.

In its revised arrangements for producing RPG, the government's advice (DETR 2000a) made the achievement of sustainable urban form a central objective. The centrality of sustainability and urban form issues can also be gleaned from the government's planning Green Paper (DTLR 2001b, p. 1, para. 1.4), which provides what is in effect a mission statement for planning:

> A successful planning system will promote economic prosperity by delivering land for development in the right place at the right time. It will encourage urban regeneration by ensuring that new development is channelled towards existing town centres rather than adding to urban sprawl. It will help to conserve greenfield land and re-use urban brownfield land. It will value the countryside and our heritage while recognising that times move on. It has a critical part to play in achieving the Government's commitment to sustainable development.

The Urban Task Force report and the urban White Paper (2000)

Shortly after the Blair government came into power in 1997, a task force chaired by the architect Lord Richard Rogers was established, charged with looking at the complex problems associated with making cities more attractive places. In the final report, *Towards an Urban Renaissance* (Urban Task Force 1999), urban form, urban design, architecture, good-quality services and crime reduction are brought together to suggest ways of making cities more attractive places to live and work in, while promoting the goals of sustainable development. This work has its roots in a long tradition of European thinking, not least the European Commission's *Green Paper on the Urban Environment* (CEC 1990). The particular importance of the urban renaissance report is that it brought about a new focus on urban design as a key element of city planning, and the need for an integrated approach to sustainable development: 'An urban renaissance should be focused on the principles of design excellence, economic strength, environmental responsibility, good governance and social responsibility' (Urban Task Force 1999, p. 25).

The findings of the Urban Task Force generated both considerable debate and widespread support across policy sectors. There was substantial sympathetic press coverage of the report's vision of vibrant and more aesthetic urban living conditions. Unsurprisingly, the CPRE, which had long advocated much of this approach (see CPRE 1994, for example), was particularly enthusiastic: 'Paradoxically the renewal of our towns and cities is the key to tackling some of our most pressing rural problems. Implementing the report is more important to rural England than new countryside legislation. Doing nothing is not an option' (Kate Parmister, CPRE, quoted in *Daily Telegraph*, 1999c). The report was also supported by development advocacy groups such as the HBF, but in this case the problems of funding development on problematic brownfield sites is emphasised, along with the consequent apparent need for public subsidy: 'To create housing markets in areas where they do not currently exist and in some of the most blighted areas this will require developments on a large scale, vision, political leadership and considerable pump-priming from the public purse' (HBF spokesman quoted in *Daily Telegraph* 1999c).

The principal criticism of the Task Force report came from those bodies which were campaigning against high-density urban living, such as the TCPA, which advocated a return to building new settlements as a response to the housing crisis (see Chapter 5). Setting out an alternative vision of urban England, it put forward the argument for new 'sustainable' settlements that 'Concentrating housing development in new and expanded settlements can make a real contribution to combating urban sprawl and protecting the countryside' (Graeme Bell [then TCPA Director], *Planning*, 15 October 1999).

The government had been waiting for the delivery of the Task Force report before finalising the first urban White Paper since 1978 (DETR 2000g). In it was set out a new vision of urban living (Box 6.2), which sought to marry a concern with promoting urban quality of life, a concern to avoid the past pitfalls of divisiveness within urban communities, and a desire not to upset the powerful countryside lobby by allowing urban sprawl. This new vision is notable for shifting the emphasis in urban policy firmly in favour of engaging with communities, rather than expecting the private sector to lead in developing new proposals. Symbolically, perhaps, bottom-up initiatives, 'people shaping the future of their community', come first in the list of priorities, while economic investment comes fourth behind urban design and environmental sustainability.

Reinforcing the government's existing commitment to compact forms of urban development, the White Paper places considerable emphasis on bringing brownfield land and empty buildings back into constructive use:

At present they are wasted assets. We have put in place measures to:

- exploit their potential so that they contribute to the quality of urban life, rather than detract from it; and

---

Box 6.2 The 2000 Urban White Paper's vision

Our vision is of towns, cities and suburbs which offer a high quality of life and opportunity for all, not just the few. We want to see:

- people shaping the future of their community, supported by strong and truly representative local leaders;
- people living in attractive, well kept towns and cities which use space and buildings well;
- good design and planning which makes it practical to live in a more environmentally sustainable way, with less noise, pollution and traffic congestion;
- towns and cities able to create and share prosperity, investing to help all their citizens reach their full potential;
- good quality services – health, education, housing, transport, finance, shopping, leisure and protection from crime – that meets the needs of people and businesses wherever they are.

This urban renaissance will benefit everyone, making towns and cities vibrant and successful and protecting the countryside from development pressures.

Source: DETR (2000g, p. 30)

- use previously developed land to prevent urban sprawl and pepper-pot developments.

(DETR 2000g, p. 9)

Regional planning and the urban renaissance agenda

The debates which took place about urban renaissance during the preparation of RPG focused on the key strategic policy issues of urban compaction and sustainable urban form, housing numbers and location, location of employment sites and transport proposals.

Elements of the urban renaissance agenda occur in all the recent regional planning documents, which all have policies that seek to achieve sustainable urban form and compact urban development. However, as an explicit, holistic concept and approach to urban development and management, urban renaissance clearly features much more strongly in some regional documents than others (Table 6.1). Interestingly, then, urban renaissance is perhaps best regarded as a political strategy and political resource in much the same way as sustainable development. It is a collection of ideas which can be drawn upon selectively by those seeking to advocate particular development approaches.

Table 6.1 The urban renaissance agenda in regional planning, as at April 2003

Region	Urban renaissance/regeneration
RPG1: North East	Does not refer to urban renaissance as such, but urban regeneration is one of four key themes in the spatial strategy. Urban renaissance issues are dealt with under separate topic headings.
RPG6: East Anglia	First policy in the development strategy is headed 'Urban renaissance'. It includes urban design; building conservation; urban open space; bringing vacant and underused sites back into use; improvement of the housing stock; tackling poverty and social exclusion; and community safety.
RPG8: East Midlands	Does not include specific reference to urban renaissance, although urban regeneration is a key element of the spatial strategy.
RPG9: South East	Chapter on quality of life begins with urban 'renaissance and concentrating development'. The policy makes urban areas the prime focus for development and redevelopment and also deals with design and restructuring.
RPG10: South West	There are no objectives or policies which specifically refer to urban renaissance, although the principal themes are covered in other policies. Nor is urban regeneration identified as a key issue.
RPG11: West Midlands[a]	Urban renaissance is one of four key themes in the spatial strategy. It is also the subject of the first objective and first policy. The policy refers to variety and choice of working and living environments; variety in employment, education and training; modern urban transport, emphasising public transport; and rejuvenation of city, town and local centres. There is a separate chapter titled 'Urban renaissance' giving more policy detail on the above themes.
RPG12: Yorkshire and the Humber	'Urban and rural renaissance' is one of four key themes in the spatial strategy, covering urban design; compact urban development; integrating land use and transportation; minimising urban transport; and tackling social exclusion, dereliction and decay.
RPG 14: North West	Urban renaissance is a key objective of the strategy, the core principles of which cover economy in the use of land and buildings; enhancing quality of life; quality in new development; and promoting sustainable economic growth, competitiveness and social inclusion.

Source: Positions taken from final versions of regional planning guidance other than in the West Midlands.

Note
a Draft prepared by the RPB.

Sustainable communities?

In early 2003 the government released its action plan *Sustainable Communities: Building for the Future* (ODPM 2003a), in the process launching some radical proposals for addressing the twin pressures of urban expansion in the South East and the East of England, and housing abandonment, particularly in northern cities. The action plan proposed new powers to intervene in areas with severe problems of housing abandonment, including the establishment of partnerships of local authorities and other key stakeholders to develop strategic plans for whole housing markets and the creation of nine low-demand pathfinder projects.

In addition, it announced the government's proposals for new housing in the south of the country, drawing on the initial findings of some sub-regional reviews commissioned as part of the regional planning process. Having reduced the proposed number of new households suggested by the South East RPG public examination panel by around 200,000 in RPG9 in 2001 (GOSE 2001), just two years later the government added back 200,000 households to the number of new households it expected to be built by 2016. The political masterstroke was to argue that the sub-regional studies suggested that many new households could be accommodated in four new 'growth areas': Thames Gateway, Milton Keynes–South Midlands, London–Stansted–Cambridge, and Ashford in Kent (Figure 6.2). In a speech following publication of *Sustainable Communities*, the Deputy Prime Minister, John Prescott, justified the decision as follows (ODPM 2003a):

> I don't want the pepperpot developments we've had in the past. And I don't want urban sprawl.
>
> That's why I've given a guarantee to safeguard the greenbelt and why I've increased the density figure for new developments.
>
> It's also why we're concentrating in the four growth areas – Ashford, Milton Keynes, Stansted and Thames Gateway.
>
> Our focus is on increasing housing supply in these areas and getting a level of critical mass and certainty into the system.
>
> (ODPM 2003a, p. 7)

There are some important developments contained in these proposals. Particularly noteworthy is the attention to addressing the problems of social housing, the clear commitment to working with communities to meet their aspirations, new funding for improving parks and open spaces, a commitment to improving local infrastructure, and the fact that local government rather than unelected business leaders appears destined to be closer to the heart of the new delivery agencies which are proposed. Perhaps most importantly, the very scale of the proposals goes some way to addressing the scale of the problems which are faced. On the other hand, whether the proposals live up to the title *Sustainable Communities* remains open to doubt, given that so little

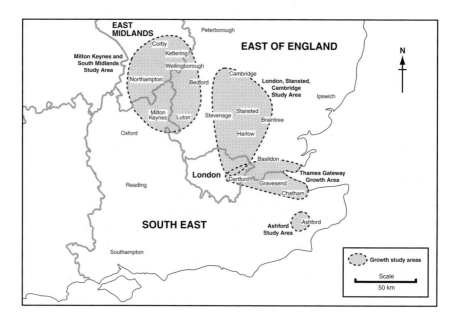

Figure 6.2 'Sustainable communities' growth study areas. (Source: Based on ODPM
2003a. Crown copyright material reproduced with the permission of the
Controller of HMSO and the Queen's Printer for Scotland (licence
number C02W0002008).)

attention is paid to issues such as water shortage in these areas, while clear
measures for improving the eco-efficiency of housing are introduced only for
social housing, not private housing (see Haughton 2003b).

Thames Gateway: rewriting the urban geography of the South East

Central to the government's *Sustainable Communities* vision for the next few
years is the Thames Gateway area, a thirty-mile-long (fifty kilometres) corridor
through east London and the neighbouring parts of Essex and Kent, where the
pace of development seems set to outstrip that of the other three growth areas
announced in the document. A budget of £446 million over the three years
2003–2006 is set aside for the Thames Gateway proposals, to be spent on land
assembly, remediation of brownfield sites, delivery mechanisms, additional
affordable housing and essential local infrastructure. In a ministerial speech
following publication of the programme, the Deputy Prime Minister said:

> The growth areas give us the chance to re-design our communities and
> move on from the way we planned new towns in the past. The

opportunity is there. The Thames Gateway alone can deliver an extra 200,000 homes and 300,000 new jobs. And virtually all on brownfield land.

(ODPM 2003b, p. 7)

The interest of this area for us is that something of its history can be traced through the regional planning process, not least as it had its own unique supplementary regional guidance released in 1995. Attempting to build on the successes of Docklands regeneration in east London in the 1980s plus the work of SERPLAN, the Conservative government in 1991 launched proposals for designating a new large-scale regeneration area in a 30-mile corridor to the east of London (Haughton *et al.* 1997; Hall 2002). This area, initially known as the East Thames Corridor but subsequently renamed Thames Gateway, suffered from severe economic and environmental problems, including large-scale industrial dereliction. That said, the area also had substantial areas of wildlife interest and ecological diversity. In social terms, the existing population had been substantially by-passed by the economic prosperity which much of the rest of the South East had enjoyed, not least the M4 corridor to the west of London.

The first RPG for the South East (DoE 1994d, para. 8–167) had argued that

> the East Thames Corridor presents the main opportunity for growth. This part of London, South Essex and Kent has the capacity over the longer term. . . to accept significant levels of housing and employment development, alongside improvements in environmental quality. The corridor will benefit particularly from planned transport and infrastructure investment, and the area's location close to the heart of London yet well related to the Channel Tunnel.

In order to promote development in the area, a planning framework for Thames Gateway (RPG9a) was published (DoE 1995). Two main centres of development were envisaged: 'The Royals and Stratford' in east London, and 'Kent Thames-side' around Dartford and Gravesend. It was hoped that these would provide the impetus for further urban regeneration in east London and the wider Thames Gateway area (Figure 6.3). Conservation areas incorporating some of the important ecological sites in the Thames estuary and marshes were identified in the framework, while areas with existing green belt protection were confirmed and supported. Improvements to the transport infrastructure of the area were seen to be critical to its success, including new river crossings and the construction of the high-speed rail link from London to the Channel Tunnel.

Though a high-level partnership was established to push forward the proposals, unlike in the earlier Docklands initiative a separate development agency was not set up to take charge of the regeneration (Haughton *et al.*

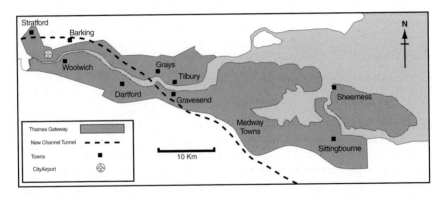

Figure 6.3 Thames Gateway area. (Source: DoE 1995.)

1997; Hall 2002), which instead largely relied on action by individual local authorities and agencies. Progress was patchy in the area, leading SERPLAN (London and South East Regional Planning Conference 1998) in its draft RPG for the South East to propose assisting it by means of an explicit policy of restricting growth in the economically buoyant areas to the west of London (these proposals are covered in Chapter 7). This proved contentious, attracting considerable debate at the public examination. The subsequent report of the public examination panel expressed its opposition to restricting growth in any part of the region (Crow and Whittaker 1999). In an attempted compromise solution, in the final version of RPG9 (GOSE 2001) central government opted to support growth in the economically buoyant areas while also providing strong support for Thames Gateway, arguing that 'The regeneration of the Thames Gateway is a regional and national priority' (p. 14). The particular attraction of regeneration in this area was that it afforded the opportunity to build large numbers of houses on brownfield sites outside the metropolitan green belt, but nevertheless fairly close to London.

Sustainable Communities (ODPM 2003a) provided a major boost to an initiative which at the time of an intermediate review had been showing mixed signs of success and some concerns about impetus and environmental impacts (Roger Tyms and Partners in association with Three Dragons, 2001). In *Sustainable Communities* a total of fourteen 'Zones of Change' are proposed within the Thames Gateway area, and these are expected to develop custom-designed delivery bodies. Although the document talks convincingly of the need to reject former models of delivery in favour of locally acceptable models, it then disconcertingly goes on to reveal that the government was negotiating with partners 'towards the establishment of new mechanisms which will use Urban Development Corporation powers in the London Thames Gateway and in Thurrock' (p. 50).

Connecting transport and urban renaissance

The reformed arrangements for regional planning which were introduced in 1998 included an expectation that each document would contain within it a summary regional transport plan, as part of the move to better integrate planning and transport policies (DETR 2000a). The critical contextual issue for regional transport planning has undoubtedly been the shift away from a strong focus on new road building during the 1980s towards a growing recognition since the mid-1990s of the need to manage the growth in road transport. During this same period there was an increased awareness of the need for better integration of land use planning and transport policy, including a brief five-year period during which the two relevant ministries were integrated within one government department. The transport White Paper (DETR 1998d) made much of the need for better integrating transport modes while also giving higher priority to more sustainable forms of transport: public transport, cycling and walking. This integration was to be brought about in part through a series of transport studies called multi-modal studies (MMSs), the first tranche of which were commissioned following the publication of *A New Deal for Trunk Roads for England* (DETR 1998e). The purpose of the multi-modal studies is to provide a new way of identifying planning and transport options (DETR 2000b), involving examining the contribution that each of the transport modes can make to meeting the objectives for the sustainable development of the region, area or corridor under consideration.

Although MMSs were intended to be a key element in the development of Regional Transport Plans (RTPs), the timing of most of these studies meant that in most regions the combined RPG/RTP process was well advanced if not completed before any of them were published. The absence of the final studies necessarily severely constrained debates about transport issues during the current policy round. It is worth noting too that improvements in transport infrastructure emerged as key objectives in all the RESs. Most stressed the need for sustainable transport, although in some regions a greater emphasis still seemed to be attached to road rather than public transport improvements. In most regional planning documents, improved transport infrastructure was also seen to be a key ingredient to promoting urban renaissance, helping support the shift to public transport in particular. This was certainly the case in the West Midlands, which is particularly interesting for the breadth of its treatment of urban renaissance themes.

Case study: a fundamental change in direction? The role of urban renaissance in the spatial strategy for the West Midlands

Urban renaissance and improved transport infrastructure comprised two of the four inter-related themes in the draft RPG for the West Midlands, the other two being rural renaissance and the diversifying and modernising of the region's economy. The West Midlands was also the only region where an MMS was published in advance of the RPG public examination, meaning that its contents could inform debates on issues such as urban renaissance.

A 'fundamental change of direction' was how draft RPG for the West Midlands (WMLGA 2001a, p. 14) described the region's new spatial strategy. In setting out its new proposals, the Regional Planning Body conceded that previous planning policies had resulted in the 'dispersal of people, jobs and investment', requiring a 'step-change' in approach (p. 14) with the new spatial strategy of 2001. The new approach was to focus more explicitly on a series of measures which would together help bring people back into the urban areas: that is, a combination of making them more attractive and restricting future growth in the outer rural areas – a strategy of urban renaissance, no less.

Policies directed towards rejuvenating the region's Major Urban Areas (MUAs) (Birmingham/Solihull, the Black Country, Coventry and north Staffordshire) provided the main focus of urban renaissance policies. Five of the eight local authorities with major urban areas in them had experienced a population decline over the period 1991–2000, providing the context for the strategy's aspiration to reverse such trends by creating 'an environment where people choose to live, work and invest' (WMLGA 2001, p. 15).

Taking on board national guidance, the regional strategy for the West Midlands proposed to address the issue of urban renaissance through an integrated policy directed towards the MUAs, promoting:

a   a variety and choice of high quality, healthy and affordable sustainable living and working environments,

b   a sufficient number and variety of jobs to meet employment needs, along with associated education and training opportunities,

c   modern urban transport networks with an emphasis on public transport, and

d   rejuvenated town and local centres to serve communities with high quality services, to promote identity and social cohesion and drive economic change.

(WMLGA 2001, p. 15)

Though the core policy on urban renaissance gave a strong commitment to making the MUAs a priority for action in the West Midlands, some regional stakeholders in interviews with us, and others at the public examination in June and July 2002, raised questions about whether draft RPG pursued this theme consistently across all policy areas. In particular, environmental groups pointed to policies on housing, economic development and transport which they felt did not always support the urban regeneration theme.

Housing levels and distribution

The draft RPG proposed a shift in policy from previous patterns of development, which favoured greenfield sites for housing in the shire counties, towards an emphasis on brownfield sites in the major urban areas, a shift heralded in the previous RPG. However, in proposing this change the document conceded that it would take time to bring about such a major shift, as a result of existing development plan allocations and planning permissions. In the longer term, though, the new strategy sought to bring about a substantial reduction in the amount of development in rural areas, specifically to assist in rejuvenating the conurbations.

Though there was universal support at the public examination for the broad concept of urban renaissance, some stakeholders (mainly pro-development interests) questioned whether the dispersal of population away from the major urban areas should or even could be reversed through land use planning policies aimed at restraining growth in the buoyant parts of the region. Typical comments at the public examination from housing developers were 'You can't move against the market' and 'Urban renaissance is being taken on board with evangelistic fervour.... We must keep our feet on the ground' (both from evidence given by Redrow Homes). The central theme of the pro-development lobby argument was that the draft RPG was too drastic in its attempts to slow down decentralisation, and should give greater recognition to the continuation, for the foreseeable future, of strong growth pressures in the shire county areas surrounding the major urban areas.

Not surprisingly, then, housing developers argued against heavy restrictions on housing growth in the buoyant shire areas, suggesting that these would stifle the housing market in the West Midlands and ultimately affect the region's economic growth. Environmental groups were also unhappy with the amount and distribution of houses, but for very different reasons. They expressed concern that the proposed spatial strategy would still result in large amounts of greenfield land being developed in the early years. Support for this position came from the sustainability appraisal (WMLGA 2001b), which had also raised this issue in suggesting that 'consideration should be given to the de-allocation of a proportion of [existing] structure plan [housing] allocations' (p. 15). It was felt that without this the policy shift towards urban renaissance in the major urban areas would be frustrated by the continuing availability of housing in the surrounding rural areas.

In its report, the public examination panel accepted the general approach towards housing provision in the draft RPG, concluding that 'WMLGA are justified in seeking to modify long-term intra-regional migration trends in support of the spatial strategy' (Swain and Burden 2002, p. 56). However, the panel also accepted that 'it would take time for there to be a marked improvement in the attractiveness of MUAs' (ibid., p. 39) and hence there would be a need to maintain a building programme outside these areas in the short to medium term.

Economic regeneration

Regeneration zones were identified in the West Midlands strategy as a mechanism by which to focus action and help reverse the decentralisation of jobs and people from the conurbations. Controversially, the concept of development in transport corridors, introduced in the previous RPG (Vigar *et al.* 2000), was also expected to play a key role in economic development policies for the region. 'High-technology corridors' (HTCs) were identified along transport routes, such as between Coventry, Solihull and Warwick, within which cluster developments would take place linked to research and development and advanced technologies. This idea arose out of the work of the Rover Task Force which had been established to look at sources of employment other than the car industry. 'Other strategic corridors' (OSCs) were also identified, justified by the need to link areas of opportunity with areas of need.

The draft strategy emphasised that developments in corridors would be focused on the MUAs, existing towns and key nodes served by public transport. Moreover, the aim was to focus new development on brownfield sites. Despite such efforts to anticipate criticisms, the proposals generated a good deal of concern among some stakeholders. Key issues included the lack of any reference to the sequential test for employment land and, even more controversially, draft RPG recognised that the use of some greenfield land would be needed for employment purposes, 'albeit as a last resort' (WMLGA 2001a, p. 68). In fact, it went so far as to suggest that some adjustment of green belt boundaries might also take place to accommodate economic development.

Policies for economic development in transport corridors, which had been first introduced in the previous version of RPG, came in for some criticism during the public examination process. For example, the Joint Statutory Conservation Agencies (the government conservation agencies, which tended to side with the environmental lobby at the public examination) described the plethora of 'corridor' policies in draft RPG as representing 'a corridor too far which will not in the longer term serve regeneration' (oral evidence to the public examination 2002). The environmental argument was essentially that too much growth was being promoted outside the major urban areas, particularly in the short to medium term, making it difficult to reverse decentralisation and therefore working against urban renaissance. Environmental groups were particularly concerned that the corridor policies would encourage car commuting, with Friends of the Earth suggesting that 'RPG made a mistake in identifying corridors [as] it encourages the thought that travel is involved' (oral evidence at the public examination 2002). The government conservation agencies also pointed to a certain naivety in thinking that linking areas of opportunity and need by corridors would mean that people would be prepared to travel long distances by public transport.

The rural lobby group CPRE also suggested that the economic development policies, and particularly the corridors, would be open to abuse, potentially resulting in ribbon development unless development was directed strongly towards brownfield land. Almost inevitably, perhaps, the CBI disagreed with this assessment, arguing that 'many brownfield sites are not attractive to employers' (oral evidence 2002). The HBF too expressed its concern about the implications of constraining development in areas of opportunity to the south and east of the region, on the grounds that 'we are a long way from making the MUAs attractive to employers'. In essence, the opposition to constraint policies was based on the belief that they would not result in development moving to the region's urban areas; rather, development might be lost to other regions or to other countries. The need to look at the external environment and the constraints within which regional planning existed was perfectly summarised by one participant who voiced the concern that 'Jobs will be sucked not just out of the region, but also out of the country, unless there is a balanced portfolio of sites" (oral evidence from planning consultants 2002).

Because some development groups argued that new employment sites needed housing sites located near them to reduce commuting, there was also disagreement between the environmental lobby and pro-development interests over whether locating jobs and houses close together would encourage shorter work-trips. The HBF was sure that it would: 'it will result in unsustainable development if employment growth is allowed without the housing to match it' (oral evidence at the public examination 2002). Others, though, pointed to studies showing that journey-to-work patterns were more complex than this: 'It is wishful thinking that where new housing and employment sites are provided together people will work in the jobs nearby' (CPRE in oral evidence at the public examination 2002).

Transport

The overarching aim of the regional transport strategy in draft RPG for the West Midlands was to create a region with an efficient network of integrated transport facilities and services which fully supported the urban renaissance aims of the spatial strategy. In particular, it identified a need to improve facilities and services in the MUAs to prevent further population decentralisation and a consequent increase in travel distances. It included a range of proposals aimed at reducing the need to travel, encouraging a modal shift to public transport, encouraging walking and cycling and demand management.

Perhaps inevitably, though, the transport strategy also identified new road proposals, plus plans for the development of Birmingham International Airport, both of which proved controversial. In addition, the government-sponsored MMS was made available to the public examination (Aspen, Burrow and Crocker 2001). The West Midlands Area MMS incorporated proposals for western by-passes to Wolverhampton and Stourbridge, reinforcing a popular feeling that it had resurrected the controversial Western Orbital Road, which had been withdrawn by the government in 1996 (Swain and Burden 2002). These by-pass proposals, which were included in draft RPG, provided 'the most controversial and hotly contested elements of draft RTS [Regional Transport Strategy] and of the whole RPG consultation, drawing some 6,000 representations' (Swain and Burden 2002, p. 105).

Our interviews with stakeholders in the West Midlands revealed that transport was widely seen to be a critical issue in bringing about urban renaissance, with existing poor accessibility brought about by congested roads and inadequate public transport services argued to be seriously undermining attempts to regenerate the major cities and towns. Preferences about what should be done to resolve these problems, though, differed substantially between different stakeholders. Business and development groups tended to emphasise the need for new road improvements, in particular pressing for a western by-pass. Advantage West Midlands (the RDA) also argued that the roads would have regeneration benefits for the sub-region, although it felt that wider benefits would be limited by the absence of high-quality routes leading eastwards into the conurbation (Swain and Burden 2002).

By contrast, the environmental lobby tended to emphasise the importance of promoting demand management and more sustainable forms of transport. Typical of the environmental case is the environmental group which argued that there was no evidence to suggest that building new by-passes would bring about regeneration: 'It won't. On the contrary it will bring about decentralisation. Wherever by-passes have been built you have got retail parks and business parks. This will not produce renaissance!' (interview 2002).

Doubts about whether major new roads would bring about the desired regeneration benefits may have influenced the public examination panel, which recommended deleting references to the western by-pass. It argued that instead more attention should be given to bringing about behavioural changes in the choice of transport modes and to a better integration between the planning and the transport elements of the regional strategy.

Environmental improvement

Environmental policies in the draft RPG focused on restoring degraded areas, managing and creating high quality new environments, and creating a high-quality built environment for all. Interestingly, it was the sustainability appraisal (WMLGA 2001b) which first highlighted a lack of recognition of the role of the natural environment in urban renaissance, arguing that 'The policy should recognise the importance of the natural environment in urban areas and the need to protect environmental assets' (p. 11).

There was widespread recognition among stakeholders in the West Midlands that environmental improvement was an important prerequisite for achieving urban renaissance. As a result, most participants at the public examination expressed support for creating a good-quality urban environment, in particular emphasising the importance of green space. This superficial consensus, though, masked a considerable range of opinions about priorities. The CBI, for example, expressed support 'for the importance of the environment in urban regeneration' but urged 'flexibility and caution' in how policies were taken forward (oral evidence to the public examination). In similar vein, a consortium of business interests pointed to 'the absolutist tendency in dealing with the environment. . . . There are economic and social assets which should over-ride environmental considerations' (oral evidence 2002).

In responding to these debates, the public examination panel considered that 'greater emphasis should be placed on improving the environment throughout the MUAs' (WMLGA 2001b, p. 24). This greater emphasis should cover 'the protection of existing environmental assets e.g. open spaces, green corridors, natural habitats and heritage aspects within MUAs. It should also highlight the importance of undertaking greening programmes' (ibid., p. 24).

Conclusions

It is salutary to be reminded of quite how much the regional approach to cities has changed over the past forty years. From the early 1970s onwards, the focus of British planning policy began to shift decisively away from the prevailing view that it was important to 'decongest' larger cities by dispersing their 'surplus' population to new and expanded towns. In its wake came a growing concern with regenerating inner-city areas by attracting jobs and people back into them. More than this, where once-large deindustrialising cities, particularly in the North and Midlands, were seen as a major problem for regional policy to address through the job creation activities of the state, now many of the larger regional cities are seen as having successfully started a process of reinvention as vibrant cultural and commercial centres in their own right. Such cities are now seen as 'drivers' of their regional economies, central to the reinvention of regions as 'world class', top ten, or whichever mantra the advertising and regeneration consultants have recommended.

But beneath the surface appearance of success in cities such as Birmingham, Bristol, Leeds, London, Manchester and Newcastle, with their vibrant city centre nightlife and daytime functions as centres of commerce, lies a continuing problem of a two-tier society and indeed a two-tier economy, in which substantial problems of social exclusion from mainstream society remain a fact of life for some communities. If planning wants to claim to be part of the successes of the positive developments in these cities, it also needs to acknowledge that it has played a role in the continuing problems they face.

In many respects, the introduction of urban renaissance policies into regional planning has filled a missing gap between national planning policy guidance and the increasing attention to such approaches within local plans and structure plans. But the regional approach has introduced a new dimension to the debate, with the greater spatial specificity of the current round of regional planning requiring greater consideration of the whole settlement pattern of a region and the ways in which policies in one area influence events in another. It is not rocket science, but in a context where regional planning was largely absent in the 1980s and quiet on spatial direction during the 1990s, it raised some profound challenges for those involved in debating alternative approaches to where growth should be focused and which planning policies and techniques might best bring this about.

On the surface, it would appear that the urban renaissance agenda ought to have a key role in such debates, with its twin emphases on regenerating urban cores and reducing out-of-town sprawl. Despite widespread agreement with the general urban renaissance approach, however, the devil has been in the detail. Central government has seen urban renaissance as a useful way of reducing the political fallout from allowing greenfield developments by encouraging high-density development on brownfield land, restricting population dispersal (with some exceptions) while claiming that attention to better urban design would mean that improvements would follow in the environmental quality of cities and towns. This leads us to think that 'urban renaissance' needs to be seen as a political strategy, not simply a set of government policies, in much the same way as we argued was the case for sustainable development. Increasingly it is necessary for those involved in regional planning to embrace something of the logic and the language of urban renaissance in order to gain central government approval, which then sets the scene for attempts to selectively use, contest and redefine the term's usage.

The clearest example of this approach was the West Midlands core strategy which gave a much stronger emphasis to urban renaissance than did regional strategies in other regions, making it a key element of the core strategy. The debates about urban renaissance in the West Midlands focused on the perennially contentious planning issues of housing and employment land, transport and the environment. Here, as elsewhere, pro-development lobby groups pointed to the problems which it associated with the 'urban renaissance' emphasis of concentrating most new development on urban brownfield sites, while rural and environmental lobby groups tended to reject 'urban renaissance'-justified approaches which would see the loss of further countryside to development. Urban renaissance, then, is a strategy, a political resource and a site of contestation, rather than simply a neutral approach benignly reshaping urban development processes.

So although a superficial consensus exists on issues such as 'sustainable development' and 'urban renaissance', in practice groups sought to use these terms selectively, in the process seeking to redefine their meaning according to their own long-standing policy preferences, while challenging the alternative readings of their opponents. In particular, when it came to how best to develop policies for taking forward the 'urban renaissance' agenda, considerable differences frequently emerged. In this way, nearly all stakeholders talk about urban renaissance in positive terms at a high level of generality, while reverting to 'business as usual' when it comes to arguing about whether they were willing to change their own stance to them. To put it another way, sustainable development and urban renaissance tend to be seen by many of those involved in seeking to influence planning policy as a means for seeking to alter other groups' preconceptions, viewpoints and preferred approaches while firmly resisting changes to their own.

7 Regional economic development, regional planning and sustainable development

Divergences and convergences in approach

> The primary task for the RPG is to provide the right land use and communications infrastructure to maximise the creation of jobs and assist economic regeneration throughout the region and especially in the region's most deprived areas.
>
> (Northern Business Forum, in written submission to the public examination of draft regional planning guidance for the North East, June 2000)

Introduction

The shift towards a greater emphasis on a regional approach to economic development and planning has found a particularly receptive audience among those concerned about the deleterious effects of the 'competitive localism' of the previous twenty years. Neoliberal policy regimes heightened and indeed reified inter-locality competition for investment in a global marketplace. Rather than waiting for government handouts to palliate the impacts of disinvestment, the new political credo was for local and regional economic development managers to create the conditions with which to retain and attract private investment: a business-friendly environment, low business costs, a range of available sites, a suitable range of skills, flexible labour markets and a good-quality environment (see Chapter 2). But for all the high-profile successes, competitive inter-locality bidding for hyper-mobile investment capital and government grants had the perverse impact of encouraging mobile firms to play localities off against each other in an effort to extract more grants, more favourable planning conditions or other concessions (Beer *et al.* 2003). At both the regional and the national levels, this form of competition resulted in a costly zero-sum game of economic development, while undermining the ability of planning authorities to impose high development standards or to bargain for more collective benefits from developers. Better regional strategic planning and collaboration between neighbouring local authorities would, it was hoped, help to reduce this counter-productive negative spiral, while encouraging higher quality of life standards.

The notion of the strategic and spatial selectivity of the state (see Chapter

2) usefully highlights the ways in which the nation-state can retain its powers through the ways in which it selectively distributes powers, responsibilities and resources across the new institutional landscapes of governance. Where new bodies are seen to be failing in some way, the state retains the right to redistribute responsibilities and resources to other actors or its own most recently designed vehicles for policy delivery. But we also argue in Chapter 2 against seeing this as a simple top-down imposition of power, mediated by local circumstances and local contingency. Instead, it is important to see how other institutions bring power to bear in their dealings with the apparatus of the state in its various local, regional and national guises. This is a theme which emerges with some force in the current chapter, which examines how local actors have sought to contest aspects of regional economic strategy, in the process influencing both regional and national policies. More than this, however, the argument here is that it is unhelpful to adopt a narrow sectoral view of regional economic development, one which is relatively blind to other regional issues, not least regional planning.

The difficult transition from 'policy silos' to integrating regional economic development and regional planning

Five features dominate recent changing approaches to regional economic development (see Table 7.1). First, there has been a shift from a patchwork geographical coverage towards a national coverage, albeit with differently resourced institutions in each region. Second, there has been a shift away from strong dominance by national civil servants towards greater devolution to a wider range of local actors. Third, there has been a shift away from national interventionist approaches for balancing out growth between regions in favour of 'catch-up' policies to encourage less well performing regions to compete better. As part of this, there has been a growing emphasis on becoming 'world class' and an awareness of competing with other regions at a global scale. Fourth, there has been fluctuating emphasis on non-economic issues, such as education, housing and quality of life. Fifth, greater attention has emerged in relation to local regeneration and community-based initiatives.

There are also some important continuities, however. Most notably, central government has retained its strong controlling influence over the mandates, resources and even the boards of regional bodies. Second, inward investment remains a strong theme when documents from the 1970s and 1990s are compared. Third, large-scale physical schemes still find favour. For instance, the proposals for maritime industries in the Humber in the Yorkshire and Humberside strategy for 1970 have their counterpart in proposals for a Humber Trade Zone in the 1999 RES. Finally, if we look beyond the strategy documents themselves, there is also still a degree of circumspection from local governments about regional bodies, which are seen as potentially eroding local autonomy.

Table 7.1 Changing approaches to regional economic development

	Characterisation of regional economic policy
Pioneering period (1930s to early 1950s)	Designation of areas requiring assistance (e.g. Development Areas); restrictions on the expansion of industry in buoyant areas (Industrial Development Certificates); state subsidies, including relocation grants for industry
Fallow period (1950s)	Continuation of previous arrangements but restrictions weakly applied and slow take-up of grants. More flexible approach to Development Areas after 1960
Regional revival (1960s through to mid-1970s)	Stronger application of regional policy including extending locational controls to offices. Regional Economic Planning Councils established. Concern to achieve balanced national economic growth through strong state direction of industry
Regional policy in retreat – second fallow period (late 1970s to early 1990s)	Large-scale dismantling of the apparatus of regional economic policy; redirection of aid to inner cities; new climate of competition for investment. 'Beggar-thy-neighbour' emphasis on 'local competitiveness' between areas
The second regional revival (1990 to present)	Strong focus on European Structural Programmes; continuing competition for inward investment; reintroduction of regional economic planning; coverage for whole country with a philosophy of 'catch up'; partial devolution of funding and programmes to Regional Development Agencies

Perhaps the most persistent feature of regional economic development since the 1940s, however, has been a concern with the 'policy silo' mentality of the approaches of successive governments to regional policy, which tended to separate out economic development from physical planning issues. New Labour's emphasis on the need for joined-up thinking and joined-up government raised expectations that these two aspects of policy might be brought closer together. And arguably they have been, in some ways. However, the fact remains that the current New Labour government has maintained the functional separation of economic development and planning by giving responsibility for regional economic development to the RDAs, while regional planning has remained the responsibility of separate Regional Planning Bodies (see Chapter 1). The tensions between these two policy communities, and in particular between the RESs and RPG, lie at the heart of this chapter. Thematically, the most important tensions have arisen over proposals to allocate large greenfield employment land sites and transport infrastructure improvements. Transport issues were introduced in Chapter 6, so in this chapter we focus on employment land sites and airport expansion proposals.

In setting up its new regional institutions, the Labour government sought to give parity of status to RPG and RES, arguing that it would be counter-productive to privilege one over the other. The two types of strategy were, however, expected to complement each other, with RDAs for instance made a statutory consultee for RPG. Despite such concerns, or perhaps because of them, there was always the potential for conflict between the different policy communities. Some of these difficulties were exacerbated by procedural differences, notably the different time-scales between the two sets of strategies and cultural differences between those preparing them.

Timing emerged as a particular issue in moving towards integrating regional economic development and regional planning. The two processes had rather different starting points (RPG was in its second round, RES in its first round), with government advice and legislation emerging at different dates. In addition, RPG took longer to prepare. One consequence of these timing issues was that in the South East and East Anglia the preparations for regional planning guidance were already well advanced when the respective economic strategies for these regions were prepared. Therefore, in these regions there was little opportunity for economic strategies to influence directly the content of draft RPG. Elsewhere, RESs and draft RPGs were developed broadly simultaneously, providing more opportunity for better integration. Nonetheless, the different time-scales for consultation and 'approval' meant that the approaches of RPG and RES sometimes subsequently diverged, as changes were made as a result of consultations and public examination. Such issues sometimes caused concern among the people we spoke to:

> A big concern for many partners has arisen from the fact that the NWDA's [the RDA for the North West] strategy came first. Many partners feel that the RPG should have set the overall framework for the NWDA strategy rather than the other way around.
>
> (interview NW8)

In the East Midlands too, one officer from a government conservation agency argued that policy integration was hampered by these timing issues: 'Well, you have this enormous problem of having the RES in place ... and they are getting on and doing the damn thing and we are still trying to get the final draft of the environmental strategy' (interview EM5). Such different procedures and different time-scales clearly presented barriers to joined up strategy preparation. As we will see in the later case study of a proposal to release land for airport-related activities in the East Midlands, there was also a timing issue in relation to the link between regional planning and other local planning processes (see Marshall 2002).

Further tensions in achieving an integrated approach can be traced to the rather different cultures of, on the one hand, the RDA boards, dominated as they are by business interests, and, on the other, those of the local authority-dominated Regional Planning Bodies. In the case of sustainable development, for instance, in their early days many RDA staff and board members had had little past experience of this issue, whereas many of the local authority planners preparing RPG had already been grappling for some time with trying to operationalise sustainable development (Benneworth 1999).

Regional Development Agencies and the business agenda

If Urban Development Corporations were the emblematic institutional component of Thatcherite approaches to 'local competitiveness', it is the Regional Development Agencies which are emblematic of New Labour's approach to 'competitive and collaborative regionalism' (Table 7.2). They formed the centrepiece of New Labour's regional policy for England when it came to power in 1997. Consultation was quickly introduced, leading to the Regional Development Agencies Act 1998, which paved the way for the creation of eight RDAs, subsequently increased to nine with the creation of the London Development Agency as part of the devolution to the GLA. The RDAs were intended to give a stronger voice to the English regions, allowing them to address regional economic differences in innovative and regionally specific ways (Tomaney and Mawson 2002).

The board members of RDAs are appointed by central government, which also decides on their funding allocations. Though private-sector interests play a central role, a wide range of other stakeholder groups are also represented on the RDA boards. In addition, the government has sought to make RDAs accountable to their regional stakeholders through giving the regional assemblies power of scrutiny over their policies, while also expecting them to be statutory consultees on the main proposals of the RDAs.

The main purposes of the RDAs, as outlined in the 1998 Act, are:

- to further economic development and regeneration;
- to promote business efficiency and competition;
- to promote employment;
- to enhance the development and application of skills relevant to employment; and
- to contribute to the achievement of sustainable development in the United Kingdom, where it is relevant to do so.

The last of these 'purposes' is of particular interest here: the RDAs have a statutory duty to contribute towards sustainable development, albeit only 'where relevant to do so'. Benneworth (1999) argues that this clause, which in effect suggests that there might be times when RDAs need not take account of sustainable development, exacerbates fault lines over different approaches to sustainable development between central government departments responsible for industry and planning. Apparently even the main government department acknowledged

Table 7.2 Local and regional economic development under the new localism and resurgent regionalism

	Competitive localism: roll-out neoliberalism 'Thatcherism'	Resurgent regionalism: second-wave neoliberalism ('Third Way')
Critiques of past policy	• Strong 'nanny state' • Red tape and bureaucracy • Planning seen as strangling jobs • No such thing as society	• Lacking policy integration • Lack of evidence base • Disenfranchised local communities • Beggar-thy-neighbour policies
Preferred rhetorics	• Market knows best • The market knows no boundaries • Discipline of the market • Global competitiveness	• Evidence-based policy and best practice • Joined-up government • Policy integration • Competitiveness and social cohesion
Scalar policy dynamics	• Rhetorics of globalisation allied to strong national steer • Wariness of any agendas from European Commission • Selective devolution to local 'quangos' • Curbing local government • Diminished role for regional and sub-regional bodies	• Rhetorics of globalisation and devolution, allied to strong national steer • Relative openness to ideas from European Commission • Reaffirmation of role of (reformed) local government • Growth of role of regional institutions and strategies
Relation to Jessop's ideal types for SWPR (see Chapter 2)	• Neoliberalism allied to neo-statism	• Neoliberalism allied to neocorporatism and neocommunitarianism
Emblematic delivery bodies for sub-national economic development policy	• Urban Development Corporations • Training and Enterprise Councils • Inner-City Task Forces • Public–private partnerships	• Regional Development Agencies • Local strategic partnerships and community plans • Urban Regeneration Companies • Neighbourhood Renewal Fund, New Deal for Communities.
Emblematic local regeneration projects	• London Docklands • Meadowhall, Sheffield and Metro Centre, Gateshead	• Millennium communities • Urban Villages • New East Manchester

that the placement of sustainable development as a fifth clause, 'after the "real" business of economic development rather than as a context for it' meant that the contribution that RDAs could make to sustainable development was in reality extremely limited.

(Benneworth 1999, p. 13)

In pursuit of their economic objectives, the RDAs are required to prepare Regional Economic Strategies (RESs), which should be integrated with other sectoral strategies. Central government advice indicated that these economic strategies should also contribute towards sustainable development (DETR 1999b), including an appraisal (sustainability appraisal) showing how the strategy will do this. The way in which the economic strategies have addressed sustainable development has been uneven, creating the potential for tension with other regional activities and with local strategies (Benneworth 1999; Gibbs and Jonas 2001).

Although considerable consultation was required in putting together RESs, to demonstrate stakeholder ownership the processes were rather different from those for RPG. Not only was the consultation period shorter, generally about six months as opposed to over two years for most regional planning documents, it was also largely conducted on the RDAs' terms, as they selected the venues, speakers, issues for consultation, and so on. Written submissions were invited but not necessarily published. More to the point, perhaps, the power dynamics of the RDAs as major funders for local authorities, business support groups and others made it impolitic to argue too strongly against their approach in public. That said, the statutory duty to consult with regional assemblies was a major step forward, and in some cases this was seen to have made a clear difference to the content of draft economic strategies (Tomaney and Mawson 2003).

Most of the first round of regional economic strategies, published in the late 1990s, lacked much in the way of clear spatial strategy. They tended to set out broad objectives and policy priorities, illustrating these with photos of local case studies. Where they were introduced, as with the Southern Crescent concept in the North West (see Chapter 6), proposals managed to get inserted with relatively little controversy. Interestingly, then, it took the formal examination processes of regional planning for some of these ideas to begin to unravel. The importance of regional planning for economic development should not be underestimated, as many of the policies for promoting regional economic development have spatial requirements, be they concerned with employment land or transport links. Consequently, some important economic policy debates, not least on employment land allocations, have risen to public prominence through the regional planning process.

Sustainable development and the 'win–win' approach to regional economic strategies

Greater regional devolution is often presented as an opportunity for greater experimentation, innovation and differentiation, but it does not always work out quite like that. In practice, the RDAs were inherently predisposed to adopt an approach to sustainable development which emphasised economic growth as a priority, given the mandate they were handed from central government, the main funding streams they were allocated, the people chosen to sit on their boards, and the staff whom they either recruited or inherited from the previous institutions whose activities they absorbed.

Perhaps inevitably, then, the vision statements of all the regional economic strategies were first and foremost oriented towards economic growth, using sustainable development to justify rather than challenge their aspirations to becoming globally competitive regions. The visions of four out of the original eight English RDAs included the aspiration to be 'word class regions', and three also aspired to be premier regions within Europe. The contradictions of all regions having similar aspirations to leap up some real or imaginary league tables seemed not to impinge very much on the thinking of those involved.

The West Midlands economic strategy provides a typical example of the broad visions proposed:

> Within 10 years the West Midlands will be recognised as a premier European location in which to live, work, invest and to visit, regarded internationally as world class and the most successful region in creating wealth to benefit everyone who lives in the area.
>
> (Advantage West Midlands 1999, p. 10)

So far so predictable perhaps. What is slightly surprising is the degree of uniformity in how these economic strategies sought to engage with sustainable development. As Benneworth *et al.* (2002) highlight in their study of this issue, the initial capacities and intelligence for dealing with sustainable development tended to differ between regions, resulting in differing treatments in the initial drafts of economic strategies. They highlight the difference between the North West, which had already been working on the links between sustainability and regional development, and the North East, where work had been slower in making an impact. However, a combination of government advice, a reluctance to upset regional partners, regional consultation and critique of draft statements, and the co-opting of experts and recruiting of new staff seemed to produce a fairly rapid movement towards a common approach to sustainable development across the regions. As Benneworth *et al.* (2002) argue, the result of such pressures was that regional economic strategies defaulted to 'lowest common denominator blandishments' (p. 210), attempting, by producing statements that were 'mainly broad-based and aspirational' (p. 208), not to stir up the conflicting interests of some stakeholders

It is worth noting that sustainability appraisals were required for RESs, providing a valuable sounding board for improving policies. As an example, the official sustainability appraisal of the North East RES picked up on the very basic issue of its understanding of sustainable development:

> There is an overall concern about the extent to which the Regional Eco-nomic Strategy (Consultation Draft) is embedded in the concept of sus-tainable development. While the strategy makes many references to it, our conclusion is that it needs to go much further, if it is to play a pivotal role in delivering sustainable development objectives. This means putting sustainable development objectives at the heart of the strategy, and making firm commitments to deliver.
>
> (One NorthEast 1999, p. 1)

Most of the first round of RESs tended to use the idea of an integrated approach to 'sustainable development' as a starting point for arguing the need for pursuing more economic growth, while taking care to address issues surrounding the local quality of life. Revised guidance on the second round of strategies seeks to reinforce the integrated approach, while stressing the strategies' role in drawing from and supporting RSDFs (Box 7.1).

Despite the undoubted tendency to conformity, it is possible to see that sustainable development was dealt with differently in the various economic strategies. In the South West (SWDA 1999), for instance, sustainable devel-opment is argued to be an integral part of the economic strategy:

> The region will make the principles of sustainable development central to its Strategy rather than a separate part of it. In taking economic decisions the region will take account of its social and environmental responsibilities, recognising the linkages between the economy, society and the environment.
>
> (section 2, p. 4)

Reflecting aspects of the government's advice (Box 7.1), however, the approach adopted tended to see the 'environment' as something able to make businesses more competitive, while the possibility that environmental con-cerns might mean some developments being unsuitable is not explicitly addressed. This was true also of the South East economic strategy, which paid considerably more attention to sustainable development and environmental issues than the RESs of most other regions, but remained largely instrumental in its perspective on the role of environment in relation to economic devel-opment (Counsell and Haughton 2003)

In contrast to these approaches, the earlier RES for the North East, *Unlocking our Potential* (One NorthEast 1999), rarely mentions sustainable

Box 7.1 Supplementary guidance for the Regional Development
          Agencies in relation to the Regional Economic Strategies

6.1 Section 4 of the Regional Development Agencies Act 1998 gives
each Regional Development Agency (RDA) a statutory purpose to
contribute to the achievement of sustainable development in the
United Kingdom where relevant to its area to do so.

6.2 Sustainable development should underpin the actions and decisions
the RDA takes in pursuance of its economic objectives. Taken
together, the RDA's purposes require it to adopt an integrated
approach to regional economic issues; bringing together economic,
social and environmental objectives.

6.3 The Regional Sustainable Development Framework (RSDF) is
developed in conjunction with partners at the regional level including
the RDA, the Government Office for the region and the regional
assembly, as well as other partners such as businesses and the voluntary
sector. The Regional Economic Strategy should take account of, and
contribute to, the agreed policies and targets set out in the Regional
Sustainable Development Framework (RSDF).

. . .

6.6 Economic growth remains vital for a better quality of life: for education, healthcare and housing, to tackle poverty and social exclusion,
and to improve standards of living through better goods and services. In
the past, economic activity tended to mean more pollution and wasteful
use of resources. We have had to spend to clean up the mess. A
damaged environment impairs quality of life and, at worst, may threaten
long-term economic growth – for example, as a result of climate
change. Also too many people have been left behind, excluded from the
benefits of development but often suffering from the side effects.

6.7 This is the challenge of sustainable development. For the future,
we need ways to achieve economic, social and environmental objectives at the same time, and consider the longer-term implications of
decisions. We need to improve the efficiency with which we use
resources. We need thriving cities, towns and villages based on strong
economies, good access to services and attractive and safe
surroundings. . . .

. . .

6.14 The Regional Development Agencies Act 1998 sets the framework for the RDA to adopt an integrated policy approach, bringing
together economic, social and environmental objectives, to produce
more effective policy-making. Taken together, promotion of these

objectives can be mutually reinforcing. For example, a region that has a properly educated work force, a supporting infrastructure and businesses that are ready to invest will also be able to provide high living standards and greater job opportunities that include all sectors of society, and produce high quality goods and services that consumers want at prices they are prepared to pay.

6.15 In turn, good environmental practices (such as energy efficiency, better environmental management and reduction in the waste of raw materials and water etc) can bring businesses significant efficiency gains. There can also be direct job creation in environmental industries. And an enhanced local environment, including the careful stewardship of the historic environment, and landscape character, can contribute to economic development and employment opportunities through encouraging tourism, inward investment and attracting a high quality workforce. . . .

. . .

6.17 In short, the Government expects the RDA in developing the integrated policy approach that will be set out in its Regional Economic Strategy, and in the delivery of the strategy, to ensure that it contributes to the policies and targets set out in the Regional Sustainable Development Framework.

Source: DTI (2002, chapter 6, paras 6.1–6.17)

development and environmental considerations after the initial vision statement, which talks about creating a sustainable society based on wealth creation. Where it does refer to sustainability issues, these frequently involve a reading which privileges the economic dimensions, in which environmental assets become relegated to an instrumental role in promoting economic growth, rather than as having value in their own right. In this way, sustainability is reduced to a reading in which its main role is sustaining economic growth rather than achieving more environmentally sustainable economic growth.

The North West RES adopted a rather wider-ranging approach, which similarly embraced the language of sustainable development. However, in this case the wording is much closer in spirit to the government's preferred integrated approach; the strategy uses this to argue that sustainable development would provide the basis for long-term competitiveness:

[Sustainable development is] a 'triple thrust' that brings together three guiding principles; competitiveness, social inclusion and environmental objectives for better resource management and environmental protection.

Sustainable development principles provide the only long-term route to competitiveness.

(NWDA 1999, p. 16)

In the most recent (Yorkshire Forward 2003) version of the RES for Yorkshire and the Humber, the RDA implies that sustainable development is at the core of its work – and indeed in most respects the second RES is more environmentally conscious than its predecessor (Figure 7.1). Interestingly enough, the second RES also drops the reference in the first RES to attempting to 'seize the opportunities for sustainable development to create "win–win" outcomes, such as creating jobs with environmental benefits' (Yorkshire Forward 1999, p. 32). In the new, 2003, version, a more measured approach advocates the benefits of integrating sustainable development into decision making, while also being clear in the strategy's commitment to supporting the (by then published) RPG for the region in reducing traffic

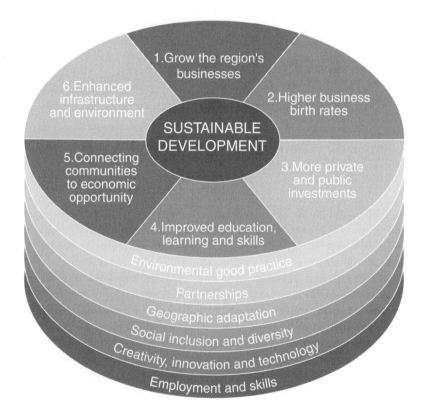

Figure 7.1 Sustainable development at the core of Yorkshire Forward's Regional Economic Strategy. (Source: Yorkshire Forward 2003. Reproduced with the permission of Yorkshire Forward.)

generation and using the sequential test to support brownfield site development, neither of which had figured prominently in the previous version.

In one of the few examples of public disagreement about environmental issues in RESs, in the East of England the regional assembly objected to an early draft version 'because of its growth targets and lack of emphasis on social exclusion and environmental protection' (EERA 2001). It subsequently endorsed the strategy after textual changes had been made to the document to address these issues.

A report on the treatment of sustainable development in the first round of RESs commissioned by the UK Round Table for Sustainable Development usefully identified a range of weaknesses, notably including a concern that the current approach was simply using sustainable development as a fig leaf for a 'business as usual' approach (Box 7.2).

Box 7.2 Weaknesses in the way Regional Economic Strategies (RESs) contributed to sustainable development

- *Balancing objectives:* Uncertainty over how the economic/employment objectives will be balanced with environmental issues in appraising individual projects.
- *Integration of sustainable development into objectives and action plans:* Regional economic strategies would be strengthened if they contained more explicit actions for ensuring that RES objectives and action plans contribute to sustainable development rather than just business as usual.
- *Environmental impacts:* There is uncertainty about the environmental and spatial impacts of development programmes (e.g. transport impacts, impacts on greenfield sites).
- *Social impacts:* There is uncertainty over the extent to which development will benefit all social groups and promote social inclusion.
- *Implementation:* The actual contribution of the strategies to sustainable development will depend on how they are implemented – which itself is determined by factors such as Regional Development Agency (RDA) culture, staff awareness, RDA development priorities, availability of tools for appraising sustainable development impacts of projects, etc.
- *Monitoring and indicators:* Monitoring mechanisms and regional indicators of sustainability are relatively underdeveloped and will need to be developed quickly if the RDAs are going to report on sustainable development progress and impact.

Source: Environmental Resources Management (2000, p. 18)

Contrasting economic development and planning approaches to regional sustainable development: differences in tenor or differences in philosophy?

The malleability and politicisation of the term 'sustainable development' which was highlighted in Chapter 3 emerged as particular issues when it came to pursuing economic goals through the RPG process. On many occasions, RDAs and various business groups sought to ground their views with the twin legitimating devices of appealing to the 'competitiveness' agenda while simultaneously situating this concern within the language of sustainable development. In the North West, for example, the North West Development Agency complained at the public examination of draft RPG that 'the RPG gives too little emphasis to the vital competitiveness and economic dimensions of sustainable development' (verbal evidence). Development pressure groups likewise tended to emphasise the importance of development: 'We don't have a problem with sustainable development inasmuch as it's got the word development in it' (interview SE7).

Of particular interest to the analysis here is the way in which local context was sometimes used quite explicitly to argue for particular approaches to sustainable development in particular regions:

> Sustainable development differs depending on what part of the country you're in . . . and so in this region we support sustainable development but are firmly of the view that economic development has to take precedence.
>
> (interview NE11)

> Sustainable development must imply that the North East region provides for a secure economic future for its people, stemming environmentally wasteful out-migration to other regions and providing the sufficient number of homes required.
>
> (HBF written submission to the public examination on draft RPG for the North East.)

In similar vein, a planner from the North East made it clear that in drafting the RPG, planners had been aware that there was a political imperative to create more jobs in the region, which meant that 'In the context of the North East, sustainable development must give a strong weight to the issue of economic growth or we would be accused of planning for decline' (interview NE1).

Such views were not necessarily prevalent throughout the northern regions, however. One local planner argued directly that the debates had become more sophisticated in Yorkshire:

> In the past there was a political will to accept almost anything which might seem to offer anyone a job. I think most of us have now moved to

a point where we don't see a future in this attitude. Because we don't want a second class region. We don't want the sort of region where anything is good enough. . . .

I think people have had their confidence dented in the notion that a Japanese company can come in and build a big factory and everything in the garden will be rosy. I don't think anyone thinks the big foreign investor is the key to sustainable development.

(interview YH13)

Given the widespread perception among their respective critics that regional planning documents tended to favour an environmental interpretation of sustainable development while economic strategies tended to support economic interests, this raised some interesting issues about which should have primacy. Not surprisingly then, one pro-development group in the North East argued strongly in favour of economic interests: 'We believe the RES should be the defining document, particularly in this region' (interview NE11). Such views fly in the face of the government's own preference for a form of parity of status between the different strategies, subject to their supporting the RSDFs. Attention to the integration of economic and spatial policy was more explicitly addressed in some regions than others. In the East Midlands, for example, the regional assembly produced an Integrated Regional Strategy (IRS) (EMRA 2000b; see Figure 7.2) which was intended to provide a common set of objectives for other regional strategy work (Box 7.3). In many ways, the IRS was a precursor to RSDFs, which were introduced in 2000. The result was apparently greater cross-fertilisation between the two strategies, although this close working was something which those involved were aware might raise concerns among others: 'There has been a spirit of partnership and cooperation [between the RDA and the regional planning body] . . . which might look on the outside like conspiracy' (interview EM9).

While being widely praised as an innovative development, the integrated strategy failed to convince some regional stakeholders, including one who argued, 'bluntly the IRS is not an IRS at all, just a series of strategies which have been put together one after the other' (interview EM3). This person also noted that in parts, the regional economic strategy and regional planning guidance appeared to be in conflict: 'in one place [the RPG] says that there is an over-supply of industrial land and in another [the RES] that we need some more! The two documents are scarcely comparable.' It is of note that these comments were made shortly after the public examination, during which the environmental group to which to person quoted belonged had opposed what it saw as the draft RPG's pro-development stance.

In Yorkshire and the Humber too, a more integrated approach was adopted in that, unusually for that time, the sustainability appraisal of the region's first RES was undertaken in parallel to that for RPG and by the same consultants. Overall, the sustainability appraisal argued that the RES provided a good basis for moving forward on sustainable development, but it

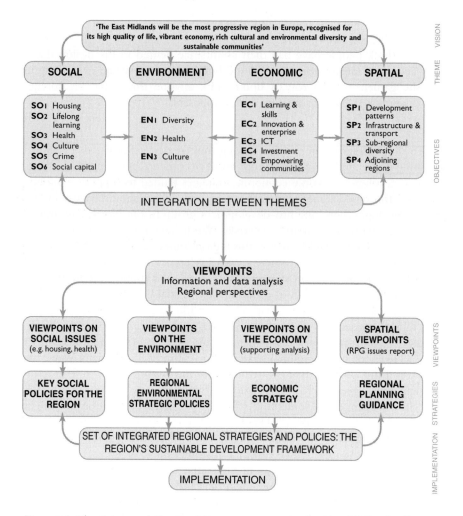

Figure 7.2 The Integrated Regional Strategy process in the East Midlands. (Source: EMRA 2000b. Reproduced by permission of the East Midlands Regional Assembly.)

did highlight a number of difficult and unresolved sustainability issues for the implementation of the strategy, including possible conflict between economic development and nature conservation in the Humber estuary. In examining the relationship between the RES and the RPG, the sustainability appraisal concluded that these were generally compatible, but on environmental protection issues it suggested that 'the thrust of the RES "in getting the best out of physical assets and conserving environmental assets" may conflict with the stronger conservationist stance of the RPG natural resource use policies'

Box 7.3 The East Midlands Integrated Regional Strategy

The Integrated Regional Strategy (IRS) concept was pioneered in the East Midlands region, where the regional assembly decided to prepare an IRS as a context for regional planning guidance (RPG), the Regional Economic Strategy (RES) and a range of other strategy work which was being undertaken in 1999 (Aitchison 2002). In doing this it had four principal purposes:

- to pursue the agreed vision for the East Midlands and provide a framework for sustainable development;
- to strengthen regional partnership working and the role of the East Midlands Regional Assembly;
- to achieve consistency, added value and the genuine integration of regional policies and strategies; and
- to help gain maximum influence for the East Midlands with external bodies.

A common vision for the future of the region was initially agreed by the main regional bodies, including East Midland Development Agency (EMDA, responsible for the RES), East Midlands Regional Local Government Association (EMRLGA, responsible for preparing regional planning guidance) and East Midlands Regional Assembly (EMRA). The work was led by the regional assembly. Eighteen regional sustainable development objectives were also agreed under four common themes – economic, social, environmental and spatial – to be used in the sustainability appraisal of regional policies. A common methodology for this was put forward in the *Step-by-Step Guide to Sustainability Appraisal* (EMRA 2000a). The IRS process is illustrated in Figure 7.2.

(ECOTEC 1999, p. 24). This neatly encapsulates something of the problem with adopting a more integrated approach, where it might lead to a seeming consensus view which represented a lowest rather than highest common denominator approach. The key point as always is that 'integration' is not of itself a neutral approach; rather, it represents a consensus view of how priorities should be managed which may well de-privilege some sectoral interests while rewarding others (Vigar *et al.* 2000).

Greenfield sites for inward investment: exploring the tensions

Disputes over approaches to economic development policies became particularly clear in the case of allocating employment land through the regional planning process. In the world of the economic development professional, an

Plate 7.1 Inward investment from the Far East: Samsung in the North East.

important tool in many areas is ensuring that large serviced sites (25 to 125-plus acres (10 to 50-plus hectares)) are available for rapid development. Many of the preferred sites tend to be located on green fields, and often close to motorway junctions, sometimes requiring adjustment to green belt boundaries (Phelps and Tewdwr-Jones 1998). Almost inevitably, this tendency, when such proposals are put forward for planning approval, causes tensions between the development community and both environmental and rural lobby groups (Vigar *et al.* 2000).

Widespread concern existed about new site designations in the light of the UK branch plant closures and retrenchments which followed the economic problems of some countries in the Far East during the late 1990s (Phelps and Tewdwr-Jones 2000). Typical of the more downbeat assessments which we encountered in discussing employment site issues were comments such as:

> We have all seen companies such as Siemens coming along and being given massive government aid . . . and as soon as the world market takes a tiny blip the whole place closes down. . . . That isn't sustainable industry, and Siemens was given carte blanche on a pristine greenfield site! You can't take land use decisions valid for twenty years on the vagaries of that sort of short-term market approach.
>
> (interview EM4)

At the institutional level, tensions sometimes emerged between planners and economic development officials, highlighting the differing discourses of development within which they tended to operate. Certainly the RDAs in all regions argued in support of the need to invest in employment land and supportive infrastructure, strongly supported by business groups such as the CBI. More variable was the support which came from local politicians and their local authority economic development officers, since in some areas there was less support for major new development than others (Beer *et al.* 2003).

The consequence of the widespread ambition to have local sites ready for incoming investors tended to be a degree of over-provision of employment sites, particularly where aggregated up to the regional-level documents. Interestingly, the revised RPG process, with its requirement for greater spatial specificity, plus its greater openness to public debate, meant that these aspirations for perhaps the first time found themselves in a forum where they could be contested. As the allocation of sites for economic development lacks the central government straitjacket imposed on housing development, there is growing recognition that the top-tier major or premium sites (125-plus acres (50-plus hectares)), should be determined at the regional scale (Vigar *et al.* 2000). But this did not necessarily reduce the problem of over-provision of such sites, since regional planning bodies, dominated by local authority representatives keen to protect their own sites, have frequently proved reluctant to rationalise provision in putting forward draft regional planning guidance.

Personnel from many different regional institutions, particularly in the Midlands and North, told us in interviews of the tensions in promoting economic development on greenfield sites and even in the green belt. As one person explained to us, he would expect that 'If a Nissan or whatever comes along and says "I want to build a car plant on a greenfield site outside Harrogate", they [the RDA] will move heaven and earth to try to ensure it happens' (interview YH5).

Clear statements from draft RPGs in the West Midlands and Yorkshire and the Humber set out the view that the allocation of employment sites might over-ride normal planning considerations in order to address growth demands:

> In order to assist in the regeneration of the West Midlands Major Urban Areas, there will be no review or adjustment of boundaries at the inner edge of the Green Belt to accommodate housing development. Some adjustment of the inner Green Belt boundaries may, however, be justified in order to provide opportunities for selective employment development.
>
> (WMLGA 2001, p. 23)

> The regeneration of the region's economy is fundamental ... and the region must compete for industrial investment in wider national and

international markets. This means that use of greenfield land is more likely to be necessary for industrial uses than for other purposes.

(YHRA 1999, pp. 30–31)

The rationale for this selectivity of approach was provided by one of those involved in formulating these policies: 'Housing is slightly different to employment, because employment can go elsewhere [out of the region], so you might want to be less restrictive in terms of where you might put employment development' (interview YH6).

These sentiments led to tensions with those opposed to any development on greenfield sites and others who wanted to see equal treatment for housing. In this sense, both environmental and housing lobbyists argued that provision of employment land without housing would be unsustainable. Environment and countryside groups used this argument to oppose any form of greenfield development, whereas pro-development lobbyists used it in support of additional allocations of housing land, arguing that balanced development required complementary provision of housing to avoid long journey-to-work trips. The inevitable consequence was that there were concerns about:

> The tricky politics of constraining housing whilst not wanting to kill off economic growth (interview EE2 housing pressure group). It will result in unsustainable development if employment growth is allowed without the housing to match it.
> (TCPA, verbal evidence to the West Midlands public examination)

> If they could have unlimited economic growth in the South East without having any more housing they would sign up straight away.
> (interview SE7 housing pressure group)

The nature, and outcomes of these debates about employment land differed between the regions, and in several regions central government exercised its powers to prevent what it saw as surplus provision where there were relatively low development pressures and substantial existing land allocations.

This was particularly noticeable in the North East, where the RES *Unlocking Our Potential* (One NorthEast 1999), placed strong emphasis on attracting inward investment. The North East has the lowest GDP per head of population and the highest rate of unemployment of all eight English regions (National Statistical Office 2000), having long suffered from decline in its traditional industries of coal mining and iron and steel. As a result, creating more jobs has tended to be a high priority in regional plans since the 1930s, as the region has sought to diversify its economic base and attract new employment. In the first version of RPG for the North East (DoE 1993b), one of the key policies was to attract employment to the North East to improve its economic base, reflecting the dominant pro-growth political aspirations in the region.

Plate 7.2 Greenfield inward investment site, North East.

These same aspirations were again in evidence in the draft RPG produced under the new arrangements (ANEC 1999), meaning that there was little contention in relation to the regional economic strategy produced in the same year. Indeed, draft RPG supported the inward investment aspirations of the RES, which had proposed four additional strategic greenfield sites without providing any great evidence of demand for this level of provision.

However, during the draft RPG consultations and the public examination, the policy on inward investment sites was contested by environmental bodies such as the CPRE and Friends of the Earth. Following these debates, the public examination panel report argued that allocating new large-scale greenfield strategic sites would undermine the urban core regeneration aspirations of both the RPG and the RES. The panel report also highlighted that there was an existing over-supply of employment land in the region and that an adequate number of existing strategic sites had already been identified in local plans. It therefore recommended deleting two of the proposed new sites and was non-committal about the other two.

The government's 'proposed changes' to RPG went even further in attempting to dilute the policy for new sites, accepting the panel's recommendation to delete two inward investment sites while itself deleting an additional site. The justification for this was that providing new sites would deflect pressure away from the existing sites, where arguably the need for jobs was greatest. Moreover, the identification of additional strategic employment sites was made a matter in future to be decided at the level of RPG, not development plans, thereby removing this issue from the direct remit of local authorities. Unsurprisingly, the regional institutions and local authorities in the North East objected to these changes, feeling that they would worsen their competitive position in relation to that of other English regions. After intense lobbying and a considerable delay in issuing the final version of RPG, central government eventually reinstated one of these sites.

Similar debates emerged in Yorkshire and the Humber. Consistent with the RES (Yorkshire Forward 1999), draft RPG for Yorkshire and the Humber (RAYH 1999) included a policy for providing regionally significant employment sites to cater for strategic developments. Different categories of sites were identified, including two major locations in the Humber estuary: up to three sites for major single users, and up to twelve sites for nationally and internationally mobile employers. This policy was criticised by environmental groups at the public examination, which pointed to an existing over-provision of employment land:

> RPG starts by correctly analysing the existing problem: that there is a very substantial over-supply of employment land. . . . However, at the same time, RPG is also proposing the allocation of employment land either to privileged sectors . . . or with a general permission that would over-ride e.g. green belt or greenfield protection in certain circumstances.
>
> (Friends of the Earth written submission to the public examination)

In reporting on the Humber estuary proposals, the public examination panel accepted the principle of two sites, but questioned their size and also whether they were already included in development plans. The proposed site on the north bank of the Humber was modified in the final version of RPG12 (GOYH 2001b) to: 'a limited number of key sites . . . which will in aggregate provide up to 100 hectares [247 acres]' (p. 54).

The public examination panel was also sceptical about some of the other sites proposed, recommending some deletions. In particular, the panel expressed concerns about the proposal that there should be a less severe attitude to the development of greenfield land for economic development than for other purposes. The argument here was that leaving the existing statement in place would water down the sequential test and the sustainability principles underlying the strategy; consequently, it was recommended for deletion. These recommendations were generally accepted in the final version of RPG12 (GOYH 2001b).

Interestingly, these debates seemed to have helped shape the revised regional economic strategy for the region released in 2003:

> In line with urban renaissance and the sequential approach in RPG, the priority will be development on brownfield sites that meet business needs and which enjoy good access by public transport for local communities.

This will increasingly mean the focus of development is on existing urban centres as well as the planned Development Zones [including the Humber Trade Zone].

(Yorkshire Forward 2003, p. 60)

Specific proposals for designating new greenfield locations for economic development were also deleted during RPG processes in the North West, the East Midlands (see p. 196, in discussion on airport development), the West Midlands and East Anglia. It is notable that some of the high-growth regions, such as East Anglia, were not exempt from government policy against green-field incursions for inward investment sites.

Emerging government policy from decisions on inward investment sites in RPG appears to be to constrain the number of greenfield incursions in support of the government's policy of compact urban development. However, in the continuing absence of any national estimates of demand for such sites, uncertainty remains about how to balance local and regional economic development aspirations against national spatial planning policy.

Contesting policies for constraining economic growth: redirecting growth in the South East

In many regions, particularly in the economically buoyant South East, parts of the South West and East Anglia/East of England but also in Cheshire within the North West, a central planning concern was whether to redirect economic development to disadvantaged parts of regions or to 'let it rip' in areas of high growth potential. These tensions about whether or not to redirect growth towards areas of greater need were particularly prominent in the South East and East Anglia.

In draft RPG for the South East, *Sustainable Development Strategy for the South East* (London and South East Regional Planning Conference 1998), SERPLAN argued that its policies for sustainable development in the region required giving priority to the less prosperous parts of the region, referred to as Priority Areas for Economic Regeneration (PAERs), for instance the Thames Gateway, which we introduce in Chapter 6. To assist in implementing this policy, it also proposed constraining development in areas of economic pressure which were also suffering significant environmental and planning constraints. A typical example of such areas, termed Areas of Economic Pressure (AEPs), is the arc to the west of London. Inevitably, perhaps, this policy, which seemed to run contrary to the national competitiveness agenda, was deeply unpopular with the business lobby. During our interviews in the South East, one pro-development supporter talked of what he saw as the naivety of planners thinking that regeneration could be supported by 'strangling the richer areas'.

There was a particularly stark contrast in this case between the proposals in the draft regional plan and those of the RDA for the South East, SEEDA, in its regional economic strategy. SEEDA's strategy was very much to sustain growth in areas of economic success, not to constrain it. Though the RES had not been published at the time of the public examination in the South East, SERPLAN's proposals nevertheless stimulated lively debates which we have described elsewhere (Counsell and Haughton 2003). The upshot was that the panel conducting the examination backed the case for supporting economic growth in areas of high demand, arguing that this was in the national and regional interest.

> Nowhere in the region should economic enterprise be frustrated save for strong and manifestly demonstrable local environmental reasons. Neither congestion nor labour supply should be used as a reason for frustrating the proper development of the regional economy to world-class.
>
> (Crow and Whittaker 1999, p. 35)

The panel also recommended weakening the policy on helping struggling areas (the PAERs), recommending that measures taken to assist them should not adversely affect and constrain the economically buoyant areas. In doing so, it was backing a shift away from the SERPLAN approach of giving priority to the regeneration of less prosperous parts of the region, in favour of the RES approach of prioritising support for economic growth in the buoyant areas. The resulting highly politicised and public debate must have led the government to consider its 'proposed changes' carefully. In the final version of RPG, RPG9 (GOSE 2001), the government adopted a middle road on the issue of PAERs. Priority is given to the deprived Thames Gateway area, but the policy on other PAERs is weakened. The public examination panel's recommendation to delete reference to AEPs was accepted, but a separate policy was included on the Western Arc, encouraging local strategies for areas where congestion or labour supply shortages are constraining growth.

Supporting economic regeneration or boosting growth? Changing regional strategies for East Anglia

East Anglia (part of the 'East of England' region since 2001) has experienced fairly rapid population and economic growth in recent years, fuelled by a booming economy in parts of the region, plus its proximity to London. Economic growth has been particularly buoyant in the Cambridge sub-region, sometimes referred to as 'Silicon Fen' or 'the Cambridge phenomenon'. With its clusters of research and high technology-based industries, this area is frequently cited as an exemplar of the potential for knowledge-based regional economic growth. It is important to emphasise, however, that this economic growth has not been evenly shared across the region, with the more isolated north and east of the region (Great Yarmouth, Lowestoft, Wisbech) in particular relatively underperforming.

This region is of particular note because until recently, regional planning guidance for East Anglia had emphasised the value of constraining growth in the Cambridge sub-region and attempting to redirect growth towards the more disadvantaged coastal towns. *Strategic Choices for East Anglia* (Department of the Environment East Anglia Regional Strategy Team 1974) was one of a national series of regional strategies produced in the early 1970s. Its main spatial strategy proposed to redirect growth from the south and west of the region to the centre, north and east. The policy involved restricting growth in those areas which were economically most buoyant in order to stimulate growth in the more remote areas, including the coastal towns, which were both losing employment in their traditional industries and suffering from a decline in seaside tourism.

This strategy of redirecting growth away from the Cambridge area was reinforced when RPG for East Anglia was published in 1991 (DoE, 1991). Specifically, the concern was that growth pressures around Cambridge were creating 'conflicts with the unique character of the city' (ibid., para. 8-083). The associated development framework was expected to provide for:

- some dispersal of investment in jobs from the prosperous and congested areas in the west, and Cambridge in particular, to those areas to the east and north where improvement in trunk roads is expected to increase their attractiveness for economic development and growth;
- the maximum use of the opportunities presented by reductions in the remoteness of the less prosperous areas to enable these areas to attract investment in jobs.

(ibid., para. 8-084)

The key to achieving the strategy was a series of proposed road improvement schemes which were intended to reduce the remoteness of the coastal areas in particular. However, the road improvements failed to materialise, following a change in national transport policy, part of the move towards a more sustainable transport policy in the mid-1990s. With the coastal areas still suffering from remoteness, the policy of redirecting growth to them became untenable, if it had ever been feasible.

Meanwhile, Cambridge continued to develop as a centre for high technology-related business, leading to growing pressures from the business community to lift the restrictions, which were seen to be both constraining the city's growth and adding to congestion problems, as more people commuted in from greater distances. Specifically, pro-growth forces argued that Cambridge's problems resulted in large part from the tightly drawn green belt around its boundaries. However, many of the local authorities in the surrounding rural areas were largely opposed to further growth, wishing to maintain the integrity of green belt protection, particularly in South Cambridgeshire (see the case study on p. 136; also While *et al.* 2002).

Not surprisingly, the amount and direction of future growth in the Cambridge sub-region featured as a prominent issue in debates during the preparation of the most recent RPG for East Anglia. The draft RPG (SCEALA 1998) abandoned the previous policy of dispersing growth away from Cambridge, but argued that selective restraint on employment growth might still be necessary for the Cambridge sub-region.

In its report on the public examination of draft RPG (Acton and Brooks 1999), the panel took issue with the statement about selective restraint, suggesting some revision of the text to 'confirm that the strategy is to plan for steady and sufficient growth at a rate that is likely to be above the national average' (p. 149). This in effect represented the removal of the last vestiges of the restraint policy pursued in previous regional strategies for East Anglia. In relation to 'the Cambridge phenomenon', the panel suggested that 'it is in the national interest for it to be nurtured and allowed to grow and evolve. It is also inescapable that the greater part of the growth will be in and close to the City' (ibid., p. 151). The panel concluded, 'we are not persuaded that growth should be restrained as a matter of principle', and went on to suggest that encouraging economic growth in Cambridge required corresponding provision for housing (see Chapter 5).

Central government in its revisions accepted the panel's recommendations on 'the Cambridge phenomenon', while also including in the revised RPG6 (GOEE 2000) a policy relating to the 'extension of the clusters of research and technology based industries'. As part of this policy, regional partners were asked to prepare a strategy which 'would identify appropriate locations and indicate how they can provide the conditions attractive to investment by research and technology based industries and their support services' (ibid., 2000 p. 20). Though most people accepted the broad shift in policy, there remained a minority who were concerned about whether it was the most appropriate strategy for the region as a whole:

> There is a question mark about whether this [concentration on Cambridge] is sustainable in social terms and whether we weren't right in the previous version [of RPG] in trying to disperse some of that growth, or manage it in a different way.
>
> (interview EE3)

Flying into trouble: new airport developments

Proposals for airport expansions frequently proved attractive to those developing regional economic strategies, being presented as drivers of wider economic growth. However, such proposals sometimes created tensions when it came to seeking to support them through the regional planning system, with planners sometimes more cautious in supporting airport developments. However as with other transport issues these concerns were not fully played out in RPG, partly because recently commissioned central government studies of airport development were still awaited and also because separate approval procedures have traditionally been in place for major infrastructure projects such as airports. In recent years, major airport developments have typically involved lengthy, acrimonious and costly public inquiries.

After the public inquiry into Terminal 5 at Heathrow had famously taken four years to complete, the government's planning reforms in 2001 sought to find other ways of dealing with such projects. The initial proposal was to deal with major projects such as airport expansion through parliamentary procedures, but widespread opposition from environmental and planning interests, plus criticism from a parliamentary select committee encouraged the government to review its proposals. The intention currently is that major infrastructure developments will be dealt with through revised public inquiry processes, keeping them separate from regional strategies (see Chapter 8).

Because of this weak role in relation to airport expansion, most regional planning debates dealt with the issue rather superficially, with an emphasis on the development of airport-related employment land. The lack of a role for RPG caused frustration for some: 'I don't see many of those big issues [referring to airport expansion] unpacked in this latest round of RPG, and yet if it [airport expansion] isn't unpacked there, where is it going to be unpacked?' (interview SE8). In fact, this issue was eventually 'unpacked' in a series of regional airport studies published by central government in 2002, too late to be taken into account by any of the public examination panels. What was always clear, however, was that government predictions suggested that air transport passenger numbers might more than double by 2020. Various options were put forward to accommodate this growth, ranging from new runways for existing airports to possible new airport sites, with Cliffe in north Kent and RAF Finningley in south Yorkshire identified as possibilities. These proposals provoked widespread concern from resident groups in the affected areas and from national environmental groups such as the CPRE. One government conservation agency official pointed to the contradictions in this approach: 'We have a system of "plan, monitor and manage" for housing, and "predict and provide" for airports. So all airports are going for growth and where is the voice telling people it is unsustainable to fly?' (interview EM7).

Reflecting the strength of its overall approach to environmental issues, the only draft RPG to pursue the line that air transport was unsustainable was the South East, which argued for a reduction in air travel, causing some tension with the RDA. The public examination panel, however, criticised the proposed approach, recommending instead that RPG provide a stronger framework for airport expansion and in particular for associated activities – high-profile sites with access to airports. Given the many other controversies surrounding regional planning in the South East, perhaps unsurprisingly central government steered clear of the airport expansion issue in the final version of RPG9, referring instead to its own proposal for a White Paper on air travel. Rather than commenting on the sustainability of further airport expansion, it argued that access to and development associated with airports should itself be guided by sustainability principles: 'Any surface access measures necessary to cater for airport growth either within existing planned limits or for further expansion, should be sustainable. Any further development associated with such airport growth should also be sustainable in nature' (GOSE 2000, p. 67).

Similar inconsistencies between attitudes to airport expansion and other aspects of transport policy can be found in the draft RPG for the West Midlands. Though the overall policy was one of 'reducing the need to travel' through demand management (WMLGA 2001a, p. 110), the policy on Birmingham International Airport was that '[It] will continue to be developed as the West Midlands' principal international airport with appropriate facilities in order to increase the extent to which it meets the region's needs for flights to all parts of the world' (p. 125). The case of airport planning is interesting here in part because of its effective absence within RPG debates, a situation which can be linked to our concerns not simply with the way in which policies come to be both contested within policy circles, but also with the ways in which certain options become excluded from consideration. The issue here is not that airport extensions are not subject to public examination; they clearly are. Rather, the issue is that a key aspect of infrastructure planning which is likely to exert a major impact on many of the concerns of sustainable development, from travel congestion in a region to global carbon emissions, was in effect excluded from strategic regional planning. Its exclusion undermined regional planning's attempts to develop holistic, integrated and indeed meaningful long-term development frameworks.

Case study: airport-related proposals for employment land near East Midlands Airport

Draft RPG for the East Midlands (EMRLGA 1999) raised the possibility of further development around Junction 23a/24a on the M1 motorway, close to East Midlands Airport. This area was identified in the RES (EMDA, 1999) as an important economic asset, and was also being heavily promoted by business interests.

It is noteworthy that this was not put forward as a firm proposal in draft RPG. However, even the possibility of development in this location was strongly opposed by East Midlands Environmental Link (EMEL, a consortium of environmental groups established specifically to engage in the RPG process). For EMEL, the concerns were several-fold. First, it felt that the proposal would in effect lead to a merging of Nottingham, Derby and Leicester into a 'super-city'. Second, it believed that the motorway location would encourage further car-borne commuting and road haulage. Third, it was worried that any development in this area would both result in the loss of open countryside and undermine urban regeneration in the three cities.

The public examination panel (in its report published in October 2000) accepted that this development would be contrary to national policy and to the sustainable development objectives of the draft guidance. It proposed that instead RPG should 'set out an alternative strategy that recognises the potential of an integrated and more polycentric approach to the attraction of inward investment' (EMRA 2000a p. 10). The Secretary of State in the 'proposed changes' to draft RPG, published in March 2001 (GOEM 2001), and in the final version of RPG8 (GOEM 2002), accepted that that there was no case for releasing further land in the foreseeable future at East Midlands Airport.

In the meantime, the draft structure plan for Leicestershire and Rutland was placed on deposit prior to its examination in public (EiP). The proposals included a policy of allowing for the development of a prestige employment site at Junction 23a/24a, subject to a number of criteria being met. Once again, strong opposition emerged from environmental groups and local people. Following on from the Secretary of State's proposed changes to RPG, a number of changes to the structure plan were put forward in advance of the EiP. These included a fairly radical shift away from favourable consideration of development at Junction 23a/24a to outright opposition: 'Beyond the boundaries of the airport in the vicinity of Junction 23a/24/24a of the M1 further large concentrations of employment development or other transport intensive uses will not be acceptable' (written submission to structure plan examination).

The structure plan EiP took place in June 2001, where the panel accepted that the change in policy represented an appropriate response from the structure plan authority to the 'proposed changes' to draft RPG. Noting some of the objections from pro-development interests and that further transport studies were under way whose outcome was uncertain, the EiP panel suggested simply deleting the policy altogether.

Conclusions

This chapter has highlighted how the tensions between regional economic strategies and regional planning guidance on how best to approach sustainable development have their own regional geographies. In broad terms, in regions experiencing strong economic growth pressures, notably in the south and east of England, the environmental aspects of sustainable development tend to be used by local planning authorities to justify constraint policies. By contrast, in the northern regions the tendency has been for planning authorities to seek to promote more economic development through RPG, with the economic aspects of sustainable development invoked as justification. These two approaches reflected some rather differently configured discourse coalitions around growth and constraint policies (Vigar *et al.* 2000; Counsell and Haughton 2003).

Three concerns come out of this chapter. The first is the problem of seeking to develop strong regional policy directions in the absence of a clear national spatial strategy (Wong 2002). So while the Regional Development

Agencies may have helped to reduce the worst aspects of zero-sum competition for inward investment projects at the inter-regional scale, it is not yet clear whether there is a sufficiently robust national framework to reduce unnecessary inter-regional bidding for projects. This concern was one which aroused some comment during our interviews, as various people argued that it was difficult to justify the selective nature of policies for constraint and restraint without a sense of national expectations on major new projects and national preferences for where these might be best channelled. The result of this lack of clarity is that most RDAs and local authorities have remained keen on identifying potential sites for large investors, seeking to use the regional planning system to allocate land in advance for such purposes.

The second concern is with the need to take into account the political dynamics of each region in seeking to understand how regional planning processes map out. For instance city-regional power alignments were being reworked in the North West as Liverpool and Manchester sought to find ways of working better together than in the past, a process which was perhaps helped by their being able to find common cause in lobbying for more attention to urban renaissance as part of fending off the Southern Crescent proposal. Likewise, Cambridge's pro-growth strategy relied strongly on support from the county council. In related vein, it was noteworthy that the continental European concern for polycentric development (European Commission 1999) did not emerge too strongly as an overt theme in this round of regional spatial strategy making, but it might be expected to be more prominent in the future as the concept becomes more widely debated.

The third concern is with the inability of regional planning to base its decisions on any sense of the likely 'quality' of future economic development. With such issues largely in the hands of regional development agencies and their local partners, regional planning is left to decide whether to allow major developments on greenfield sites without being clear whether the resulting employment will create local jobs, long-term jobs, or jobs in 'clean and green' industries. This was a concern which we met in one form or another from environmental groups in particular, which tended to accept the importance of jobs but worried about being asked to trade off known environmental qualities against an unknown quality of economic development. Interestingly, this was also a concern which was beginning to worry some RDAs as they sought to come to terms with their mandate on sustainable development: 'What we need is to find the right kinds of economic growth rather than seeking a lower level of growth' (interview: regional development agency, south of England). The fundamental contradiction here is that planning is increasingly seen as engaged in collaborative work on 'place making', helping to design better-quality places for people to live, work and invest in, yet in many ways the reconfiguration of strategic powers to the regional level runs the risk of producing 'decontextualised' strategic decision making.

We can also begin to unpick some other tensions and contradictions in the new regional governance systems in their support for economic development. In the case of regional economic strategies, for instance, national policy makers have been able to demonstrate a 'light touch' in approving regional economic strategies. Yet they have managed to retain for themselves a certain amount of central control not only through their role in allocating budgets and choosing RDA board members, but also by the indirect mechanism of using the regional planning system. This is not to suggest that this is a deliberate strategy, but rather that it is a simple fact of the way in which centralised control has been maintained so far over regional planning guidance, ensuring that the final documents tended to reflect national priorities rather better than regionally expressed preferences. In effect, regional planning has become a back-door way of constraining some of the more expansionist aims of the RDAs, and in some cases of scaling back the ambitions of local authorities.

In addition to a geography of regional debates on how best to interpret sustainable development in relation to economic development, it is possible to see that there has been a geography to the government's interventions on this issue. On the one hand, it has tended to rein in proposals for large greenfield employment land sites, especially but not exclusively in the northern regions. As part of this approach, the government has also tended to support arguments in favour of restraining economic development sites where these might undermine 'urban renaissance' efforts in the existing urban areas. Alternatively, when it has come to proposals to use constraint policies in areas such as Cambridge and the west of London area, the government has intervened to undermine them.

At first glance this seems to be regional policy in reverse, restricting growth in the least prosperous regions while wanting to support it in already congested areas. It is possible that this is simply part of the fundamental contradictions of the national neoliberal approach to economic management. But it also reflects something of the way in which neoliberalism has required regions to cope with these contradictions in regionally specific ways which sometimes go against the national project. The result is some intriguing tensions emerging between national growth policies, national planning policies, and their regional counterparts.

8 Looking to the future

Regions, spatial strategies and sustainable development

The governance of current and future regional complexity

Strategic regional planning is essentially the governance of complexity, where preferences are debated and decisions made about the shaping of future regional development. It is a process whose legitimacy derives from a mixture of statutory purpose and the collective 'ownership' which emerges from being developed in open, creative and collaborative ways. An essential feature of regional planning procedures, therefore, is that they provide the scope for debates involving a multiplicity of ideas, values, facts and counter-facts, claims to moral certainties and concerns about conceptual uncertainties. But it is also a forum for examining competing priorities, not least geographical and sectoral ones. For fear of drowning in the detail and ambiguities of all this, regional planning is also continuously on the search for simplicity and transparency in bringing about agreement about how best to guide future development.

Debates in regional planning tend to focus less on the detail of place making, much more on the underlying principles about how development should take place, on whose terms and to what end. Behind the often high-profile disputes about how much and what types of development regional planning should allow, there is therefore also a less trumpeted continuing search for meaning and truth in sometimes seemingly bland principles, concepts, techniques and even just words. These debates are important, however, since control over the meaning and truth of concepts and words can be a means of altering power relations and power possibilities. It is in this context that the analysis in this book has sought to unpick some of the ways in which the meaning of the term 'sustainable development' has been defined, developed, debated, mobilised and resisted.

One of the starting points for the analysis was that the processes of argumentation surrounding regional planning and sustainable development often drew from ideas which tended to get represented in fairly simple ways for public consumption, for instance in media debates about 'concreting the countryside' or competing claims that jobs are being given preference over nature conservation. Alternatively, within the more formal and technical apparatus of the regional planning systems (e.g. written submissions and verbal statements at public examinations), more complex understandings of the underlying issues inevitably prevailed, as groups sought to gain legitimacy by grounding their arguments in more nuanced and sophisticated understandings of the complexities involved.

In a sense, many of the debates in regional planning over recent years have revolved around attempts to move away from overly simplistic binaries such as economy versus environment, instead developing more subtle, more sophisticated policy understandings. Intriguingly, central government itself has been centrally involved in undermining 'purist' or single issue approaches in English planning by virtue of introducing the integrated approach to planning, which has quite explicitly set out to challenge the previously dominant mindset of trading off economic and environmental issues against each other (see Chapter 3). Yet the integrated approach has brought with it a new set of tensions and even contradictions, as planners have sought to grapple with the multiplicity of sustainabilities which have been invoked in the name of sustainable development: environmental sustainable development, sustainable urban or rural regeneration, and sustainable economic development. More than this, it is still clear that integrated approaches to sustainable development have been instrumental in allowing the UK government to consolidate its own particular set of objectives for sustainable development.

Regional planning and competing sustainabilities

As Chapters 3 and 6 argue, sustainable development and urban renaissance are essentially political strategies open to continuing contestation, rather than neutral concepts. We have sought to examine the way in which sustainable development in particular was used within regional planning debates, focusing on the various selectivities involved.

Chapter 2 highlights two ways of looking at processes of selectivity: one looking at the strategic selectivity of the state, the other involving a more decentred analysis of how the behaviour patterns of individuals and institutions can be shaped by the way in which concepts such as sustainable development are generated, debated, assimilated, normalised, policed and disputed. In many ways this involved looking at similar issues from two different standpoints, one stressing the hegemonic tendencies of powerful bodies, expressed through the state, the other stressing the multiplicities of ways in which powerful tendencies might be enacted, resisted and reworked.

Ideas about 'the strategic and spatial selectivity of the state' were helpful in understanding how and why regional planning was used by central government to consolidate its preferred objectives-led approach to sustainable development, with its emphasis on high and stable economic growth. As this definition was inserted into and policed within the various aspects of the planning apparatus, it became near impossible to argue for alternative policy forms which strayed from this particular understanding. 'Urban renaissance' was used in a similar way as a tactic for enforcing a particular approach to development, drawing legitimacy from its strong links to the parallel planning debates on sustainable development. Despite such strong centralising tendencies, which saw a uniformity in formal visions for regions and sustainable development, in practice there was a marked geography in how sustainable development was worked into regional planning issues. The result was some interesting tensions between the differing stakeholders in the process at all levels of the system, as ideas were put forward, countered and reworked. Examples examined here include the role of central government in increasing the proposed allocation of new housing development in the South East, while reducing the proposed allocations in the North East, in each case over-riding regional protests that their initial allocations had been the best 'sustainable' option (see Chapter 5). In the case of employment land allocations too, central government over-rode attempts to constrain new developments in 'hot spots' in the South East, while also overturning proposals to create major new employment sites in the North East, where demand was much lower (see Chapter 7).

But it is important not to read these actions as simple manifestations of the power tactics and hegemonic tendencies of the state, since doing so would miss many of the complexities involved. For instance, there was the conscious 'positioning' of groups at different levels of the system in these debates. From local planning authorities through to regional bodies and national planners, all were involved in power-plays and mind-games, which could be seen as a process of making 'offers', counter-offers and concessions through the various stages of the drafting process. But more than this constant iteration across the scales of planning, there were complex interplays with other actors within the system, for instance local, regional and national environmental, housebuilding and economic development advocacy groups.

Certainly the orchestration of media protest over housing in the South East drew from the combination of local, regional and national lobbying voices and tactics. These were often politically targeted on issues where the government was known to be sensitive, from accusations of 'concreting over the countryside' to the loss of marginal parliamentary seats or councils. But this was far from a uniform phenomenon across the country. In practice, different dominant regional groupings sought to mobilise 'sustainable development' rhetorics in rather different ways to support their preferred positions, in the process marginalising differing opposing voices. So in the North East, planners and developers were largely at one in promoting the case for more development as the 'sustainable' option, while environmental groups were residualised. In the South East, on the other hand, it was planners and environmentalists who found common cause in resisting development pressures as 'unsustainable'. This geography of selective sustainabilities left the government seeking to mediate in what it saw to be the national interest, in the process ensuring that the development voice was better heeded in the South

East and the environmental voice paid greater attention in the North East. This was far from a simple imposition of top-down preferences, therefore.

The analysis here highlights how concepts and techniques emerged through what were often complex interconnecting processes of development, experimentation, disputation and then either rejection, acceptance or reformulation. In the case of environmental capital for instance, the debates involved a wide range of actors, government conservation agencies and lobby groups promoting particular approaches; consultancies and academics honing or critiquing particular ideas and techniques; and local governments seeking to adapt them to local circumstances. Adding spice to this mix were the public examinations of draft plans, providing an arena in which ideas and techniques had to be justified in public to peers who might well contest them as favouring certain interests over others. Central government presence was certainly felt through these debates through its support, be it warm, tepid or cold. Planning debates in the different fora, from working groups through to public examination, served to embed and 'normalise' particular values and approaches. For instance, in the current round of regional planning debates it was largely counter-productive to argue against the very concept of brownfield-site targets, with debate instead reduced to technical aspects of how high targets should be set, the use of supporting techniques such as urban capacity studies, and the need to display greater sensitivity to local conditions.

While this brief overview is suggestive of the value of looking at the normalising and counter-hegemonic tendencies which emerge at the local and regional levels, on its own this approach runs the risk of missing the ways in which these debates do still remain subject to powerful state-strategic selectivities. This is particularly apparent in the multiplicity of ways in which central government can suggest that it regards certain approaches as unacceptable, warning the key players in regional debates away from devoting too much time to them. Favoured approaches, alternatively, can quickly become concreted into the planning system, whether through the statutory system or by being inserted into the professional arena with guides to good practice and the like.

In all of this, our analysis has come to recognise not simply the selectivities over alternative environmental and planning knowledges, but also the powerful pulsing mechanisms and disjunctures in the flows of knowledge and ideas. In the case of planning, new ideas and new techniques tend to be closely monitored as they are formulated, advocated, practised and contested, with the professional planning press playing a key role in this. In addition, there are a substantial group of paid planning consultants and professional advisers who work with planning authorities and other planning stakeholders, all of whom seek to spot precedents which might be used to help reinforce or refute particular arguments (see Chapter 4). This might seem to be a process which would simply lend a deadening hand to processes of innovation, but in practice the process was more varied and quixotic than that, as ideas which appeared to have been discredited in one context might emerge elsewhere, with supporting arguments strengthened or techniques reformulated in order to counter previous objections. In this way, attempts to introduce new techniques created some powerful disjunctures and uncertainties in the system, and thereby required participants to re-examine continuously their own viewpoints and preferences, in the process serving to clarify what was deemed acceptable or not, or where priorities lay.

The analyses of sustainability appraisal (Chapter 3), environmental capital (Chapter 4) and urban capacity (Chapter 5), for instance, revealed the ways in which stakeholders had to come to terms with these new techniques, which in turn required examining the underpinning assumptions and values involved. These techniques all purported to be supporting sustainable development in one way or another, yet each was subject to critique, refinement and the pursuit of clarity.

All this might seem a long way from the concerns of institutionalist literature and communicative planning, the dominant theoretical approach in planning for well over a decade (Tewdwr-Jones and Allmendinger 2003). Though social capital was undoubedly built up with the recent turn to a more colloborative approach to regional planning, nonetheless conflict and lack of trust remain rife within the system. With its emphasis on promoting idealised form of deliberative argumentation, collaborative planning proved helpful in examining planning against an idealised form of system of open and constructive debate, respectful of differing viewpoints and knowledges. Yet in practice, the reality of how debates were conducted in regional planning was very different from the ideal, being an exercise in power dynamics rather than simple social capital formation and consensus building. On the surface, there was considerable open, rational and respectful debate in the formal fora, but these modes of behaviour are probably best seen as tactical power positionings, reflecting how institutions wanted to be perceived as legitimate, fair-minded and open. The reality was that after many hours of participating in working groups, writing formal submissions, and presenting at public examinations, very few of those involved ever seemed to change their minds very much. The process was essentially one of seeking first to influence those drafting RPG, then the public examination panel inspectors. Once past this stage, the focus of lobbying was largely on national government itself.

Worse still, the process seemed unable to generate widespread agreement on many key issues, even after two years of work. It perhaps took the South East RPG to bring home quite how ineffective the process had been as a colloborative venture. In this case, central government felt it had to mediate between the sharply divided viewpoints of some of the key stakeholders, in the process imposing many of its own solutions to issues such as housing numbers and economic constraint policies (see Chapters 5 and 7). But not having won over the hearts and minds of developers and local planning authorities has militated against this being a workable solution, leaving a compromised RPG respected by few (Lock 2002). The continuing housing crisis, particularly the problems in achieving even the lowest forecasts of future demand, ultimately required the government to step in to break the deadlock which it had itself been partly responsible for creating.

It is interesting in this respect to return to the criticisms of earlier approaches to regional planning guidance – that it was insufficiently spatial and strategic, that it tended largely to reflect national guidance and that it was not open and transparent. In some senses, there has been improvement on all these grounds, yet perhaps far less than advocates of the new system might have hoped for. The new approach to regional planning guidance continued to produce draft RPG which ducked many of the main issues about where to guide growth within each region, and in the lack of a national spatial framework, there remained a lack of integration across regions (Wong 2002). In terms of providing a strategic approach, again many difficult issues tended to be sidestepped, not least the main decisions on infrastructure provision, from public transport, roads and airports, to health and education, to water supply. Indeed, many of the most problematic decisions were deferred to commissioned sub-regional studies or structure plan deliberations. In addition, attempts to provide more decisive actions within RPG, such as in housing allocations, almost inevitably ran into some form of opposition, at its most extreme breaking out into heated media campaigns.

The quiet and noisy spaces of regional planning

There were other selectivities at work in the new regional planning system, notably over which subjects were covered and which were not, and which subjects were intensely scrutinised and which were not. More than this, there were important issues of whose voices got heard or paid regard to in the new governance systems, and whose didn't, reflecting their positioning within broader societal power dynamics and institutional structures. In the current round of regional planning, the noisy spaces of regionalism were occupied by those debating housing issues, with the lobbying activities of environmental and development groups particularly prominent. As we have already intimated, the discursive techniques tended to vary according to the forum in which views were being aired, with simpler storylines developed for media consumption, grounded in claims to moral authority. By contrast, more complex forms of argumentation were carried out in the formal deliberative processes of plan formation, which produced more subtle positionings within debates and also greater recourse to claiming or contesting legitimacy through the shaping of both concepts such as sustainable development and urban renaissance and their associated planning techniques.

The quiet spaces of regionalism in planning are by their very nature less dramatic, with particular silences surrounding the role of social infrastructure provision. This was important in many ways. For instance, there was little guidance on where new hospitals and clinics might be built, as these were generally deemed to be either local planning issues or issues which were largely for the health authorities to determine. This is more problematic than it might seem, with major new hospitals sometimes being built on the edge of built-up areas to replace older central hospitals whose sites were sold off for redevelopment. Too often, such decisions seemed to emerge without full consideration of the environmental and traffic implications, being driven more by the financial logic of the health service and the Private Finance Initiative (a UK system for getting private developers to develop a facility then lease it back) than the overall needs of areas.

The most notable silence, though, was the one noted in Chapter 5, the limited attention given to social housing provision in the early stages of the current round of regional planning guidance. This in part reflected the lack of a regional tier of organisation for many groups in this sector, which, initially at least, made it difficult for their interests to be reflected fully in each region. Part of the issue here was again the sectoralisation of responsibilities within UK local and national government, with local authority housing departments appearing to be largely disengaged from their local planning counterparts when it came to shaping future planning guidance.

Devolution and the future of the English regions

New Labour's 'devolution project', which has already seen new devolved political responsibilities in Scotland, Wales, Northern Ireland and London, is set to continue with devolution to the English regions. This will not, though, involve a simple one-off transfer of state responsibilities, as devolved status will be granted only to those regions whose people vote in favour of it in a referendum (see Chapter 1).

The government's devolution proposals for the English regions, published in the White Paper *Your Region, Your Choice* (Cabinet Office and DTLR 2002), are being taken forward in the Regional Assemblies (Preparations) Bill published in November 2002. In presenting the proposals to the public, the Deputy Prime Minister, John Prescott, argued that this represented a long-awaited break from centralism in English government:

> This Bill takes forward our commitment to provide England's regions with their own elected assemblies. Giving the regions their own democratic voice will enable them to provide the solutions that meet the needs of individual regions and communities – breaking away from the 'Whitehall knows best' attitude. This is part of our wider agenda to transform our communities – making them better places to live and work.
>
> (ODPM 2002c)

As regionalism is stronger in some regions than others, there will almost inevitably be different institutional arrangements in place in different regions in the foreseeable future. At the moment, the strength of pro-regional feeling tends to be strongest, or at least most vocal, in the northern regions, so it is likely that they will be the first to use referenda to determine whether they should move towards regional devolution.

It is not our intention here to explore the wider governance implications of the devolution proposals so much as to consider what they mean for the future of regional planning and sustainable development. Where regions elect for devolved status, they will be given wide responsibilities for strategic planning, including taking the lead role in the preparation and implementation of Regional Spatial Strategies (see p. 208) and regional housing strategies, and accountability for the RDAs. The White Paper proposes: 'giving assemblies important functions in key areas such as economic development, spatial planning and housing, and the flexibility they need to develop innovative solutions. This means they will have the powers to drive improvements in their regions' (Cabinet Office and DTLR 2002, p. 34). The White Paper goes on to identify a range of issues for which the assemblies will be expected to prepare regional strategies: sustainable development, economic development, skills and employment, spatial planning, transport, housing, health improvement, culture and biodiversity. So the regions themselves will become responsible for strategic planning within the context of national legislation and advice, subject to agreeing with central government a number of high-level targets against which they would be required to report progress.

New Labour's planning reforms

For planning, and in particular strategic planning, the period 2000–2003 was a major period of experimentation as New Labour implemented many of the ideas for reform initially flagged up in consultation papers issued during 1998 (see Chapter 1). In pursuing its modernising planning agenda, the government shifted the main scale for strategic planning from county structure plans to the region. It also altered planning guidance to reflect the broader agenda of spatial planning as opposed to land use planning, aiming to achieve greater integration between related policy sectors. The government also opened up regional planning to a wider range of stakeholders in place of what had previously been a local authority-dominated process. What emerged was a shift in the balance of power away from county councils, a tier of local government which New Labour had frequently been at political odds with, towards new regional arrangements as the seat of strategic planning policy, even though these currently lack direct regional democratic accountability.

Building on these early reforms, the government has embarked on a further round of modernising planning with the publication of the planning Green Paper, *Planning: Delivering a Fundamental Change* (DTLR 2001b) and associated proposals for reforming the way planning deals with major infrastructure developments. As part of a broader concern to make planning more transparent and more efficient, the main proposals were:

- to make planning work better for business through measures such as delivery contracts and Business Planning Zones, where there would be a relaxation of planning restrictions;
- to replace local plans with simplified Local Development Frameworks (LDF);
- to create a single tier of statutory strategic plans called Regional Spatial Strategies, replacing county structure plans and regional planning guidance; and
- to bring major infrastructure proposals, such as airport developments, directly under the control of Parliament in order to avoid lengthy planning inquiries.

The consultation on the proposed planning reforms generated considerable interest, with 15,489 responses received. According to the government (ODPM 2002b), these were generally 'supportive of the need for reform and the broad aims behind the government's proposals'. This broad statement, which few would dispute, masked an array of concerns and supporting statements which had been expressed in press releases and on the Web sites of environmental groups, business and housebuilder interests, professional planning bodies and others. A flavour of these mixed responses can be gleaned from the following quotations from press releases issued in the wake of the Green Paper:

> Planning proposals are good news for the economy, jobs and people – says CBI.
>
> (CBI 2001)

> Government planning changes a disaster for environment says FOE.
>
> (Friends of the Earth 2001)

> The stripping away of time consuming, costly and confusing tiers of bureaucracy should be welcomed by everyone.
>
> (HBF 2001b)

> Gaping hole in government's proposals for planning reform.
>
> (CPRE 2001c)

For the environmental lobby, the issues of greatest concern were the abolition of county structure plans, the creation of Business Planning Zones where there would be a relaxation of planning regulations, and the proposals to remove regulation of major infrastructure projects from the planning system. These changes were opposed because of fears that they would weaken the regulatory apparatus of planning, exposing countryside nature in particular to greater threats.

The same issues were also perhaps the aspects of the reforms most *favoured* by business interests which had been lobbying the government to speed up the planning process, removing what they considered to be unnecessary constraints in the present system. As the CBI put it, changes which improved the speed of planning applications were welcomed, since 'Our present planning system undermines competitiveness and discourages firms from expanding here' (CBI 2001). As with the discourses of lobby groups during the preparation of RPG, though, these are public positions for media consumption. In practice, the main lobby groups all responded to the government's consultation in a more balanced way, clearly preferring to remain 'engaged' in the process of planning reform rather than being excluded from it.

The most damning indictment of the reforms came not from a lobby group, but from the House of Commons Select Committee on Transport, Local Government and the Regions, following its investigation of the Planning Green Paper:

> We conclude that the Government's proposals are unworkable as a whole. We share the Government's enthusiasm for clearing the stuffy air which surrounds planning. We wish to encourage innovation and enthusiasm for the immense positive contribution which planning can make to public life. Yet the Green Paper shows a lack of grasp of the real issues over outward appearances
>
> (Thirteenth Report of the Select Committee on Transport Local Government and the Regions, July 2002, para. 210).

Despite the Select Committee's views, the government decided to go ahead with most of its reforms – the only significant change being that it dropped the proposal for removing infrastructure developments from planning control. The other main proposals are going forward, at the time of writing, in the Planning and Compulsory Purchase Bill. In effect, central government has retained its strong control over the statutory framework for planning, despite bringing a wide range of stakeholders into consultations about what form this should take.

In terms of the future of strategic planning, it appears that the new system of Regional Spatial Strategies (RSSs) will continue the shift towards greater integration with other scales of planning activity and other policy sectors, and will have the benefit of statutory status. But in the absence of devolution to the English regions (see p. 206), the Secretary of State will retain the role of issuing the new RSSs, as was the case with RPG, raising questions of whether they will be any more strategic or regional than their predecessors. Nor do the new proposals adequately address the integration of regional economic planning and regional spatial planning, since RSSs and RESs will continue to be prepared separately and to have equal status. However, as something of a concession to concerns about tensions between these documents, RESs are intended in future to be better integrated and prepared within the spatial development framework provided by the RSS: '[The government intends] to integrate the RSS more fully with other regional strategies. Each RSS should provide the long term planning framework for the Regional Development Agencies' strategies and those of other stakeholders, and assist in their implementation' (DTLR 2001b, para 4.42).

The Planning and Compulsory Purchase Bill also includes proposals for the reform of planning in Wales which are different in some respects from those in England. Planning reforms are also under way in Scotland and Northern Ireland (see Chapter 1), which means that the overall picture of planning in the United Kingdom can perhaps be seen as one of diverging planning systems and institutional arrangements. Indeed, the government appears keen to *encourage* diversity among the different territorial administrations of the United Kingdom, creating competitive pressures to improve policy performance. These changes will not, though, radically alter the hierarchical nature of British planning: central control will still be exerted through devices such as national guidance, national housing projections, central policy on sustainable development and economic development, national indicators and targets, and so on.

The implications of these changes for sustainable development are probably mixed. Groups concerned about environmental protection such as Friends of the Earth and the CPRE feel that the proposed reforms will not help deliver sustainable development:

> Overhauling the planning system was a golden opportunity to deliver sustainable development. But New Labour has blown it. And with plans to fast track major infrastructural projects still to be published, things can only get worse
>
> (Friends of the Earth 2001).

> We needed an improved, more effective planning system which enjoys the confidence of business and public alike. The Government should make it clear that the purpose of planning is to promote sustainable development and ensure that land is managed in the wider public interest. Instead it is offering a recipe for alienation, confusion, conflict and delay.
>
> (CPRE 2002b)

The business and housebuilding lobbyists were more sanguine in their comments on the reforms. Although not directly referring to sustainable development, they did use more moderate language to suggest that the reforms would deliver a more integrated, socially responsible approach to regional policy:

> We also welcome the renewed emphasis on regional strategies to ensure that the pressing need for housing is put into action. Many areas need

more housing to ensure they remain economically and socially viable. It is the under supply of housing that has created problems of affordability resulting in the break up of communities.

(HBF 2001b)

Business and the community are not separate entities. Both want a system that allows objectors to be heard while ensuring applications are judged quickly and transparently. A system that serves business better is also good for the economy, jobs and people.

(CBI 2001)

What these changes mean for planning policy and for the achievement of sustainable development could well be mixed. The clearer separation of national and regional policy will remove the anomaly of regional spatial strategies being prepared in the region but issued by central government. This could reduce the opportunities for central government in the future to enforce national policies over regional aspirations. As suggested in Chapter 7, though, this could be a mixed blessing for those stakeholders opposed, for example, to aspirations for growth in regions such as the North East, since they will no longer be able to rely on central government exercising its restraining influence.

Devolution in this sense may not provide a simple picture of benefits emerging under the new system for those groups pursuing approaches to sustainable development which involve a strong emphasis on environmental protection. As we discussed earlier, the North East region, which many place at the forefront in seeking devolution, perhaps had the least 'integrated' approach to sustainable development, giving a strong emphasis to the economic pillar over and above the environmental one. Alternatively, the South East, which initially at least placed a stronger emphasis on the environmental pillar of sustainable development, is likely to be one of the last regions to seek devolution. It is far from certain, then, that regionalism in the short term at least will be a better thing for those seeking to promote environmental priorities.

In most respects, however, the government's proposals are likely to improve the legitimacy and the outcomes of future regional planning processes, in particular where the link is made to democratic regional institutions. There are areas of concern in all this, however, some of which have already been alluded to. First, there is considerable potential for regional mechanisms to lead to a deregulatory race to the bottom, especially in aspects of environmental protection. Second, and related, it remains to be proven that the local protectionist instincts will be overcome, which is important in that they have led to many of the more contentious aspects of regional planning being either sidestepped or reduced to a lowest common denominator approach. Third, it will be difficult to move beyond an already introspective regional system towards a greater awareness of how regional strategies might exercise wider impacts. Fourth, though they are meant to be long-term plans, most regional planning exercises rarely make decisions for the long term, largely instead working out short-term compromises to try to deal with long-term problems. It remains to be seen whether the new system is likely to be any better on this score than the existing system. Fifth, there is a concern that powerful regional growth machines will marginalise dissenting voices and agendas, steamrollering through policies for achieving short-term political and economic advantage at uncertain future social and environmental cost.

Sustainable development for the regions?

Throughout this book, the emphasis has been on sustainable development as the vehicle for multiple ambitions, a political resource for those wishing to use and adapt part of the agenda which the term encompasses in order to pursue often partisan objectives. This has seen sustainable development defined in many different ways, including the UK government's own pre-ferred objectives-led approach. Our unease with the government's object-ives-led approach to sustainable development has perhaps been apparent already, not least the way in which the need for 'high and stable economic growth' is asserted so strongly, whereas the other three objectives are more passively framed. It is a useful exercise in this context to return to the defini-tion of sustainable development which generated the current interest in the concept, namely that it is development which meets the needs of the present without compromising the ability of future generations to meet their needs. In previous work drawing from the wide-ranging debates on sustainable development, five key principles were highlighted, two of which feature in most accounts of sustainable development: inter- and intra-generational equity (see Haughton 1999c). To conclude our analysis, we want to examine briefly the performance of recent regional planning in England against these principles. Necessarily this assessment focuses on strategic intent more than on-the-ground impacts, which may yet take some time to take effect, and, equally necessary in a brief overview, the coverage is partial. How does regional planning measure up against the *principle of inter-generational equity*, or futurity? As with all the principles introduced here, views on whether it is being achieved will very much depend on how sustainable development is being interpreted, so different groups will come to differing assessments.

The provision of adequate shelter for all is a recurrent theme in sustainable development debates, which, looked at from the perspective of the house-building and social housing advocacy groups lobby, might well raise concerns about whether the planning system is delivering the amount of development needed to satisfy future demand for houses. So, developers might well argue that planning is failing the principle of futurity by constraining their ability to build enough houses, in the process fuelling price increases and contributing to homelessness.

Alternatively, environmental groups might argue that planning best serves the principle of futurity by maintaining strict controls on urban development, thus protecting countryside for the benefit of future generations. Not surprisingly, therefore, many environmental groups are not happy with aspects of the government's proposals for the future of planning, which they consider pay too little attention to their view of what sustainable development entails.

Inevitably, then, there are different perspectives on whether the planning system is achieving the principle of futurity, reflecting different attitudes towards the relative importance of providing adequate supplies of housing land to meet future needs and protecting the countryside from development for the enjoyment of future generations. In some respects, most parties seem to feel that planning policy is failing aspects of this principle at the moment, albeit for very different reasons. For ourselves, this is a key finding: how difficult it is to find an approach which meets the aspirations of all for what is handed on to future generations, and the degree to which these aspirations vary across regions, across stakeholder groups and across different professional groups.

Has regional planning guidance helped in meeting the needs of the present generation, the *principle of intra-generational equity*? The main losers in regional planning debates have perhaps been the lower-income groups, which have suffered most from the problems of housing abandonment in the North and overheated housing markets in the South East, both of which recent planning policies have contributed to. It is also low-income groups which are likely to suffer most from the loss of brownfield sites to development in areas where existing residential densities are high and the provision of local amenities low. The main winners have probably been those who live in prosperous suburbs and smaller settlements, who have seen measures retained which protect their property values and safeguard their access to open country, notably the decision to retain the green belt and the general presumption against developing on greenfield sites.

Has regional planning helped address *geographical equity*, or transfrontier responsibility? This principle requires that regional policies are geared to addressing extra-regional and global issues as well as regional ones. For the most part, regional planning has been a largely introspective affair, though it is probably fair to say that it has attempted to address global issues indirectly. This is evident in the range of compaction policies which have as part of their rationale the aim of reducing carbon emissions. Alternatively, with the emphasis of regional planning on economic growth and consumption, those who see sustainable development as a largely environmental issue would probably say that regional planning is working against this principle because it is based on assumptions about the value of greater international trade in goods and resources.

Has regional planning contributed to the *principle of procedural equity*, which holds that regulatory and participatory systems should be devised and applied to treat all people openly and fairly? Changes made to the planning system since 1997 have continuously emphasised the need for greater involvement by stakeholders in planning processes. Whether the new arrangements have been effective in bringing about greater participation is debatable, however (Haughton and Counsell 2002). For example, though the post-1997 system for producing RPG has generally been welcomed by stakeholders as being more transparent than previous arrangements, encouraging greater participation from a wide range of groups, there are still tensions requiring resolution. Our work suggests that while regional planning may well have moved from tokenism in consultation towards more genuine engagement with a wider range of interest groups, the system remains some way from fully engaging with a wide range of groups at all stages of preparing regional planning documents. At the moment, the system tends to favour those well-organised and well-resourced groups which have traditionally been involved in the planning process, such as the CPRE and HBF.

The final principle is that of *environmental or inter-species equity*, which can be interpreted in many ways, but broadly speaking it is about placing the survival of other species of plants and animals on a more equal basis to the survival of humans. Changes from an environmental bottom line to a triple bottom line ('win–win–win') have resulted in a more human-centred approach to sustainable development which focuses more on the quality of (human) life than on protecting the natural environment. This shift to a triple bottom line might be seen as a weakening in the approach to inter-species equity, but in practice (see chapter 4) the current round of regional planning has resulted in stronger policies on biodiversity, for example. Overall, then, though the approach to sustainable development has perhaps become more anthropocentric in recent years, regional planning policy does appear to be adopting a stronger approach towards issues such as biodiversity and habitat conservation, driven in part by EU requirements.

Though using these five principles is undoubtedly a crude analytical device, it is helpful in drawing attention to the uneven progress of regional planning in promoting what many people would see as the key underlying features of sustainable development. Overall, there is evidence of what most planning participants would see as positive steps in some areas, such as procedural and inter-species equity, but less clear progression in other areas. But the key issue here, as throughout this book, is that different people interpret sustainable development in very different ways. In choosing our criteria for judging progress on 'sustainable development' we reveal something of our own selectivities and preferences, while accepting that what we might regard as progress others might well regard as moving backwards. We do not claim to have the definitive answer, but we hope that we have helped in understanding why different people within the planning system would have arrived at different conclusions to ours.

Appendix
Method matters

The empirical material on which this book is based has several sources. First, 121 interviews were conducted, involving 137 key actors and covering each of the eight English regions and a number of local case study areas. At the regional level, interviewees included people involved in preparing draft regional planning guidance, both officers and politicians, regional government office officials responsible for preparing the final versions of RPG, local planners who contributed to RPG debates, RDAs, active business lobby groups such as chambers of commerce, CBI regional groups, the HBF and consultants employed on behalf of development groups, government statutory agencies (e.g. the Environment Agency, the Countryside Agency, English Heritage), local and regional environmental groups, community groups, social housing groups, plus academics engaged in regional planning debates, including members of our panel of regional experts. In the case study areas a smaller range of people were interviewed, principally local planners and pro-development and environment lobby groups.

People associated with significant national-level responsibilities were also interviewed, ranging from central government officials to representatives of key lobby groups. In some cases, particularly influential players were revisited at a later stage of the RPG process, in order for us to get a better sense of how events had worked out. Each interview was given a unique reference beginning with the initials of the region it took place in. This reference is used with quotations in the text, usually linked to the key actor group that the interviewee represented, although it is omitted where it might breach confidentiality. Because interviewees were likely to have different dominant concerns at different stages of the RPG process, information is also provided on which month and year interview information was obtained in. To avoid lengthy references in the text, these dates are given in the list of interviewees at the end of this appendix. More interviews were undertaken in some regions than others, depending on the particular issues we were exploring, the key stakeholders involved, and the location of the case study areas.

In all but a handful of cases, permission was given for interviews to be taped, with a condition of confidentiality, providing a rich source of quotes for this book. The general approach here is to select quotations which typified the general view of either a particular respondent or a particular group of respondents. On other occasions, quotations are chosen to represent views which were not representative of a general viewpoint, in which case this is made clear in the text.

Although two of the public examinations had concluded by the time this project started (those in East Anglia and South East), members of the research team were able to attend parts of six of the public examinations of draft RPG documents simply by joining the public section of the audience. In addition, on one occasion during the Yorkshire and the Humber examination, one of us presented pre-prepared evidence on behalf of the TCPA. Notes were made of the general discussions during the public examinations, including the direct transcribing of some quotations from participants. As these comments were made in public, they are not treated as confidential, so when our transcripts of the public examinations are used, individuals or their organisations are usually named.

A considerable amount of secondary source material was compiled and analysed during the course of the project, including all the drafts of RPG produced for public comment and all the sustainability appraisals of RPG which were published. The drafts of RPG were all subject to a form of content analysis. Drawing on reports from national government and international bodies in particular, we identified a range of issues which we might have expected to see covered in RPG and then made a simple summary of how many of these issues were covered in RPG. We also compiled and analysed copies of local planning documents in a number of case study areas to explore the two-way flow of planning policy between the regional and the local scales.

Other documents used here included many of the submissions made by different interest groups about the draft RPG and submitted to the public examination panels, plus the panel reports themselves. The submissions were in many cases, but by no means all, rather dry commentaries being made to a professional audience, often in fairly technical terms. While these documents were part of the formal 'internal' process of engaging in debate about how RPG should be shaped, many of the key actors were also engaged in a form of 'external' debate as they sought to influence government officials, professional bodies, and also, in many cases, public perceptions and media debates about particular issues. These came in many forms: reports commissioned from (usually sympathetic) advisers, often academics, internally produced reports, and press releases. All these sources provided helpful insights into the discursively constructed nature of planning ideas, requiring that the various submissions, reports and press releases were treated as 'position' statements – as partial, and often far from impartial, attempts to influence the direction of the debates surrounding particular regional planning issues.

In addition, aspects of the media coverage of regional planning issues were analysed as part of the project. Throughout the study period, considerable media coverage was attracted to housing issues in particular, with employment and environment issues sometimes appearing in supportive roles to these debates, more rarely emerging in their own right. The media coverage extended to television news items and documentaries, but by their nature it was difficult to obtain anything but a partial coverage of these, especially regional television programmes. The focus in this book is on two aspects of the media's interpretation of regional planning: the press releases published by the main lobby groups on their Web sites; and the use of these and other materials by national newspaper groups, in particular the *Guardian, The Times* and the *Daily Telegraph*, plus the BBC Web site.

The analysis examines some of the ways in which key actors seek to insert their views into the public domain, through written and verbal presentation at planning inquiries, through press releases and lobbying documents. The approach is to use quotations which seemed particularly powerful articulations of a given 'storyline', which sometimes means that these lack some of the subtleties of understanding which might underlie them. Their value to the analysis, though, is that it is precisely such powerful quotations which can help set the tenor of public debates. It is worth noting too the potential for differences between views for public and private consumption, and between views put over in interviews with us as opposed to through media outlets.

At the outset of the project, a network of academic experts was established, one from each region, who were asked for advice on who to speak to in each region. As these people are regional activists in their own right, we also formally interviewed six of them as part of our work. As each process of RPG preparation reached its conclusion, a working paper was produced for each region summarising our main findings to that point. Drafts of these were provided to the relevant regional experts, who were in most cases able to help improve our understanding of events in their region. Copies of the regional reports can be viewed at the University of Hull Web site: http://www.hull.ac.uk/geog/research/html/hg1crp.html.

Interviews

North East

NE1   Regional planner: February 2000
NE2   Government Office: February 2000
NE3   Government Office: February 2000
NE4   Academic: February 2000
NE5   Academic: February 2000
NE6   Pro-development lobbyist: March 2000
NE7   Economic development officer: February 2000
NE8   Environmental NGO: April 2000

Public examination June 2000

NE9   Environmental NGO: September 2000
NE10   Environmental NGO: September 2000
NE11   Business interest group: September 2000
NE12   Environmental NGO: October 2000
NE13   Government Office: October 2000
NE14   Local planner: October 2000

'Proposed changes' April 2001

NE15   Regional planner: May 2001
NE16   Environmental NGO: July 2001
NE17   Environmental NGO: October 2001
NE18   Environmental NGO May 2001
NE19   Government Agency: May 2001
NE20   Local planner: May 2001
NE21   Local planner: May 2001
NE22   Pro-development lobbyst: May 2001
NE23   Local planner: May 2001
NE24   Local planner: May 2001

South East

Public examination, May/June 1999

'Proposed changes', March 2000

SE1   Academic: March 2000
SE2   Professional body: March 2000
SE3   Planning consultant: March 2000
SE4   Government Office: March 2000
SE5   Regional planner: March 2000
SE6   Environmental NGO: April 2000
SE7   Pro-development group: April 2000
SE8   Planning NGO: October 2000
SE9   Environmental NGO: October 2000
SE10   Local planners: December 2000
SE11   Government Agency: December 2000
SE12   Academic: February 2001
SE13   Economic development officer: February 2001
SE14   Government Office: July 2000
SE15   Civil servants: July 2000
SE16   Civil servant: July 2000
SE17   Civil servant: July 2000

East Midlands

EM1   Government Office: May 2000
EM2   Local planner: May 2000

Public examination, June/July 2000

EM3   Environmental NGO: August 2000
EM4   Environmental NGO: August 2000
EM5   Government Agency: October 2000
EM6   Local planner: October 2001
EM7   December 2000: Government Agency
EM8   Pro-development group
EM9   Regional planner: February 2001
EM10   Regional planner: February 2001

'Proposed changes', March 2001

Yorkshire and the Humber

YH1   Academic: April 2000
YH2   Local planner: May 2000
YH3   Government Office: May 2000
YH4   Local planner: May 2000
YH5   Government Office: June 2000
YH6   Government Office: June 2000

Public examination, July 2000

YH7   Social housing group: June 2000
YH8   Health authority: June 2000
YH9   Government Agency: October 2000
YH10   Pro-development group: October 2000
YH11   Government Agency: October 2000
YH12   Local planner: November 2000
YH13   Local politician: November 2000
YH14   Local planner: November 2000
YH15   Economic development officer: December 2000
YH16   Government Agency: December 2000
YH17   Government Office: May 2000
YH18   Government Office: May 2000

'Proposed changes', March 2001

YH19   Local planner: July 2001
YH20   Economic development officer: November 2001

South West

SW1   Academic: February 2000
SW2   Government Office: March 2000
SW3   Academic: February 2000

Public examination March 2000

SW4   Local planner: July 2000

'Proposed changes' December 2000

SW5   Environmental NGO: February 2001
SW6   Regional NGO: February 2001
SW7   Government Office: February 2001
SW8   Planning consultant: February 2001
SW9   Planning consultant: February 2001
SW10   Government Office: November 2001
SW11   Pro-development lobbyist: November 2001
SW12   Local planners: November 2001

East Anglia/East of England

Public examination, February 1999

'Proposed changes', March 2000

EE1   Government Office: July 2000
EE2   Regional planner: July 2000
EE3   Local planner: July 2000
EE4   Government agency: December 2000
EE5   Economic development officer: December 2000
EE6   Government agency: February 2001
EE7   Regional planner: March 2000
EE8   Pro-development lobbyist: March 2000
EE9   Government agency: March 2000
EE10   Local planner: November 2001
EE11   Environmental NGO: November 2001
EE12   Government Office: November 2001
EE13   Pro-development lobbyist: November 2001

North West

NW1   Regional NGO: December 2000
NW2   Government Office: December 2000
NW3   Academic December 2000
NW4   Regional planner: December 2000

Public examination, February 2001

NW5   Local planners: April 2001
NW6   Environmental NGO: April 2001
NW7   Pro-development lobbyist: May 2001
NW8   Government Agency: May 2001
NW9   Local planners: May 2001
NW10   Regional planner: May 2001
NW11   Environmental NGO: July 2001
NW12   Environmental link group members: July 2001

'Proposed changes', June 2002

West Midlands

WM1   Environmental NGO: March 2001
WM2   Local planner: March 2001
WM3   Government Office: March 2001
WM4   Regional planner: June 2001
WM5   Business interest group: June 2001
WM6   Economic development officer: June 2001
WM7   Government Agency: June 2001
WM8   Environmental NGO: January 2002
WM9   Government Office: January 2002
WM10   Local planner: February 2002
WM11   Local Planner: February 2002
WM12   Environmental network member: February 2002
WM13   Academic: June 2002

Public examination, June 2002

Bibliography

Abercrombie, P. (1945) *The Greater London Plan, 1944*, HMSO, London.

Acton, J.E. and Brookes, R.P. (1999) *Draft Regional Planning Guidance for East Anglia: Report of the Panel Conducting the Public Examination*, Government Office for the East of England, Cambridge.

Acton, J.E., Mattocks, J.R. and Robins, D.L.J. (2001) *Draft Regional Planning Guidance for the North West: Report of the Panel*, Government Office for the North West, Manchester.

Advantage West Midlands (1999) *Creating Advantage: The West Midlands Economic Strategy*, AWM, Birmingham.

Aitchison, T. (2002) 'The South West: lessons for the future', in T. Marshall, J. Glasson and P. Headicar (eds) *Contemporary Issues in Regional Planning*, Ashgate, Aldershot.

Alden, J. (2001) 'Planning at the national scale: a new planning framework for the UK', in L. Albrechts, J. Alden and A. da Rosa Pires (eds) *The Changing Institutional Landscape of Planning*, Ashgate, Aldershot.

Alden, J. and Morgan, R. (1974) *Regional Planning: A Comprehensive View*, John Wiley, New York.

Allen, J., Massey, D. and Cochrane, A. (1998) *Rethinking the Region*, Routledge, London.

Allmendinger, P. (2001) *Planning in Post-modern Times*, Taylor and Francis, London.

Allmendinger, P. and Tewdwr-Jones, M. (2000) 'New Labour, new planning? The trajectory of planning in Blair's Britain', *Urban Studies* 37 (8), 1379–1403.

Amin, A. (1994) 'Post-Fordism: models, fantasies and phantoms of transition', in A. Amin (ed.) *Post-Fordism: A Reader*, Blackwell, Oxford.

Amin, A. and Hausner, J. (1997) 'Interactive governance and social complexity', in A. Amin and J. Hausner (eds) *Beyond Market and Hierarchy: Interactive Governance and Social Complexity*, Edward Elgar, Cheltenham.

Amin, A. and Thrift, N. (1994) 'Living in the global', in A. Amin and N. Thrift (eds) *Globalization, Institutions, and Regional Development in Europe*, Oxford University Press, Oxford.

Amin, A. and Thrift, N. (1995) 'Globalisation, institutional "thickness" and the local economy', in P. Healey, S. Cameron, S. Davoudi, S. Graham and A. Madani-Pour (eds) *Managing Cities: The New Urban Context*, John Wiley, Chichester.

Aspen, Burrow and Crocker (2001) *The West Midlands Area Multi-modal Study: Final Report*, Governmental Office for the West Midlands, Birmingham.

Association of North East Councils (ANEC) (1999) *Draft Regional Planning Guidance for the North East*, North East Regional Assembly, Newcastle.

Baker, M. (1996) 'Viewpoint: rediscovering the regional approach', *Town Planning Review* 67, iii–vi.

Baker, M. (1998) 'Planning for the English regions: a review of the Secretary of State's regional planning guidance', *Planning Practice and Research* 13 (2): 153–169.

Baker, M. (2002) 'Governmental Offices of the Regions and regional planning', in T. Marshall, G. Glasson and P. Headicar (eds) *Contemporary Issues in Regional Planning*, Ashgate, Aldershot.

Baker, M., Deas, I. and Wong, C. (1999) 'Obscure ritual or administrative luxury? Integrating strategic planning and regional development', *Environment and Planning B: Environment and Design* 26, 763–782.

Baker Associates (2001) *Regional Planning Guidance for the North East (RPG1): Sustainability Appraisal of the Proposed Changes to draft RPG1*, Baker Associates, Bristol.

Barlow, J., Bartlett, K., Hooper, A. and Whitehead, C. (2002) *Land for Housing: Current Practice and Future Options*, Joseph Rowntree Foundation, York.

Barton, H., Davies, G. and Guise, R. (1995) *Sustainable Settlements: A Guide for Planners, Designers and Developers*, University of the West of England and LGMB, Luton.

Beer, A., Haughton, G. and Maude, A. (eds) (2003) *Developing Locally: Comparing Local Economic Development across Four Nations*, Policy Press, Bristol.

Benneworh, P. (1999) 'Sustainable development, regional economic strategies and the RDAs', *Regions: The Newsletter of the Regional Studies Association* 222, 10–19.

Benneworth, P., Conroy, L. and Roberts, P. (2002), Strategic connectivity, sustainable development and the new English regional governance', *Journal of Environmental Planning and Management* 45, 199–218.

Bishop, K. (1996) 'Planning to save the world? Planning's green paradigm', in M. Tewdwr-Jones (ed.) *British Planning Policy in Transition*, UCL Press, London.

Blowers, A. (1980) *The Limits of Power*, Pergamon Press, Oxford.

Blowers, A. (1997) 'Society and sustainability', in A. Blowers and B. Evans (eds) *Town Planning into the 21st Century*, Routledge, London.

Blowers, A. (ed.) (1993) *Planning for a Sustainable Environment*, Earthscan, London.

Blowers, A. and Evans, B. (eds) (1997) *Town Planning into the 21st Century*, Routledge, London.

Braun, B. and Castree, N. (1998) 'The construction of nature and the nature of construction', in B. Braun and N. Castree (eds) *Remaining Reality: Nature at the Millennium*, Routledge, London.

Breheny, M. (1991) 'The renaissance of strategic planning?', *Environment and Planning B* 18, 233–249.

Breheny, M. (1992) 'Emerging constraints in the South East', in P. Townroe and R. Martin (eds) *Regional Development in the 1990s: The British Isles in Transition*, Jessica Kingsley, London.

Breheny, M. (ed.) (1992) *Sustainable Development and Urban Form*, Pion, London.

Breheny, M. (1997) 'Urban compaction: feasible and acceptable?', *Cities* 14, 209–219.

Breheny, M. (1999) 'People, households and houses: the basis to the "great housing debate" in England', *Town Planning Review* 30, 275–293.

Breheny, M. and Hall, P. (eds) (1996) *The People – Where Will They Go?*, Town and Country Planning Association, London.

Brenner, N. (2000) 'The urban question as a scale question: reflections on Henri

Lefebvre, urban theory and the politics of scale', *International Journal of Urban and Regional Research* 24, 361–378.

Brenner, N. and Theodore, N. (2002) 'Cities and the geographies of "actually existing neoliberalism"', *Antipode* 34, 347–379.

Brindley, T., Rydin, Y. and Stoker, G. (1989) *Remaking Planning: The Politics of Urban Change*, Unwin Hyman, London.

Brindley, T., Rydin, Y. and Stoker, G. (1996) *Remaking Planning: The Politics of Urban Change*, 2nd edn, Routledge, London.

British Broadcasting Corporation (BBC) (2001) 'Tories pledge to protect greenbelt', 30 April, http://news.bbc.co.uk/1/hi/uk_politics/1305209.stm, accessed 3 December 2002.

BBC (2002) 'Prescott unveils £1bn housing plan', http://news.bbc.co.uk/1/hi/uk_politics/2135057.stm, accessed 21 November 2002.

Bryant, R. (2002) 'Non-governmental organisations and governmentality: consuming biodiversity and indigenous people in the Philippines', *Political Studies* 50, 268–292.

Buchanan, C. (1972) *The State of Britain*, Faber and Faber, London.

Bunce, M. (1994) *The Countryside Ideal: Anglo-American Images of Landscape*, Routledge, London.

Burchell, R. and Shad, N. (1998) 'A national perspective on land use policy alternatives', paper given at National Public Policy Education Conference, Portland, OR, 22 September 1998.

Burden, T. and Campbell, M. (1985) *Capitalism and Public Policy in the UK*, Croom Helm, London.

Burningham, K. (2000) 'Using the language of a NIMBY: a topic for research, not an activity for researchers', *Local Environment* 5 (1), 55–68.

Burton, E. (2000) 'The potential of the compact city for promoting social equity', in K. Williams, E. Burton and M. Jenks (eds) (2000) *Achieving Sustainable Urban Form*, E. & F.N. Spon, London.

Cabinet Office and Department for Transport, Local Government and the Regions (DTLR) (2002) *Your Region, Your Choice: Revitalising the English Regions*, The Stationery Office, London.

CAG Consultants and University of Hull (2003) 'Sustainable development tools for regional policy: output 2 – final report to the English Regions Network', unpublished.

Calthorpe, P. and Fulton, W. (2001) *The Regional City: Planning for the End of Sprawl*, Island Press, Washington, DC.

Castells, M. and Hall, P. (1994) *Technopoles of the World: The Making of the 21st Century Industrial Complexes*, Routledge, London.

Cherry, G. (1972) *Urban Change and Planning: A history of urban development in Britain since 1750*, G.T. Foulis, Henley-on-Thames.

Colin Buchanan and Partners (2001) *Cambridge Sub-Regional Study Draft Final Report*, Colin Buchanan and Partners, London.

Commission of the European Communities (CEC) (1990) *Green Paper on the Urban Environment*, EUR 12902, CEC, Brussels.

Confederation of British Industry (CBI) (2001) 'Planning proposals are good news for the economy, jobs and people – says CBI', press release, 12 December, http://www.cbi.org, accessed 8 January 2002.

Connell, R. (1999) 'Accommodating development: a view from West Sussex', paper given at ESRC Seminar 'Planning, Space and Sustainability', Department of City and Regional Planning, University of Cardiff.

Cooke, P. (1983) *Theories of Planning and Spatial Development*, Hutchinson, London.

Cooke, P. and Morgan, K. (1998) *The Associational Economy: Firms, Regions and Innovation*, Oxford University Press, Oxford.

Council for the Protection of Rural England (CPRE) (1994) *Urban Footprints*, CPRE, London.

CPRE (2001a) 'Green Belts – still working under threat', briefing, June, http://www.cpre.org.uk, accessed 5 April 2002.

CPRE (2001b) 'Prescott's greenfield housing curb thwarted', press release issued 1 March, http://www.cpre.org.uk, accessed 8 March 2001.

CPRE (2001c) 'Gaping hole in government's planning reforms', press release issued 12 December, http://www.cpre.org.uk, accessed 17 December 2001.

CPRE (2002a) *Even Regions, Greener Growth*, London, CPRE.

CPRE (2002b) 'Government planning proposals set to fail communities, business and the countryside', press release issued 18 March, http://www.cpre.org.uk, accessed 19 March 2002.

Counsell, D. (1998) 'Sustainable development and structure plans in England and Wales: a review of current practice', *Journal of Environmental Management and Planning*, 41 (2), 177–194.

Counsell, D. (1999a) 'Sustainable development and structure plans in England and Wales: operationalising the themes and principles', *Journal of Environmental Planning and Management* 42, 45–61.

Counsell, D. (1999b) 'Attitudes to sustainable development in the housing capacity debate: a case study of the West Sussex Structure Plan', *Town Planning Review* 70, 213–229.

Counsell, D. (1999c) 'Attitudes to sustainable development: policy integration, participation and Local Agenda 21, a case study of the Hertfordshire Structure Plan', *Local Environment* 4, 23–33.

Counsell, D. (2001) 'A regional approach to sustainable urban form?', *Town and Country Planning* 70, 322–335.

Counsell, D. and Bruff, G.E. (2001) 'Treatment of the environment in regional planing: a stronger line for sustainable development?', *Regional Studies* 35 (5): 486–492.

Counsell, D. and Haughton, G. (2001) *Sustainable Development in Regional Planning Guides, 4: The South East*, http://www.hull.ac.uk/geog/research/html/hg1crp.html.

Counsell, D. and Haughton, G. (2002a) *Sustainability Appraisal of Regional Planning Guidance: Final Report*, Office of the Deputy Prime Minister, London. http://www.hull.ac.uk/geog/research/html/hglcrp.html.

Counsell, D. and Haughton, G. (2002b) 'Sustainability appraisal: delivering more sustainable regional planning guidance?', *Town and Country Planning* 71, 4–18.

Counsell, D. and Haughton, G. (2002c) 'Complementarity or conflict? Reconciling regional and local planning systems', *Town and Country Planning* 71, 164–168.

Counsell, D. and Haughton, G. (2003) 'Regional planning in transition: planning for growth and sustainable development in two contrasting regions', *Environment and Planning C* 21, 225–239.

Counsell, D., Haughton, G.F., Allmendinger, P. and Vigar, G. (2003) 'New directions in UK strategic planning: from development plans to spatial development strategies', *Town and Country Planning* 72, 15–19.

County Planning Officers' Society (1993) *Planning for Sustainability*, Hampshire County Council, Winchester.

Cowell, R. (2000) 'Environmental compensation and the mediation of environmental change: making capital out of Cardiff Bay', *Journal of Environmental Planning and Management* 43 (5), 689–711.

Cowell, R. and Murdoch, J. (1999) 'Land use and the limits to (regional) governance: some lessons from planning for housing and minerals in England', *International Journal of Urban and Regional Research* 23 (4), 654–669.

Cox, K. (2002) 'Globalization, the regulation approach, and the politics of scale', in A. Herod and M. Wright (eds) *Geographies of Power: Placing Scale*, Blackwell, Oxford.

Cox, K. and Mair, A. (1991) 'From localised social structures to localities as agents', *Environment and Planning A* 23, 197–214.

Crow, S. and Whittaker, R. (1999) *Regional Planning Guidance for the South East of England: Report of the Panel*, Government Office for the South East, Guildford.

Crowther and Bore (2000) *Draft Regional Planning Guidance for the South West: Report of the Panel*, Government Office of the South West, Bristol.

Daily Telegraph (1999a) 'All party revolt at homes betrayal', 10 October, http://www.telegraph.co.uk, accessed 23 February 2000.

Daily Telegraph (1999b) 'Report destroys Prescott pledge on countryside', 9 October, http://www.telegraph.co.uk, accessed 23 February 2000.

Daily Telegraph (1999c) 'A hundred ways to improve our cities'. 30 June, http://www.telegraph.co.uk, accessed 14 May 2003.

Davies, W.K.D. (1997) 'Sustainable development and urban policy: hijacking the term in Calgary', *GeoJournal* 43, 359–369.

Davoudi, S. (2000) 'Sustainability: a new vision for the British planning system' *Planning Perspectives* 15, 123–137.

Dean, M. (1999) *Governmentality: Power and Rule in Modern Society*, Sage, London.

Deas, I. and Ward, K. (2000) 'From the "new localism" to the "new regionalism"? The implications of regional development agencies for city-regional relations', *Political Geography* 19, 273–292.

Deluce, P. (1998) 'Take action for social housing and defend the green belt ...', *Corporate Watch*, Issue 7, Spring, www.corporatewatch.org/magazine/issue7, accessed 3 October 2002.

Department of the Environment (DoE) (1991) RPG6 *Regional Planning Guidance for East Anglia to 2016*, HMSO, London.

DoE (1992a) PPG1 *General Policies and Principles*, HMSO, London.

DoE (1992b) PPG12 *Development Plans and Regional Planning Guidance*, HMSO, London.

DoE (1993a) *A Guide to the Environmental Appraisal of Development Plans*, HMSO, London.

DoE (1993b) RPG1 *Regional Planning Guidance for the North East*, HMSO, London.

DoE (1994a) *Sustainable Development: The UK Strategy*, HMSO, London.

DoE (1994b) *Biodiversity: The UK Action Plan*, HMSO, London.

DoE (1994c) PPG9 *Nature Conservation*, HMSO, London.

DoE (1994d) RPG9 *Regional Planning Guidance for the South East*, HMSO, London.

DoE (1995) RPG9A *The Thames Gateway Planning Framework*, HMSO, London.

DoE (1996a) PPG6 *Town centres and retail development*, HMSO, London.

DoE (1996b) *Household Growth: Where Shall We Live?*, HMSO, London.

Department of the Environment East Anglia Regional Strategy Team (1974) *Strategic Choices for East Anglia*, HMSO, London.

Department of the Environment, Transport and the Regions (DETR) (1997) *Building Partnerships for Prosperity: Sustainable Growth, Competitiveness and the English Regions*, The Stationery Office, London.

DETR (1998a) *The Future of Regional Planning Guidance*, The Stationery Office, London.

DETR (1998b) *Regional Development Agencies' Regional Strategies*, The Stationery Office, London.

DETR (1998c) *Planning for Communities of the Future*, The Stationery Office, London.

DETR (1998d) Transport White Paper, *A New Deal for Transport*, The Stationery Office, London.

DETR (1998e) *A New Deal for Trunk Roads for England*, The Stationery Office, London.

DETR (1999a) *A Better Quality of Life: Strategy for Sustainable Development for the UK*, The Stationery Office, London.

DETR (1999b) PPG12 *Development Plans*, The Stationery Office, London.

DETR (2000a) PPG11 *Regional Planning*, The Stationery Office, London.

DETR (2000b) *Guidance on Preparing Regional Sustainable Development Frameworks*, The Stationery Office, London.

DETR (2000c) PPG3 *Housing*, The Stationery Office, London.

DETR (2000d) *Good Practice Guide on Sustainability Appraisal of Regional Planning Guidance*, The Stationery Office, London.

DETR (2000e) *Strategic Gap and Green Wedge Policies in Structure Plans*, The Stationery Office, London.

DETR (2000f) *Guidance on the Methodology for Multi-modal Studies*, The Stationery Office, London

DETR (2000g) *Our Towns and Cities: The Future – Delivering an Urban Renaissance*, The Stationery Office, London.

Department of Trade and Industry (DTI) (2002) *Supplementary Guidance for the Regional Development Agencies in Relation to the Economic Strategies*, DTI, London.

Department for Transport, Local Government and the Regions (DTLR) (2001a) PPG25 *Development and Flood Risk*, The Stationery Office, London.

DTLR (2001b) Planning Green Paper, *Planning: Delivering a Fundamental Change*, The Stationery Office, London.

DTLR (2001c) Lord Falconer's speech to the Town and Country Planning Summer School, http://www.detr.gov.uk/about/ministers/speeches, accessed 23 April 2002.

DiGiovanna, S. (1996) 'Industrial districts and regional economic development: a regulation approach', *Regional Studies* 30, 373–388.

Dow, S. (1998) 'Beyond dualism', *Cambridge Journal of Economics* 14, 143–158.

Doyle, T. and McEachern, D. (2001) *Environment and Politics*, 2nd edn, Routledge, London.

Duncan, J. (1990) *The City as Text: The Politics of Landscape in the Kandyan Kingdom*, Cambridge University Press, Cambridge.

East of England Development Agency (EEDA) (2001) *East of England 2010*, EEDA, Cambridge.

East of England Regional Assembly (EERA) (2001) 'Assembly endorses new Economic Development Strategy', press release, http://www.eelgc.gov.uk, accessed 14 May 2003.

East Midlands Development Agency (EMDA) (1999) *Prosperity through People: Regional Economic Strategy for the East Midlands*, EMDA, Nottingham.

East Midlands Regional Local Government Association (EMRLGA) (1999) *Draft Regional Planning Guidance for the Spatial Development of the East Midlands: public examination draft*, EMRLGA, Melton Mowbray.

East Midlands Regional Assembly (EMRA) (2000a) *Step-by-Step Guide to Sustainability Appraisal*, EMRA, Melton Mowbray.

EMRA (2000b) *East Midlands Integrated Regional Strategy*, EMRA, Melton Mowbray.

ECOTEC Research and Consulting (1999) *Sustainability Appraisal of the Draft Regional Economic Strategy for Yorkshire and the Humber*, ECOTEC, Leeds.

Eden, S. (1996) *Environmental Issues and Business*, John Wiley, Chichester.

Eden, S. (1999) '"We have the facts": how business claims legitimacy in the environmental debate', *Environment and Planning A* 31, 1295–1309.

Eden, S., Tunstall, S.M. and Tapsell, M. (2000) 'Translating nature: river restoration as nature-culture', *Environment and Planning D* 18, 257–273.

Elson, M. (1999) 'Green belts: the need for reappraisal', *Town and Country Planning* 68 (5), 156–158.

Elson, M. (2002) 'Modernising green belts: some recent contributions', *Town and Country Planning* 71, 266–267.

Elson, M. (2003) 'A "take and give" green belt?', *Town and Country Planning* 72, 104–105.

Elson, M., Walker, S. and Macdonald, R. (1993) *The Effectiveness of Green Belts*, HMSO, London.

English Nature (1992) *Sustainable Development in Structure Plans*, English Nature, Peterborough.

English Nature, Countryside Agency, English Heritage and Environment Agency (2001) *Quality of Life Capital: What Matters and Why?*, http://www.qualityoflife-capital.org.uk.

Environmental Resources Management (2000) *Sustainable Development through Regional Economic Strategies*, ERM, Oxford.

European Commission (1999) *European Spatial Development Perspective: Towards Balance and Sustainable Development of the Territory of the European Union*, Office for Official Publications of the European Communities, Luxembourg.

Evans, A. (1991) '"Rabbit hutches on postage stamps": planning, development and political economy', *Urban Studies* 28 (6), 853–870.

Evening Standard (1999) 'New homes gobble up green belt', 11 October, http://www.thisislondon.co.uk, accessed 23 December 2000.

Eversley, D. (1975) *Planning without Growth*, Fabian Research Series 321, Fabian Society, London.

Fairclough, N. (1998) 'Political discourse in the media: an analytical framework', in A. Bell and P. Garrett (eds) *Approaches to Media Discourse*, Blackwell, Oxford.

Fairclough, N. (2000) *New Labour, New Language*, Routledge, London.

Faludi, A. (2002) 'Positioning European spatial planning', *European Planning Studies* 7, 897–909.

Flyvbjerg, B. (1998) 'Empowering civil society: Habermas, Foucault and the question of conflict', in M. Douglass and J. Friedmann (eds) *Cities for Citizens*, John Wiley, Chichester.

Foucault, M. (1991a) 'Questions of method', in G. Burchell, C. Gordon and P. Miller (eds) *The Foucault Effect: Studies in Governmentality*, Harvester Wheatsheaf, London.

Foucault, M. (1991b) 'Governmentality', in G. Burchell, C. Gordon and P. Miller (eds) *The Foucault Effect: Studies in Governmentality*, Harvester Wheatsheaf, London.

Freudenberg, W.R. and Pastor, S.K. (1992) 'NIMBYs and LULU: stalking the syndromes', *Journal of Social Issues* 48, 39–61.

Friedmann, J. (1998) 'The political economy of planning: the rise of civil society', in M. Douglass and J. Friedmann (eds) *Cities for Citizens*, John Wiley, Chichester.

Friedmann, J. and Weaver, C. (1979) *Territory and Function: The Evolution of Regional Planning*, MIT Press, Cambridge, MA.

Friends of the Earth (1999a) 'Housing nightmare for South East', press release issued 8 October, http://www.foe.co.uk, accessed 20 November 2002.

Friends of the Earth (1999b) 'Housing: South West next under the bulldozer', press release issued 22 November, http://www.foe.co.uk, accessed 21 November 2002.

Friends of the Earth (2001) 'Government planning changes a disaster for environment says FOE', press release issued 12 December, http://www.foe.co.uk, accessed 8 January 2002.

Geddes, P. (1915) *Cities in Evolution*, Williams and Norgate, London.

Gibbs, D. (2002) *Local Economic Development and the Environment*, Routledge, London.

Gibbs, D. and Jonas, A. (2001) 'Rescaling and regional governance: the English Regional Development Agencies and the environment', *Environment and Planning C: Government and Policy* 19, 269–288.

Girardet, H. (1992) *The Gaia Atlas of Cities: New Directions for Sustainable Urban Living*, Gaia Books, London.

Glasson, J. (1974) *An Introduction to Regional Planning*, Hutchinson Educational, London.

Gobbett, D. and Palmer, R. (2002) 'The South West: lessons for the future', in T. Marshall, J. Glasson and P. Headicar (eds) *Contemporary Issues in Regional Planning*, Ashgate, Aldershot.

Goodwin, M. and Painter, J. (1996) 'Local governance, the crises of Fordism and the changing geographies of regulation', *Transactions of the Institute of British Geographers* 21, 635–648.

Government Office for the East of England (GOEE) (2000) Draft RPG6 *Regional Planning Guidance for East Anglia to 2016 (incorporating Secretary of State's Proposed Changes)*, The Stationery Office, London.

GOEE (2001) RPG6 *Regional Planning Guidance for East Anglia to 2016*, The Stationery Office, London.

Government Office for the East Midlands (GOEM) (2001) Draft RPG8 *Regional Planning Guidance for the East Midlands (incorporating Secretary of State's Proposed Changes)*, The Stationery Office, London.

GOEM (2002) RPG8 *Regional Planning Guidance for the East Midlands*, The Stationery Office, London.

Government Office for the North East (GONE) (2001) Draft RPG1 *Regional Planning Guidance for the North East (incorporating Secretary of State's Proposed Changes)*, The Stationery Office, London.

GONE (2002) RPG1 *Regional Planning Guidance for the North East*, The Stationery Office, London.

Government Office for the North West (GONW) (2002) Draft RPG13 *Regional Planning Guidance for the North West (incorporating Secretary of State's Proposed Changes)*, The Stationery Office, London.

GONW (2003) RPG13 *Regional Planning Guidance for the North West*, The Stationery Office, London.

Government Office for the South East (GOSE) (2000) Draft RPG9 *Regional Planning Guidance for the South East (incorporating Secretary of State's Proposed Changes)*, The Stationery Office, London.

GOSE (2001) RPG9 *Regional Planning Guidance for the South East*, The Stationery Office, London.

Government Office for the South West (GOSW) (2000) Draft RPG10 *Regional Planning Guidance for the South West (incorporating Secretary of State's Proposed Changes)*, The Stationery Office, London.

GOSW (2001) RPG10 *Regional Planning Guidance for the South West*, The Stationery Office, London.

Government Office for Yorkshire and the Humber (GOYH) (2001a) Draft RPG12 *Regional Planning Guidance for Yorkshire and the Humber (incorporating Secretary of State's Proposed Changes)*, The Stationery Office, London.

GOYH (2001b) RPG12 *Regional Planning Guidance for Yorkshire and the Humber*, The Stationery Office, London.

Graham, S. (1999) 'Constructing premium networked spaces: reflections on infrastructure networks and contemporary urban society', *International Journal of Urban and Regional Research* 24, 183–200.

Greater London Authority and the Mayor of London (2001) *Towards the London Plan*, GLA, London.

Greater London Authority and the Mayor of London (2002) *The Draft London Plan*, GLA, London.

Grigson, W.S. (1995) *The Limits of Environmental Capacity*, The Barton Wilmore Partnership, London.

Hajer, M. (1995) *The Politics of Environmental Discourses: Ecological Modernization and the Policy Process*, Clarendon Press, Oxford.

Hall, J. (1982) *The Geography of Planning Decisions*, Oxford University Press, Oxford.

Hall, P. (1980) 'Regional planning: directions for the 1980s', *Town Planning Review* 41, 253–256.

Hall, P. (1988) *Cities of Tomorrow: An Intellectual History of Urban Planning and Design in the Twentieth Century*, Blackwell, Oxford.

Hall, P. (2000) 'The centenary of modern planning', in R. Freestone (ed.) *Urban Planning in a Changing World: The Twentieth Century Experience*, E. and F.N. Spon, London.

Hall, P. (2002) *Urban and Regional Planning*, 4th edn, Routledge, London.

Hall, P. and Ward, C. (1998) *Sociable Cities: The Legacy of Ebenezer Howard*, John Wiley, Chichester.

Hall, P., Gracey, H., Dewett, R. and Thomas, R. (1973) *The Containment of Urban England*, vol. 2, George Allen and Unwin, London.

Hall, S., Critcher, C., Jefferson, T., Clarke, J. and Roberts, B. (1978) *Policing the Crisis: Mugging, the State, and Law and Order*, Macmillan, London.

Harding, A. (1996) 'Is there a new community power and why should we need one?', *International Journal for Urban and Regional Research* 20, 637–655.

Hardy, D. (1991) *From New Towns to Green Politics: Campaigning for Town and Country Planning, 1946–1990*, E. and F.N. Spon, London.

Harrison, C.M. and Burgess, J. (1994) 'Social constructions of nature: a case study of conflicts over the development of Rainham Marshes', *Transactions of the Institute of British Geographers* 19, 291–310.

Harvey, D. (1996) 'The environment of justice', in A. Merrifield, and E. Swyngedouw (eds) *The Urbanization of Injustice*, Lawrence and Wishart, London.

Haughton, G. (1990) 'Targeting jobs to local people: the British urban policy experience', *Urban Studies* 27 (2), 185–198.

Haughton, G. (1999a) 'Trojan horse or white elephant? The contested biography of the life and times of the Leeds Development Corporation', *Town Planning Review* 70 (2), 173–190.

Haughton, G. (1999b) 'Searching for the sustainable city: competing philosophical rationales and processes of "ideological capture" in Adelaide, South Australia', *Urban Studies* 36, 1891–1906.

Haughton, G. (1999c) 'Environmental justice and the sustainable city', *Journal of Planning Education and Research* 18, 233–242.

Haughton, G. (2003a) ' "Scripting" sustainable settlement', in C. Freeman and M. Thompson-Faucett (eds) *Living Space*, University of Otago Press, Dunedin, New Zealand.

Haughton, G. (2003b) 'City-lite: planning for the Thames Gateway', *Town and Country Planning* 72 (3), 95–97.

Haughton, G. and Counsell, D. (2002) 'Going through the motions? Transparency and participation in English regional planning', *Town and Country Planning* 71 (4), 120–123.

Haughton, G. and Hunter, C. (1994) *Sustainable Cities*, Jessica Kingsley, London.

Haughton, G. and Roberts, P. (1990) 'Government urban economic policy, 1979–89: problems and potential' in M. Campbell (ed.) *Local Economic Policy*, Cassell, London.

Haughton, G. and While, A. (1999) 'From corporate city to citizen's city? Urban leadership *after* local entrepreneurialism in the UK', *Urban Affairs Review* 35 (1), 3–23.

Haughton, G., Rowe, I. and Hunter, C. (1997) 'The Thames Gateway and the re-emergence of regional planning: the implications for water resource management', *Town Planning Review* 68 (4), 407–422.

Haughton, G., Lloyd, P. and Meegan, R. (1999), 'The re-emergence of community economic development in Britain: the European dimension to grassroots involvement in local regeneration', in G. Haughton (ed.) *Community Economic Development*, The Stationery Office, London.

Hay, C. (1995) 'Restating the problem of regulation and re-regulating the local state', *Economy and Society* 24, 387–407.

Healey, P. (1990) 'Structure and agency in land and property development processes', *Urban Studies* 27, 89–104.

Healey, P. (1997) *Collaborative Planning: Shaping Place in Fragmented Societies*, Macmillan, London.

Healey, P. (1998) 'Collaborative planning in a stakeholder society', *Town Planning Review* 69, 1–21.

Healey, P. (1999) 'Sites, jobs and portfolios: economic development discourses in the planning system', *Urban Studies* 36, 27–42.

Healey, P. and Shaw, T. (1993) 'Planners, plans and sustainable development', *Regional Studies* 27, 769–776.

Healey, P. and Shaw, T. (1994) 'Changing meanings of the environment in the British planning system', *Transactions of the Institute of British Geographers* 19 (4), 420–437.

Herington, J. (1991) *Beyond Green Belts: Managing Urban Growth in the 21st Century*, report for the Regional Studies Association, London, Jessica Kingsley, London.

Hertfordshire County Council (1998) *Hertfordshire County Structure Plan Review, 1991–2011*, HCC, Hertford.

Hertfordshire County Council (2001) *The Hertfordshire Town Renaissance Campaign: Campaign Report, Stage 1*, HCC, Hertford.

Hillier, J. (2000) 'Going around the back? Complex networks and informal action in local planning processes', *Environment and Planning A* 32, 33–54.

HMSO (1990) *This Common Inheritance*, HMSO, London.

HMSO (1994) *Sustainable Development: The UK Strategy*, HMSO, London.

Holland, S. (1976a) *The Regional Problem*, Macmillan, London.

Holland, S. (1976b) *Capital versus the Regions*, Macmillan, London.

Hough, M. (1990) *Out of Place: Restoring Identity to the Regional Landscape*, Yale University Press, New Haven, CT.

House Builders Federation (HBF) (2001a) 'London and South East housing crisis deepens'. press release issued on 30 November, http://www.hbf.co.uk, accessed 27 June 2002.

HBF (2001b) 'Planning Green Paper: a response', press release issued 12 December, http://www.hbf.co.uk, accessed 8 October 2002.

HBF (2002) 'Building a crisis "homes shortage"', press release issued 1 May, http://www.hbf.co.uk, accessed 21 November 2002.

House of Commons Select Committee on Transport, Local Government and the Regions (2002) *Thirteenth Report – Planning Green Paper*, http://www.publications.parliament.uk, accessed 5 July 2002.

Howard, E. (1898) *Tomorrow: A Peaceful Path to Real Reform*, Swan Sonnenschein, London. A revised edition was published in 1902 as *Garden Cities of Tomorrow*, Swan Sonnenschein, London.

Howes, H.R. (2002) 'The South West: lessons for the future', in T. Marshall, J. Glasson, and P. Headicar (eds) *Contemporary Issues in Regional Planning*, Ashgate, Aldershot.

Hull, A. (1997) 'Restructuring the debate on allocating land for housing growth', *Housing Studies* 16, 379–382.

Humber, R. (1990) 'Prospects and problems for private housebuilders', *The Planner* 76 (7), 15–19.

Hunter, C., Rowe, I. and Haughton, G. (1996) 'Supply augmentation or demand management? Two case studies of the challenges of meeting water demands in south east England', Sustainable Urban Development Working Paper Series, Leeds Metropolitan University.

Hutton, W. (2002) 'Cities shouldn't loosen their green belts', *Observer*, 12 May, p. 30.

Imrie, R. and Thomas, H. (1999) *British Urban Policy*, Sage, London.

Independent (1999) 'Mutiny in Middle England', 19 October, http://www.independent.co.uk, accessed 28 February 2000.

Innes, J. (1995) 'Planning theory's emerging paradigm: communicative action and interactive practice', *Journal of Planning Education and Research* 14, 183–190.

International City/County Management Association with Anderson, G. (1998) *Why Smart Growth: A Primer, Executive Summary*, cited on the Web site Smart Growth Online, http://www.smartgrowth.org.

Isard, W. (1960) *Methods of Regional Analysis: An Introduction to Regional Science*, MIT Press, Cambridge, MA.

Jackson, P. (1991) 'Mapping meanings: a cultural critique of locality studies', *Environment and Planning A* 23, 215–228.

Jacobs, M. (1997) *Making Sense of Environmental Capacity*, Council for the Protection of Rural England, London.

Jessop, B. (1982) *The Capitalist State*, Martin Robertson, Oxford.

Jessop, B. (1990) *State Theory: Putting the Capitalist State in Its Place*, Polity Press, Cambridge.

Jessop, B. (1994) 'Post-Fordism and the state, in A. Amin (ed.) *Post-Fordism: A Reader*, Blackwell, Oxford.

Jessop, B. (1995) 'The regulation approach, governance and post-Fordism: alternative perspectives on economic and political change?' *Economy and Society* 24, 307–333.

Jessop, B. (1997) 'The entrepreneurial city: re-imaging localities, redesigning economic governance, or restructuring capital?', in N. Jewson and S. MacGregor (eds) *Transforming Cities: Contested Governance and New Spatial Divisions*, Routledge, London.

Jessop, B. (1998) 'The rise of governance and the risks of failure: the case of economic development', *International Social Science Journal* 155, 29–45.

Jessop, B. (1999) 'Reflections on globalization and its (il)logics', in P. Dicken, P. Kelley, K. Olds and H. Young (eds) *Globalization and the Asia Pacific: Contested Territories*, Routledge, London.

Jessop, B. (2000a) 'Governance failure', in G. Stoker (ed.) *The Politics of British Urban Governance*, Macmillan, Basingstoke.

Jessop, B. (2000b) The crisis of the national spatio-temporal fix and the ecological dominance of globalizing capitalism', *International Journal of Urban and Regional Studies* 24 (2), 273–310.

Jessop, B. (2001) 'Bringing the state back in (yet again): reviews, revisions, rejections and redirections', placed on the Web on 10 May 2001: http://www.comp.lancs.ac.uk/sociology/soc070rj.html.

Jessop, B. (2002) 'Liberalism, neoliberalism and urban governance: a state-theoretical perspective', *Antipode* 34 (2), 452–472.

Joint Strategic Planning and Transportation Unit (1998) *Joint Replacement Structure Plan: Deposit Plan*, JSPTU, Bristol.

Jonas, A. (1994) 'The scale politics of spatiality', *Environment and Planning D* 12, 257–264.

Jones, M. (1997) 'Spatial selectivity of the state? The regulationist enigma and local struggles over economic governance', *Environment and Planning A* 29, 831–864.

Jones, M. (2001) 'The rise of the regional state in economic governance: 'partnerships for prosperity; or new scales of state power?', *Environment and Planning A* 33, 1185–1211.

Jones, M. and MacLeod, G. (1999) Towards a regional renaissance? Reconfiguring and rescaling England's economic governance', *Transactions of the Institute of British Geographers*, 24, 295–314.

Jones, M. and Ward, K. (2002) 'Excavating the logic of British urban policy: neoliberalism as the "crisis of crisis management"' *Antipode* 34, 473–494.

Krugman, P. (1997) *Pop Internationalism,* MIT Press, Cambridge, MA.

Latour, B (1993) *We Have Never Been Modern*, Harverster Wheatsheaf, Hemel Hempstead.

Leadbetter C. (2000) *Living on Thin Air: The New Economy (with a Blueprint for the 21st Century)*, Penguin, London.

Lee, R. (1977) 'Regional relations and economic structure in the EEC', in D.B. Massey and P.W.J. Batey (eds) *Alternative Frameworks for Analysis*, London Papers in Regional Science 7, Pion, London.

Lock, D. (2002) 'RPG – the government can't let go', *Town and Country Planning*, June, p. 155.

Lockwood, M. (1999) 'Humans valuing nature: synthesising insights from philosophy, psychology and economics', *Environmental Values* 8, 381–401.

London and South East Regional Planning Conference (SERPLAN) (1998) *A Sustainable Development Strategy for the South East*, SERPLAN, London.

Lösch, A. (1954) *The Economics of Location*, trans. W.H. Woglom, Yale University Press, New Haven, CT.

Lovering, J. (1999) 'Theory led by policy: the inadequacies of "the new regionalism" (illustrated from the case of Wales)', *International Journal of Urban and Regional Research* 23, 379–395.

McCormick, J. (1995) *The Global Environmental Movement*, 2nd edn, John Wiley, Chichester.

McGregor, A. (2000) '"Warm, fuzzy feelings": discursive explorations into Australian environmental imaginations', PhD thesis, University of Sydney.

McGuirk, P. (2001) 'Situating communicative planning theory: context, power, and knowledge', *Environment and Planning A* 33, 195–217.

MacLeod, G. (2001) 'New regionalism reconsidered: globalisation and the remaking of political economic space', *International Journal of Urban and Regional Research* 25, 804–829.

MacLeod, G. and Goodwin, M. (1999) 'Space, scale and state strategy: rethinking urban and regional governance', *Progress in Human Geography* 23, 503–527.

Macnaghten, P. and Urry, J. (1998) *Contested Natures*, Sage, London.

Marsden, T., Murdoch, J., Lowe, P., Munton, R. and Flynn, A. (1993) *Constructing the Countryside*. UCL Press, London.

Marshall, T. (2001) 'Regional planning and regional politics: political dimensions of regional planning guidance in two English regions, 1996–2001', mimeo.

Marshall, T. (2002) 'The re-timing of regional planning', *Town Planning Review* 73 (2), 171–196.

Marvin, S. and Guy, S. (1997) 'Creating myths rather than sustainability: the transition fallacies of the New Localism', *Local Environment* 2, 311–318.

Massey, D. (1979) 'In what sense a regional problem?', *Regional Studies* 13, 231–241.

Massey, D. and Meegan, R. (1978) 'Industrial restructuring versus the cities', *Urban Studies* 15, 273–288.

Mills, S. (1997) *Discourse*, Routledge, London.

Ministry of Housing and Local Government (1964) *The South East Study: 1961–1981*. HMSO, London.

Mittler, D. (2001) 'Hijacking sustainability? Planners and the promise and failure of Local Agenda 21', in A. Layard, S. Davoudi and S. Batty (eds) *Planning for a Sustainable Future*, Spon Press, London.

Mordue, T. (1999) 'Heartbeat country: conflicting values, coinciding visions', *Environment and Planning A* 31, 629–646.

Morgan, K. (2001), 'The new territorial politics: rivalry and justice in post-devolution Britain', *Regional Studies* 35, 343–348.

Mumford, L. (1938) *The Culture of Cities*, Harcourt, Brace, New York.

Murdoch, J. (2000), 'Space against time: competing rationalities in planning for housing', *Transactions of the Institute of British Geographers*, 25, 503–519.

Murdoch, J. and Abram, S. (2002) *Rationalities of Planning: Development versus Environment in Planning for Housing*. Ashgate, Aldershot.

Murdoch, J. and Norton, A. (2001), 'Regionalisation and planning: creating institutions and stakeholders in the English regions', in L. Albrechts, J. Alden and A. da Rosa Pires (eds) *The Changing Institutional Landscape of Planning*, Ashgate, Aldershot.

Murdoch, J. and Tewdwr-Jones, M. (1999), 'Planning and the English regions: conflict and convergence amongst the institutions of regional governance', *Environment and Planning C: Government and Policy* 17, 715–729.

Myerson, G. and Rydin, Y. (1996) (eds) *The Language of Environment: A New Rhetoric*, UCL Press, London.

Nagar, R., Lawson, V., McDowell, L. and Hanson, S. (2002) 'Locating globalization: feminist (re)readings of the subjects and spaces of globalization', *Economic Geography* 78, 285–306.

National Assembly for Wales (NAW) (2001) *Planning: Delivering for Wales*, NAW, Cardiff.

Newby, L. (2001) 'Yorkshire Forward: integrating sustainability, investment and business development', in C. Hewett (ed.) *Sustainable Development and the English Regions*, IPPR and the Green Alliance, London.

Newman, J. (2001), *Modernising Governance*, Sage, London.

Northern Ireland Assembly (2001) *Shaping Our Future: The Regional Strategy for Northern Ireland 2025*, Northern Ireland Assembly.

North West Development Agency (NWDA) (1999) *England's North West: A Strategy towards 2020*, NWDA, Warrington.

NWDA (2003) *Regional Economic Strategy 2004*, NWDA, Warrington.

North West Regional Assembly (NWRA) (2000) *People, Places and Prosperity: Draft Regional Planning Guidance for the North West*, NWRA, Wigan.

Observer (2002) 'Developers use crisis to invade green belt'. 12 May, http://society.guardian.co.uk/housing/story/, accessed 21 November 2002.

O'Connor, J. (1988) 'Capitalism, nature, socialism: a theoretical introduction', *Capitalism, Nature, Socialism* 1, 11–38.

O'Connor, M. (1993) 'On the misadventures of capitalist nature', *Capitalism, Nature, Socialism* 4 (3), 7–40.

O'Connor, M. (1994) 'The material/communal conditions of life', *Capitalism, Nature, Socialism* 5 (4), 105–114.

Offe, C. (1975) 'The theory of the capitalist state and the problem of policy formation', in L.N. Lindberg, R. Alford, C. Crouch and C. Offe (eds) *Stress and Contradiction in Modern Capitalism*, D.C. Heath, Lexington, MA.

Offe, C. (1984) *Contradictions of the Welfare State*, Hutchinson, London.

Offe, C. (1985) *Disorganised Capitalism*, Polity Press, Cambridge.

Office of the Deputy Prime Minister (ODPM) (2002a) *Sustainable Communities, Housing and Planning*, http://www.odpm.gov.uk/about/ministers/speeches, accessed 18 July 2002.

ODPM (2002b) *Planning Green Paper: Summary of Responses*, http://www.odpm.gov.uk, accessed 21 June 2002.

ODPM (2002c) 'Bill paves way for England's first', http://www.odpm.gov.uk, accessed 9 May 2003.

ODPM (2003a) *Sustainable Communities: Building for the Future*, The Stationery Office, London.

ODPM (2003b) Speech by the Deputy Prime Minister to the Guardian Urban Regeneration Conference, 8 April 2003, http://www.odpm.gov.uk/about/ministers/speeches, downloaded 21 April 2003.

Office for National Statistics (ONS) (2000) *Regional Trends*, The Stationery Office, London.

One NorthEast (1999a) *Unlocking Our Potential: Regional Economic Strategy for the North East*. One NorthEast, Newcastle.

One NorthEast (1999b) *Sustainability Appraisal of the Consultation Draft of the North East's First Regional Economic Strategy*. One NorthEast, Newcastle.

Organisation for Economic Cooperation and Development (OECD) (1976) *Regional Problems and Policies in OECD Countries*, vol. 2, OECD, Paris.

Owens, S. (1986) *Energy, Planning and Urban Form*, Pion, London.

Owens, S. (1994) 'Land, Limits and sustainability: a conceptual framework and some dilemmas for the planning system', *Transactions of the Institute of British Geographers*, 19, 439–456.

Owens, S. and Cowell, R. (2002) *Land and Limits: Interpreting Sustainability in the Planning Process*, Routledge, London.

Painter, J. (2002) 'Governmentality and regional economic strategies', in J. Hillier and E. Rooksby (eds) *Habitus: A Sense of Place*, Ashgate, Aldershot.

Parke, J. and Travers, M. (2000) *Draft RPG for the East Midlands: Report of The Public Examination Panel*. GOEM, Nottingham.

Peck, J. (2002) 'Political economies of scale: fast policy, interscalar relations, and neoliberal workfare', *Economic Geography* 78, 331–360.

Peck, J. and Tickell, A. (1994) 'Too many partnerships. . . the future for regeneration partnerships, *Local Economy* 9 (3) 251–265.

Peck, J. and Tickell, A. (1995a), 'Business goes local: dissecting the "business agenda" in Manchester', *International Journal of Urban and Regional Research* 19 (1), 55–78.

Peck, J. and Tickell, A. (1995b) 'The social regulation of uneven development: regulatory deficit, England's South East and the collapse of Thatcherism'. *Environment and Planning A* 27, 15–40.

Peck, J. and Tickell, A. (2002) 'Neoliberalizing space', *Antipode* 34, 380–404.

Pennington, M. (2002) *Liberating the Land: The Case for Private Land-Use Planning*, Institute of Environmental Affairs, London.

Phelps, N. and Tewdwr-Jones, M. (1998) 'Institutional capacity building in a strategic policy vacuum: the case of Korean company LG in South Wales', *Environment and Planning C: Government and Policy* 16, 735–755.

Phelps, N. and Tewdwr-Jones, M. (2000) 'Globalisation, regions and the state: exploring the limitations of economic modernisation through inward investment', *Urban Studies* 38, 1253–1272.

Pierre, J. and Peters, B.G. (2000) *Governance, Politics and the State*, Macmillan, Basingstoke.

Piore, M. and Sabel, C. (1984) *The Second Industrial Divide: Possibilities for Prosperity*, Basic Books, New York.

Porter, M. (1990) *The Competitive Advantage of Nations*, Macmillan, London.

Potter, J. and Wetherell, M. (1994) 'Analyzing discourse', in A. Bryan and R. Burgess (eds) *Analyzing Qualitative Data*, Routledge, London.

Powell, A.G. (1978) 'Strategies for the English regions: ten years of evolution', *Town Planning Review* 49, 5–13.

Power, A. (2001) 'Social exclusion and urban sprawl: is the rescue of cities possible?', *Regional Studies* 35, 731–742.

Rabinow, P. (1984) *The Foucault Reader*, Pantheon Books, New York.

Raco, M. (1998) 'Assessing "institutional thickness" in the local context: a comparison of Cardiff and Sheffield', *Environment and Planning A* 30, 975–996.

Raco, M. and Imrie, R. (2000) 'Governmentality and rights and responsibilities in urban policy', *Environment and Planning A* 32, 2187–2204.

Rees, W. (1995) 'Achieving sustainability: reform or transformation?', *Journal of Planning Literature* 9, 343–361.

Regional Assembly for the North West (2000) *People, Places and Prosperity: Draft Regional Planning Guidance for the North West*, RANW, Wigan.

Regional Assembly for Yorkshire and the Humber (RAYH) (1999) *Advancing Together. Towards a Spatial Strategy: Draft Regional Planning Guidance*, RAYH, Wakefield.

Richardson, A.F. and Simpson, E.A. (2000) *Draft Regional Planning Guidance for the North East: Panel Report*, GONE, Newcastle.

Richardson, R., Bradley, D., Jones, I. and Benneworth, P. (1999) 'The North East', in M. Breheny (ed.) *The People: Where Will They Work?* Town and Country Planning Association, London.

Roberts, P. (1996) 'Regional planning guidance in England and Wales: back to the future?' *Town Planning Review* 67, 97–109.

Roberts, P. (1999) 'Strategic connectivity', in *The New Regionalism: Strategies and Governance*, Centre for Local Economic Strategies, Manchester.

Roberts, P. and Lloyd, M.G., (2000) 'Regional Development Agencies in England: new regional planning issues?' *Regional Studies* 34, 75–80.

Robinson Penn (1999) *Sustainability Appraisal of the Consultation Draft of the North East's First Regional Economic Strategy*, Robinson Penn, Newcastle.

Robson, B., Peck, J. and Holden, A. (2000) *Regional Agencies and Area-Based Regeneration*, Policy Press, Bristol.

Roger Tym and Partners in association with Three Dragons (2001) *Thames Gateway Review*, www.planning.odpm.gov.uk/thamesgateway/01.htm, downloaded 16 December 2002.

Rogers, R. (1997) *Cities for a Small Planet*, Faber and Faber, London.

Rogers, R. and Power, A. (2000) *Cities for a Small Country*, Faber and Faber, London.

Roseland M (1998) *Towards Sustainable Communities,* New Society Publishers, Gabriola Island, BC, Canada.

Royal Commission on Environmental Pollution (RCEP) (2002) *Twenty Third Report: Environmental Planning*, The Stationery Office, London.

Royal Town Planning Institute (RTPI) (2000) *Green Belt Policy: A Discussion Paper.* RTPI, London.

RTPI (2002) *Modernising Green Belts*, RTPI, London.

Rydin, Y. (1998a) 'Land use planning and environmental capacity: reassessing the use of regulatory policy tools to achieve sustainable development', *Journal of Environmental Planning and Management* 41 (6), 749–765.

Rydin, Y. (1998b) *Urban and Environmental Planning in the UK*, Macmillan, Basingstoke.

Rydin, Y. (1999) 'Can we talk ourselves into sustainability? The role of discourse in the environmental policy process', *Environmental Values* 8, 467–484.

Rydin, Y. and Thornley, A. (2001) 'An Agenda for the New Millennium', in Y. Rydin and A. Thornley (eds) *Planning in the UK: Agendas for the New Millennium*, Ashgate, Aldershot.

Satterthwaite, D. (1997) 'Sustainable cities or cities that contribute to sustainable development?', *Urban Studies* 34 (10), 1667–1691.

Saxenian, A.-L. (1994) *Regional Advantage: Culture and Competition in Silicon Valley and Route 128*, Harvard University Press, Cambridge, MA.

Sayer, A. (1989) 'Dualistic thinking and rhetoric in geography', *Area* 21, 301–305.

Scott, A.J. (1988) *Metropolis: From the Division of Labor to Urban Form*, University of California Press, Berkeley.

Scott, A.J. (1998) *Regions and the World Economy: The Coming Shape of Global Production, Competition and Political Order*, Oxford University Press, Oxford.

Scottish Executive (2002) *Review of Strategic Planning: Conclusions and Next Steps*, Scottish Executive, Edinburgh.

Self, P. (1982) *Planning the Urban Region*. George Allen and Unwin, London.

Selman, P. (1996) *Local Sustainability: Managing and Planning Ecologically Sound Places*, Paul Chapman, London.

Shaffer, F. (1970) *The New Town Story*, MacGibbon and Kee, London.

Shaw, D. and Sykes, O. (2001) *Delivering the European Spatial Development Perspective*, University of Liverpool.

Shelter (2002) 'Most needy must benefit from Government housing investment', press release on 17 July 2002, downloaded from www.shelter.org.uk on 4 October 2002.

Shirley, P. (1998) *Urban Task Force Prospectus: The Wildlife Trusts' and the Urban Wildlife Partnership's Response*, The Wildlife Trusts, Newark.

Shucksmith, M. (1990) *House Building in Britain's Countryside*, Routledge, London.

Simmons, M. (1999) 'The revival of regional planning', *Town Planning Review* 70, 159–172.

Smith, N. (2003) 'Remaking scale: competition and cooperation in prenational and postnational Europe', in N. Brenner, B. Jessop, M. Jones and G. MacLeod (eds) *State/Space: A Reader*, Blackwell, Oxford.

Smith, S.P. and Sheate, W.R. (2001a) 'Sustainability appraisals of regional planning guidance and regional economic strategies in England: an assessment'. *Journal of Environmental Planning and Management* 44 (5) 735–755.

Smith, S.P. and Sheate, W.R. (2001b) Sustainability appraisal of English regional plans: incorporating the requirements of the EU Strategic Environmental Assessment Directive', *Impact Assessment and Project Appraisal* 19, 263–276.

South East England Development Agency (SEEDA) (1999) *Building a World Class Region: An Economic Development Strategy for the South East of England*, SEEDA, Guildford.

South West Development Agency (1999) *Regional Strategy, 2000–2010*, SWDA, Exeter.

South West Regional Planning Conference (SWRPC) (1999) *Draft Regional Planning Guidance for the South West*, SWRPC, Taunton.

Standing Conference of East Anglian Local Authorities (SCEALA) (1998) *Regional Strategy for East Anglia, 1995–2016* SCEALA, Bury St Edmunds.

Stead, D. (2000) 'Unsustainable settlements', in H. Barton (ed.) *Sustainable Communities*, Earthscan, London.

Stoker, G. (2002) 'Life is a lottery: New Labour's strategy for the reform of devolved governance', *Public Adminstration* 80, 417–434.

Storper, M. (1997) *The Regional World: Territorial Development in a Global Economy*, Guilford Press, New York.

Storper, M. (1998) 'Civil society: three ways into a problem', in M. Douglass and J. Friedmann (eds) *Cities for Citizens*, John Wiley, Chichester.

Strange, I. (1997) 'Directing the show? Business leaders, local partnership and economic regeneration in Sheffield'. *Environment and Planning C* 15, 1–17.

Swain, C. and Burden, W. (2002) *West Midlands RPG: Panel Report*, Government Office West Midlands, Birmingham.

Swain, C. and Rozee, L. (2000) *Regional Planning Guidance for Yorkshire and the Humber: Public Examination Panel Report*, GOYH, Leeds.

Swyngedouw, E. (1997) 'Neither global nor local: "glocalization" and the politics of scale', in K.R. Cox (ed.) *Spaces of Globalization: Reasserting the Power of the Local*, Guilford Press, New York.

Tewdwr-Jones, M. (ed.) (1996) *British Planning Practice in Transition: Planning in the 1990s*, UCL Press, London.

Tewdwr-Jones, M. (2001) 'Complexity and interdependency in a kaleidoscopic spatial planning landscape in Europe', in L. Albrechts, J. Alden and A. da Rosa Pires (eds) *The Changing Institutional Landscape of Planning*, Ashgate, Aldershot.

Tewdwr-Jones, M. and Allmendinger, P. (1998) 'Deconstructing communicative rationality: a critique of Habermassian collaborative planning', *Environment and Planning A* 30, 1975–1989.

Tewdwr-Jones, M. and Allmendinger, P. (2003) 'Conclusion: communicative planning and the post-positivist planning theory landscape', in P. Allmendinger and M. Tewdwr-Jones (eds) *Planning Futures: New Directions for Planning Theory*, Routledge, London.

Thomas, D. (1975) 'United Kingdom', in H.D. Clout (ed.) *Regional Development in Western Europe*, John Wiley, London.

Thomas, K. and Kimberley, S. (1995) 'Rediscovering regional planning? Progress on regional planning guidance in England', *Regional Studies* 29, 414–422.

Thornley, A. (ed.) (1993) *Urban Planning under Thatcherism: The Challenge of the Market*, Routledge, London.

Times, The (2000) 'Concrete is for ever'. 28 February.

Tomaney, J. and Mawson, J. (eds) (2002) *England: The State of the Regions,* Bristol, Policy Press.

Tomaney, J. and Ward, N. (eds) (2001) *A Region in Transition: North East England at the Millennium*, Ashgate, Aldershot.

Town and Country Planning Association (TCPA) (2002a) *Green Belts: TCPA Policy Statement*, TCPA, London.

TCPA (2002b) *New Towns and Town Extensions: TCPA Policy Statement*, London, TCPA.

UK Government (1990) *This Common Inheritance*, HMSO, London.

Urban Task Force (1999) *Towards an Urban Renaissance*, The Stationery Office, London.

Urry, J. (1995) *Consuming Places*, Routledge, London.

Valler, D.C., Wood, A. and North, P. (2000) 'Local governance and local business interests: a critical review', *Progress in Human Geography* 24 (3), 409–428.

Vigar, G. and Healey, P. (1999) 'Territorial integration and "plan-led" planning', *Planning Practice and Research* 14 (2), 153–169.

Vigar, G., Healey, P., Hull, A. and Davoudi, D. (2000) *Planning, Governance and Spatial Strategy in Britain*, Macmillan, Basingstoke.

Wackernagel, M. and Rees, W. (1996) *Our Ecological Footprint: Reducing Human Impact on the Earth*. New Society Publishers, Gabriola Island, BC, Canada.

Wacquant, L. (1996) 'The rise of advanced marginality: notes on its nature and implications', *Acta Sociologica* 39, 121–139.

Wannop, U. (1995) *The Regional Imperative: Regional Planning and Governance in Britain, Europe and the United States*, Jessica Kingsley, London.

Wannop, U. and Cherry, G. (1994) 'The development of regional planning in the United Kingdom', *Planning Perspectives* 9, 29–60.

Ward, K. (1997) 'Coalitions in urban regeneration: a regime approach', *Environment and Planning A* 29, 1493–1506.

Ward, S.V. (1994) *Planning and Urban Change*, Paul Chapman, London.

West Midlands Local Government Association (WMLGA) (2001a) *Draft Regional Planning Guidance*, WMLGA, Birmingham.

WMLGA (2001b) *Sustainability Appraisal of Draft RPG policies for the West Midlands*, WMLGA, Birmingham.

West Sussex County Council (WSCC) (1996) *West Sussex Structure Plan, Third Review: Environmental Capacity in West Sussex*, WSCC, Chichester.

WSCC (1997) *West Sussex Structure Plan, Third Review: Examination in Public Panel Report*, WSCC, Chichester.

Whatmore, S. and Boucher, S. (1993) 'Bargaining with nature: the discourse and practice of environmental gain', *Transactions of the Institute of British Geographers* 18, 166–178.

Wheeler, S.M. (2002) 'The New Regionalism: key characteristics of an emerging movement', *Journal of the American Planning Association* 68, 267–278.

While, A., Gibbs, D.C. and Jonas, A.E.G. (2002) 'Unlocking the city? Growth pressures and the search for new spaces of governance in Greater Cambridge, England', mimeo.

Wildavsky, A.B. (1973) 'If planning is everything maybe it's nothing', *Policy and Sciences* 4 (2), 127–153.

Williams, C.M. (2002) 'The South West: lessons for the future', in T. Marshall, J. Glasson and P. Headicar (eds) *Contemporary Issues in Regional Planning*, Ashgate, Aldershot.

Williams, K., Burton, E. and Jenks, M. (eds) (2000) *Achieving Sustainable Urban Form*, E. & F.N. Spon, London.

Williams, R. (1973) *The Country and the City*, Oxford University Press, Oxford.

Wilson, A.G. (1974) *Urban and Regional Models in Geography and Planning*, John Wiley, Chichester.

Wong, C. (2002) 'Is there a need for a fully integrated spatial planning framework for the United Kingdom?', *Planning Theory and Practice* 3, 277–300.

World Commission on Environment and Development (WCED) (1987) *Our Common Future*, Oxford University Press, Oxford.

Yorkshire Forward (1999) *Regional Economic Strategy for Yorkshire and the Humber*, Yorkshire Forward, Leeds.

Yorkshire Forward (2003) *Regional Economic Strategy for Yorkshire and the Humber 2003–2011*, Yorkshire Forward, Leeds.